FAULKNER

Crowell's Handbook of

FAULKNER

By DOROTHY TUCK

LEWIS LEARY, *Advisory Editor*

THOMAS Y. CROWELL COMPANY

New York, Established 1834

The sources of the short illustrative quotations from
Faulkner's works are indicated in "Abbreviations Used
in the Text"; complete publishing data are given in
the "Selected Bibliography" at the back of the book.

8 / 3
Juc

For HARRIET BLUM and EDWARD TRIPP
with appreciation

Introduction

MOST PEOPLE who care about literature agree that William Faulkner has taken a place beside Nathaniel Hawthorne, Herman Melville, and Henry James as one of the rare artists in fiction produced in the United States. Yet, perhaps more than any of these others, he has become also an international novelist, admired, honored, and imitated in many lands. His reputation, large in his own country, grows even larger abroad, where his books are found in translation in most of the major literary centers of the world. Throughout much of Europe, especially in France, he has been named among the first of novelists, with Dostoevski, Tolstoi, Proust, or Sartre, nor is he less admired in Tokyo or New Delhi, Cairo or Rio de Janeiro, where readers have long responded to his way of regarding people and his way of using words which seem extraordinarily his own, yet catch and hold the imagination of readers everywhere.

Faulkner's reputation outside the United States is different from that of many other native writers who have become popular abroad. He is not read, as Theodore Dreiser or Sinclair Lewis, for examples, are read, because he reveals or satirizes the faults of his countrymen; nor is his appeal that of Ernest Hemingway, whose brittle, brilliant, but restricted, style, and whose stoic passivity, are much admired. Many readers abroad do not think of Faulkner as a foreign writer at all—he certainly does not seem to them simply an American who reveals shortcomings of life in the United States or who uncovers idiosyncrasies of native provincial character. Faulkner strikes them rather as a world-embracing writer, because he speaks to them of the plight of man everywhere, with compassion and outrage, even with insinuations of tragedy in an old and understandable sense of that word, but conditioned by his humanity to an indomitable, comic, and sorrowful quest toward values necessary for survival.

Blinded by what they must be, the people whom Faulkner presents in his fiction do not always discover these values, and the mistakes they make as they search for them are often hideously grotesque. They stumble toward death, as Joe Christmas does, or toward success, like Flem Snopes, or toward brief, almost illusionary understanding, like Ike McCaslin, never without the uncomfortable necessity of overcoming difficulties which they or other men place in their way, and seldom without the heretical and never quite plausible belief that each man may somehow work his way toward happiness or security or salvation. Theirs is not in strictest sense a tragic plight, for though each is pitted against natural forces, implacable but inherently beneficent, his principal antagonist is himself and what his obedience to the demands of other men has made him. As much as Emerson's, Faulkner's age, he might have said, is retrospective, dwelling within sepulchers of its fathers, giving lip-service to creeds which stultify and misdirect.

1

For all his universality, Faulkner can be discovered to have been shaped by several native traditions, so that he appeared among us, not as a new man entirely, but as a talented successor to others. His allegiance to the spirit of Nathaniel Hawthorne, for one, rests on more than the circumstance that each man was, almost apologetically, descended from a family once prominently a part of the history of its region; that each on becoming a writer changed the spelling of his name—Falkner to Faulkner, Hathorne to Hawthorne; that each tacitly encouraged other people to think of him as an isolated man, removed from conversation with other writers; or that Faulkner titled his first book *The Marble Faun*. Each may be remembered as a romancer, less interested in the rational and realistic than in the nebulous and inexpressible reachings of the human heart, so that his characters expand into psychological archetypes, more recognizable for what they suggest of people everywhere than as exactly defined individuals.

Faulkner spoke much as Hawthorne might have spoken when he told a class of young writers at the University of Virginia that "it's the heart that has the desire to be better than man is; the up here can know the distinction between good and evil, but it's the heart that makes you want to be better than you are. That's what I mean by to write from the heart. That it's the heart that makes you want to be brave when you are afraid you might be a coward, that wants you to be generous, or wants you to be compassionate when you think that maybe you won't. I think that the intellect, it might say, 'Well, which is the more profitable—shall I be compassionate or shall I be uncompassionate? Which is most profitable? Which is most profitable—shall I be brave or not?' But the heart wants to be better than man is."

Right or wrong, and anti-intellectual as they may be, statements such as that are familiar to any reader of older American writings. They underline and rephrase distinctions on which Emerson insisted, between Understanding, which is man-devised and very likely to be wrong, and Reason, which is intuitive and which can be divine. They explain again what Melville had Plotinus Plinlimmon explain in *Pierre* about differences between chronometrical and horological time—the one, man-made and useful, but incorrect; the other, eternal, often inconvenient, but everlastingly true.

They say again, with less economy of words, almost exactly what Hawthorne often said about the superiority of heart over head, or what Whittier said, or even Longfellow when he had anything to say. They represent an adaptation and extension of what Coleridge said in England, and Goethe in Germany, about man's allegiance beyond all knowledge to what he recognized without thought as good. They have been found to echo Jonathan Edwards' earlier certainty that people are better when they place love, which is intuitive understanding and compassion and admiration of those things which are by divine right true, above the presumptions of creeds invented by man.

And they are far older than that, reflecting Biblical injunction and a humanistic tradition seldom without advocates in Europe or the East, but which became in the United States in the nineteenth century a view of knowledge and a way of thinking about facts that lie beneath appearances, which has given to much American writing since certain identifiable characteristics. Most of us agree that Richard Chase is correct in saying that the tradition of fiction among us is the tradition of romance, and that Northrop Frye is correct in explaining that the romance "radiates a glow of subjective intensity that the novel lacks," so that "a suggestion of allegory is constantly creeping about its fringes." We have become accustomed to agreement with D. H. Lawrence, who many years ago instructed us that fiction in the United States is characterized by an unwillingness to take off its clothes in order to show what is underneath, with the result that many American writers often seem to mean something quite different from what they say.

We are likely to call such writers symbolists, though perhaps they might be more truly designated as allegorists manqué, and to present Faulkner as chief among them. Like the Melville whom Lawrence Thompson once disclosed as having so intense a "quarrel with God" that he dared not express it directly, like Hawthorne whose *The Scarlet Letter* has been interpreted in a dozen ways, like the Henry James whom Quentin Anderson has discovered to be a devious deviser of parables, or like Katherine Anne Porter who delights with indirection, Faulkner also suggests more than he ever says. He once described himself as a "failed poet," forced against his will to prose, much as Emerson once spoke of himself as a poet maimed. Robert Penn Warren, also a poet, first reminded us, I think, that if we read Faulkner as if he were a poet, many difficulties would disappear.

For, more than most writers of his time, Faulkner tempts readers toward discovering something like allegorical meanings in his fiction. But one suggestion of allegory tumbles so fast after another which seems to hint at something quite different from the first that even many of his most devoted readers have difficulty in determining what Faulkner in that sense really intends. If he says this, they are likely to ask, how can he say that? The truth may be that Faulkner intends few of the meanings ascribed to him. In

/

social matters he seems the least programmatic of writers, and that has been supposed to be one of the reasons why in the 1930s he was unpraised by many contemporary critics, most of whom during that decade were sure that an important responsibility of literature was to help people recognize improvements in the way they might assist one another. Hardly anything that Faulkner has written seems to inspire reform in a social sense. It is even unlikely that many people have been led to wanting to be better people as a result of reading him. To those who require of literature what it is not always capable of producing, this lack of what used to be called social consciousness has sometimes made Faulkner difficult to understand. How can a person have such fun or relate such horrors without serious civic purpose?

But to those who cherish literature as a pinwheel throwing off a profusion of sparks, Faulkner has provided luxurious opportunities for adventures in interpretation. Catching at one spark or another, enchanted by its single glowing brightness, readers have pursued Faulkner to gloomy or luminous areas where he may never have intended to be found. He has tempted with symbols which dart toward meaning and then fall short, to be replaced by other symbols, equally undefining, until the attentive reader's mind, teased from one intimation to another, becomes a kaleidoscope of impressions, as chaotic as the fables which Faulkner has set before him. Without attention, any reader can become lost in any Faulkner book.

He can become confused by Faulkner's manner of talking and the way he tells a story. First things do not always come first. Events do not progress in simple chronological order. Late in any narrative, the reader may discover something about a character which, if he had known it earlier, would have quite changed his former estimate of that character. Many of Faulkner's sentences seem interminably long, with one parenthetical aside dangling from another, and others dangling from that, until the weight of digression may seem to submerge what grammatically the sentence is about. Faulkner may frequently seem compulsively a talker, so fond of his flow of words that he forgets what he had set out to say. He may seem to become, as someone has said, hopelessly involved in his own technical virtuosity. He speaks so profusely that he does not always speak carefully.

Some have supposed that Faulkner insists on experimenting with new ways of saying things because old ways have been so smudged by use that they no longer reflect what is meant to be said. Others have supposed him to be an incorrigible tease who plays games with his readers and sets traps for them. Time is often snapped quite out of joint, so that it becomes difficult to determine, not only when a thing happens, but whether it really has happened at all or is only an hallucination in the mind of some character. Nor is it always possible to understand what his characters are up to. They are treated, it has been said, "in such a way that while their motives are apparently crystal clear to each other, the reader has to work like the very devil to find out why they do what they do." Most of them seem motivated, observes Wilbur Frohock, "by obscure obsessive neuroses, and tortured by anxieties which the reader does not share and which lead to actions which take place outside the normal order of events at abnormal speed."

But in spite of these difficulties, and perhaps in recognition of the universality of these obscure anxieties, thoughtful readers have responded to the challenge of Faulkner's writings. They have agreed with Robert Penn Warren that the evaluation of these writings presents "the most challenging single task in contemporary American literature for criticism to undertake," because "in mass of work, in scope of material, in range of effect, in reportorial accuracy and symbolic subtlety, in philosophical weight," Faulkner proves himself worthy of testing beside any master of the past.

Among the more popular early interpretations were those which found Faulkner an apologist for problems unique to the American South. The familiar lore or local gossip which he had heard recounted in kitchen or country store or beside the evening fire on hunting trips had been "elaborated, transformed, given compulsive life by his emotions," explained Malcolm Cowley, "until by the simple intensity of feeling, the figures in it became a little more than human, became heroic or diabolical, became symbols of the old South, of war and reconstruction, of commerce and machinery destroying the standards of the past." In doing this, Cowley continued, "Faulkner performed a labor of imagination that has not been equalled in our time, and a double labor: first, to invent a Mississippi county that was like a mythical kingdom, but was complete and living in all its details; second, to make his story of Yoknapatawpha County stand as a parable or legend of the Deep South."

Others, recognizing Faulkner as a writer who speaks best of what he knows most intimately in scene and character, so that his stories are of course Southern and his people inhabitants of that legend-filled region, find him nonetheless in theme and situation quite transcending locality, to speak of kinds of people who might be found anywhere, and of motives and tensions which are shared by all. Yoknapatawpha County is often explained as a microcosm of the modern world, a Spenglerian nightmare filled with violence and greed, without an ethical center, and driving fast toward disaster. It is seen as a cheap, tawdry, and soulless world, a wasted land in which the Snopeses and their kind, little men of niggling morality, inspired by no standards except those set by ambition and self-admiration, scheme and cheat and fawn their way toward success. It has been called a weaseling world, dominated by hollow men who stamp on every human decency as they climb. But it is also a world in which love and honor and pity and pride and compassion and sacrifice—these are Faulkner's words—still quietly prevail as man's bulwarks against disaster.

"It took us a long time," says one of the characters in *The Wild Palms*, "but man is resourceful and limitless in inventing too, and so we have got rid of love at last just as we have got rid of Christ. We have the radio in place of God's voice, and instead of having to save emotional currency for months and years to deserve to spend it all for love we can now spread it out thin into coppers and titillate ourselves at any newsstand, two to a block like sticks of chewing gum or chocolate from the automatic machines. If Jesus returned today we would have to crucify him quick in our own defense, to justify and preserve the civilization we have worked and suffered and died shrieking and cursing in rage and impotence and terror for two thousand years to create and perfect in man's own image; if Venus returned she would be a soiled man in a subway with a palm full of French postcards."

It is not only of Mississippi, nor the American South, nor even the United States, of which Faulkner writes, though it is of these also; it is the whole of Western civilization which he sees in dreadful vision as "paying the price for having erected its economic edifice not on the rock of stern morality but on the shifting sands of opportunism and moral brigandage." So perhaps it is with the poets, with T. S. Eliot and Ezra Pound, Wallace Stevens and E. E. Cummings, that Faulkner is to be remembered, and in the climate of whose opinions he must be read. His iconoclastic vision of the world is filled, like theirs, with bitterly nostalgic reminders of what could have been, of what can be, and of what must be, if the world is not to torment itself to physical as well as moral destruction. When Faulkner is violent in action or rhetoric, he portrays a world in which violence seems to lead man toward what he most desires. But it never does, nor does despair.

2

Again, Faulkner is discovered to be within a familiar American literary tradition, which insists that particulars rightly seen become universals, so that any man is the microcosm of all men. In this view, which Emerson and Thoreau and many of their nineteenth-century compatriots inherited from and shared with other men in other lands, nature is recognized as symbol of spirit. When Faulkner has Doc Peabody in *As I Lay Dying* speak of "our land: opaque, slow, violent; shaping and creating the life of man in its implacable and brooding image," he is approaching an attitude similar to that of earlier Americans. Only when Ike McCaslin, after initiation and trial, gives himself wholly to nature by divesting himself of man-devised, distracting instruments—like watch and gun and compass—does he glimpse truth, which is all truth, and which he can experience but never explain.

Nature is more than a backdrop for the drama which Faulkner's fiction reveals. It looms, never completely personified, as an irrational, primal force, at once beautiful and ominous. "God created man," Ike McCaslin explains in "Delta Autumn," "and He created the world for him to live in and I reckon he created the kind of world He would have wanted to live in if He had been man—the ground to walk on, the big woods, the trees and water, and the game to live in it." Nature is lush, amoral, fecund, implacably competent, "with woods for game and streams for fish and deep rick soil for seed and lush springs to sprout it and long summers to mature it and serene falls to harvest it." But the land also contains people who make it a "doomed wilderness . . . constantly and punily gnawed at by men with plows and axes." Bright meadows become golf courses, cities encourage corruption.

For man disfigures nature—no conservationist could be more explicit on this than Faulkner. As the wilderness vanishes under macadam and steel, it becomes part of a native adaptation of the Christian myth of a vanished paradise which Fenimore Cooper recognized and struggled to explain. Hacked at and mutilated, nature continues to menace the ambitions of men. Eden is lost because man is man, impatient and ruthless, falsely ambitious, and without the wisdom to know his ordered place. Nature is despoiled, yet, uncorrupted and timeless, she ultimately takes her revenge, as she does in *Moby Dick* and less violently in *Huckleberry Finn*. But once, long ago, so the fable familiarly begins, there had been a time when people lived in truer relationship with nature—until mortal sin brought death into the world, with all its woe.

That perhaps is every poet's theme—the relationship of man to forces which cripple or exalt him. As an American, Faulkner shared old certainties with earlier native writers about beauty and truth in essential unity, though he preferred to quote Keats's familiar formulation which spoke of them more satisfyingly. He shared immensely with Thoreau in recognition of the awful loveliness of nature and its inscrutable demands. With Emerson and Henry James, he shared a brooding sense of history—how past infiltrates present until time becomes at once eternal and contemporary, so that man's contentment where he is depends on knowledge of where he has been. Apprehension of the past cannot be reached out for, nor can it be limited to that which is convenient or pleasant or prideful to recall. To passive and receptive people, like the boy in "The Bear" or Dilsey in *The Sound and the Fury*, it comes all at once as an informing vision which needs no explanation. To Hightower in *Light in August*, it is hallucination of which he must talk incessantly.

Recognition of Faulkner's attitude toward time is often thought to be central to an understanding of his work. But this central area is where

Faulkner is usually least explicit. He cannot be said to have an articulated theory of history, only a brooding sense of the importance of the past. It impinges on the present, distorting or clarifying. As tradition or recorded fact, as legend or myth, it weaves a web in which all men are entangled. Sometimes beneficial, sometimes harmful, it relentlessly molds man's opinions and actions. If Faulkner is to be found to any degree a tragic writer, it is in his attitude toward man's absorption in the continuum of time.

"Faulkner's vision of the world," Jean-Paul Sartre has said, "can be compared to that of a man sitting in a convertible looking backward. At every moment shadows emerge on his right, and on his left flickering and quavering points of light, which become trees, men, and cars only when they are seen in perspective. The past here gains a surrealistic quality; its outline is hard, clear, and immutable. The indefinable and elusive present is helpless before it; it is full of holes through which past things, fixed, motionless, and silent, invade it." All that exists is a pattern, that web which the past has woven. A sense of present time can only be expressed in terms of the past, in concepts and images which the past has provided. Thus Sartre speaks of the feeling of suspension in Faulkner's writing, as if man was poised now as the cumulation of a series of events which had all been in the past—poised momentarily, waiting for the past to thrust him, willy-nilly, into a future of which his imperfect knowledge of the past allows him no foreknowledge.

In thus presenting historical fictions which treat of the past as story, anecdote, fable, and myth, none completely told, but each shaping some part of the web which is the present, not flowing but intertwined, sometimes grotesquely, Faulkner draws on a remarkable and apparently uncontrolled flow of rhetoric. It is not unusual to find—as, for example, in some of those unforgettable interchapters in Requiem for a Nun—single sentences which speak all in one breath of historical or actual past, traditional or commonly accepted past, and legendary or mythic past, piling suggestions of meaning layer on layer, until the sentence seems to catch up and hold suspended the whole of time. Conrad Aiken has described Faulkner's style as fluid, slippery, and heavily mannered, overelaborated and involuted, as if the writer, "in a sort of hurried despair, had decided to tell us everything, absolutely everything, every last origin or source or quality or qualification, and every future permutation as well, in one terrifically concentrated effort: each sentence to be, as it were, a microcosm."

The extravagance of William Faulkner, who fills sentences so abundantly, is related also to the extravagance of the American tall tale. It presents the view of an alert but ruminative countryman on whom events and memories impinge with such rapidity that he has no time to sort them to simplicity. He must talk, and endlessly talk, about what he knows and sees and remembers, because he is sure that if he stops talking to order them to system, other sights and memories will pass him by. Faulkner is the talk-ingest man in modern literature. He can talk simply and well, can tell an exciting story with casual directness, as he does in the slapstick tale of the spotted horses, or in recounting Senator Snopes's curious adventures in Memphis. He often sounds as if he were speaking from the depths of a great chair set before an open fire, with glass in hand and friends around him, all comfortable and a little sleepy, oblivious of time and the necessity for hurry. His voice drones on, lavishly and discursively, as he elaborates on familiar twice-told tales.

Faulkner's voice inevitably reminds us then of that native oral tradition which Mark Twain once spoke of as "a high and delicate art," in which the narrative flows "as flows the brook down through the hills and leafy woodlands, its course changed by every boulder it comes across and by every grass-clad gravelly spur that projects into its path, its surface broken but its course not stayed by rocks and gravel on the bottom in shoal places." Rambling and disjointed, these slowly voiced excursions do however have a destination, "a nub, point, snapper, or whatever you like to call it." To recognize this, "the listener must be alert," Mark Twain warns, "for in many cases the teller will divert attention from the nub by dropping it in a careful casual and indifferent way, with the pretence that he does not know it is a nub."

Faulkner's leisurely voice may not always seem attractive. It moves on in circles, slowly, obtusely, delaying expectations. Little is ever simplified for the convenience of fast reading. Time is made to stand still for page after page, while past time crowds up on it, disfiguring and obscuring as often as it clarifies. Faulkner requires of each reader a willingness to sit with him a long time, until from the mesmeric rhythms of his speaking something emerges of understanding of the complicated meshing of humor and pathos and misdirected good intentions which make up the substance of most men's lives.

He is an American writer certainly, in tone, in themes, in attitude. His native origins are certified by his insistence on the preeminence of the human spirit, even when that spirit is crippled or deformed; by his attitude toward nature as a balm, a corrective, and a kaleidoscope of elusive symbols; by his sense of the past; by his sophisticated development of native lore and his drawling, laconic or tensely excited, manner of telling a story. He is in the line of frontier humorists, as extravagant as Sut Lovingood or Mark Twain, as extra-vagant as Thoreau. No section other than the American South could have produced him.

3

Yet in none of his characteristics is Faulkner more native than in his refusal to be limited by section or nationality. From the first raising of voices in the wilderness of the Western world, Americans have insisted on their right to speak for all men. Their experience was not exclusive, but provided a mirror in which all mankind might see its own. One man's sin became humanity's burden, and one man's glory a beacon for all. When they sang to celebrate themselves, they welcomed universal recognition that what belonged to them or was discovered by them, belonged as well to others. America opened its arms wide to strangers, and then often did not treat them well. The way they acted and their reasons for it were determined by local situations and contemporary events, complicated by each man's inevitable entanglement with what his people had been. As a result, they sometimes had some explaining to do.

But to read Faulkner as a social or political or explanatory novelist in a regional or sectional sense is to read him incompletely. As a man of his time, living where he did, he had opinions and attitudes, with some of which not all of his contemporaries could agree. His characters more than once speak with disrespect or lack of understanding about other characters who differ from them in race or religion or education or social class. It may even be true that Faulkner is condescending toward Negroes, just as he is condescending toward women and bankers and lawyers. If the faithful family retainer, Dilsey, is a stereotype, so also is Jason Compson or Colonel Sartoris. Joe Christmas' problem, that he could not determine who he was, quite transcends the terms of black and white in which Faulkner presented it. The swarming, grasping people of Yoknapatawpha County, whether morally deteriorated or spiritually uplifted, are real people, in a real locality, in the United States, because Faulkner has placed them there; but they are other people also, who live or have lived anywhere in a world disrupted. These things never happened and these people never lived, except as Faulkner created them.

"As one reads about them," says Steven Marcus, "one gets a renewed sense of how one of the primal powers of literature is to raise mythology to the level of history, to treat the material of the imagination as if it were indistinguishable from the actuality it invades and transcribes. Faulkner is the only contemporary American writer who has a facility for this; perhaps he is the only modern writer who has it at all. The stories he wrote over twenty-five years have become part of the given; he takes a past which he has created himself and deals with it as recorded reality. It is 'out there,' independent of his ministrations, waiting for him to record and recreate rather than invent. And as the degree of Faulkner's conviction about the historicity of his imagination seems positive, so, too, does the degree to which he seems able to represent concretely the deterioration in American life of those institutions and values which allow for the cultivation of the imagination and the spirit."

It is not necessary to stop there, nor have Faulkner's readers over the world so limited their interpretation of Faulkner's vision. By an incredibly complex series of creative acts Faulkner has transformed the particular to the universal, so wrenching geography from moorings that Yoknapatawpha County becomes the place where any reader lives; and Joe Christmas and Dilsey and Jason Compson and Flem Snopes become, not distorted representations of people who are known and disliked or admired, but recognizable fragments of every reader's opportunity or doom.

This transformation has little to do with what Faulkner intended or with the burdens which critics have placed upon him. Perhaps because he has until recently been actively with us, his own statements so greatly a part of our estimation, Faulkner has not yet been seen in his complex entirety by any single commentator. Olga Vickery may come closest, for she puts aside more successfully than most the temptation to make Faulkner an apologist for some favorite view. For Faulkner does tease readers to find meanings of their own in what he has written, to the point where Irving Howe, in intelligent exasperation, has accused him of "failure of intellect" because he failed to supply a "high order of comment and observation *within* the structure of his work," and because of his inability "to handle general ideas with a dramatic cogency equal to his ability to render images or conduct."

Others, however, suppose that Faulkner's success derives precisely from his refusal to give allegiance to any but the simplest of meanings. To them, his writing, at its best, presents a series of dialogues in which this view is presented, then that, and then another, leaving resolution to each reader. People who hold this view do not say there is no center in Faulkner, only that there is no ideological center. No more than most of his literary contemporaries, or his American literary antecedents, was Faulkner, they would say, a thoughtful, idea-expanding man. He flew, as old-time aviators used to express it, by the seat of his pants, observant, resourceful, quick at maneuvering, skilled at balance, looping or diving just for the sport of it, or to thrill spectators, but never quite able to explain his movements on charts, although he did know, in a general way, and with confidence no charts could challenge, what he was about and where he was going. If other people did not care to follow, so much the less fun for them.

Most commentators pull Faulkner up short by dividing his career into three, sometimes four, carefully charted segments: the first, a period of trial and error, when as a young man he learned his trade; the second and most significant, beginning in 1929 and extending into the later 1930's, when Faulkner in his thirties did not quite know what he was about, but produced in quick succession *Sartoris, The Sound and the Fury, Sanctuary, As I Lay Dying, Light in August, Pylon,* and *Absalom, Absalom!*; the third, beginning in 1938 with *The Unvanquished* (some would begin this period with *The Hamlet* in 1940, and slip in a brief catch-all period between), when for the rest of his life Faulkner, as if disappointed that his earlier books

had been misunderstood, attempted through patient and simplified restate-
ment, especially in "The Bear" and *The Fable*, and in iterative public comments at Stockholm, Nagano, and Charlottesville, to put forward an explanation of what all the time he had intended. However convenient such
a division may be, it can be thought of as representing exactly the kind of
orderly commentary which Faulkner particularly distrusted. He never
really admitted what he was up to.

But he never had to, for critics from the first have been eager to provide
that service to Faulkner which D. H. Lawrence once explained that every
critic owed to each author—to rescue the author from himself, by explaining to him what he must have meant. At first, Faulkner was explained as
a salesman of vice, a deliberate and scandalous exploiter of sensational,
often erotic, devices, whose perverts, degenerates, and introverts identified
him as one of those writers who "set themselves up in a literary business,
with unmitigated cruelties and abnormalities as their stock in trade," a forerunner of Mickey Spillane in the novel of violence, a deftly elusive John
O'Hara. His apocalyptic vision—in Faulkner's case the paradise lost in the
American South—placed him beside Brockden Brown and Poe and, as if
in afterthought, Melville. People like Clifton Fadiman spoke of his anti-
narrative techniques, as if Faulkner, like a perverse child, had gone to work
with a pair of scissors to cut a good yarn to shreds. Sociological writers,
Marxist or worse, found him a master dissector of aristocratic mores, with
the Southern gentleman's no longer elegantly concealed hatred of all
women and all Negroes. He became a man of perverse, exasperating sug-
gestiveness, who "crowds symbols in" until

> There is a hidden meaning
> In every glass of gin.

At other extremes, he has become known as a kind of redeemer, who
borrows religious imagery and symbolic suggestions of the continuing
efficacy of the Christian mythos, set forth through phrases reminiscent of
the Sermon on the Mount, to suggest that man may become better than he
has been. Sometimes salvation is explained as willingness humbly to submit
one's self as an innocent companion to other creatures who inhabit and
do not mutilate the good land which has been given as gift to all. Again,
with compulsive modernity, Faulkner's gift to a reader's enthusiasm for the
explicit is explained, most recently by Cleanth Brooks, as a subtle reinforce-
ment of an American yearning toward community. We are all in this together. Let us then take hands and have compassion one for another.

All of these things may be in Faulkner, and more besides, but a statement of them does not exhaust his curious multiplicity. "I wish I could
have managed him," Ernest Hemingway is once said to have said, thinking
of Faulkner as if he were a prize fighter who could be taught feints and jabs

and delicately controlled footwork. Faulkner was a wild swinger who missed many marks, and sometimes, it has been supposed, fell flat on his face. He admired, or pretended to admire, the even wilder swinging of Thomas Wolfe, because Wolfe dared to put all of himself into everything he ever wrote, in a tremendous effort, said Faulkner, "to put all of the history of the human heart on the head of a pin." When Faulkner's characters are careful contrivers, proud of the effectiveness of their footwork, they become wealthy, like Flem Snopes, but impotent.

Searching for meaning in Faulkner's writing probably results in each searcher's finding meaning in himself, and that is usually a good thing, if it is not taken too seriously. For meanings slither and swerve and turn about on themselves, especially when suggested by so thoughtless but so thought-provoking a writer as Faulkner. If he does often seem uncertain of ideas, he is observant and insightful and honest, fundamentally simple. The simplicity is not of surface, because the surface which Faulkner presents is a slippery surface, roughened by people who act strangely, compulsively, and self-consciously, or with so much lack of self-consciousness that they fail in humanity, restrained by being what they have to be from becoming what they could.

His fools and knaves and retrospective people, his tin men (like Popeye), his hollow men (like Jason Compson), his scarecrows (like Horace Benbow—headpiece stuffed with straw, alas!); his popinjays, his sacrificial Lee Goodwin and his self-righteously avenging Percy Grimm, his virtuous and self-congratulatory virgins and his lush, fecund female destroyers who consume as they create; his proud Snopeses and his humble Snopeses, his idiots and lawyers, sewing-machine salesmen, farmers and woodsmen—Melville might have noticed that there is not a poet among them—are all caught and held, not in logical association one to another, but in a net of language which reaches out, with many a breathtaking swerving, finally to bind them in a series of relationships greatly more human than tragic.

4

To understand living, Faulkner may seem to say, one must live. Only then, when errors have been made, can experience be examined to discover, perhaps too late, what life intended. The words in which other men have wrapped creed or tradition can be misleading: "words go straight up in a thin line, quick and harmless," Faulkner has one character explain, so that "sin and love and fear are just sounds that people who never sinned nor loved nor feared have for what they never had and cannot have until they forget the words." Hot-blooded, rash, ambitious man rushes through time, pursued or pursing, with his mouth open wide, shouting explanations for what he must do: to "people to whom sin is just a matter of words, to them salvation is just words too." Even the best of words are caught and marred by time: when most explicit, they are likely to be most wrong. They have been used as spurious counters, as counterfeits of spirit.

Yet Faulkner's own large achievement as an artist has been in the manipulation of words. Weaving them to massively intricate patterns in which one element counterbalances another, so that meaning in any usual sense becomes confused, he evoked suggestions of meanings which no words express. Any attempt to explain him, explains him only in part; for what Faulkner wrote is not meant to be explained, only experienced. Each tale is complete, yet each comments on every other, until the whole becomes an intricate reflection of men and women entangled in living. Whether with conscious aesthetic purpose or as a brooding, questioning, haphazard recorder of what he has seen and heard, Faulkner thus has created a montage of people stumbling and constantly talking, a world disordered within which most readers inevitably discover themselves.

By some it is cherished as a tragic world, meaningless and damned, and Faulkner more than once, perhaps teasingly, seems to encourage this view, even to giving dark characters such tragedy-suggesting names as Clytemnestra or Christmas. Sad things happen in many of the tales, and people die, sometimes violently and unnecessarily, as people do. Yet, unless living itself is tragic because it must end without fulfillment of all it has desired, Faulkner's view may be recognized as comic, as he speaks with affectionate compassion of people who are human enough to make their own mistakes. Tragedy, he may seem to say, is devised by man as a simple explanation—such as Shreve McCannon devises in Absalom, Absalom!— of why he does not do better than he does. It is neither necessary nor final, only an expedient, comforting because it eases a burden. The comic view, more difficult to sustain, requires recognition of the "old verities and truths of the heart, the old universal truths lacking which any story is ephemeral or doomed"—the love and honor and pity and pride and compassion and sacrifice which guarantee that "man will not merely endure, he will prevail."

Unlike many of his contemporaries, Faulkner seems to have withstood the dour Central European invasion of Western culture by men like Conrad and the Russian novelists, to hold fast to an older, perhaps ultimately more realistic, and not at all simple, but optimistic, view of man. In this also he reveals the influence of native predecessors who gave allegiance to attitudes borrowed from abroad, which Faulkner now returns in generous measure.

To know him, he must be read, and such a guide as this which Dorothy Tuck has provided may make that reading easier for people who come at Faulkner now, all at once, for the first time. They are to be envied for the opportunity of making his acquaintance.

Columbia University   LEWIS LEARY

Abbreviations Used in the Text

PAGE NUMBERS following quotations within the text refer to the novel under discussion, unless otherwise indicated. When the quotation is taken from another book the initials of the title are given. Page numbers in Faulkner's novels refer to the editions listed below. Inexpensive paperback and Modern Library editions have been used wherever possible.

AA	Absalom, Absalom! (Modern Library)
ALID	As I Lay Dying (Modern Library)
CS	Collected Stories (Random House)
EP&P	Early Prose and Poetry (Atlantic-Little, Brown)
F	A Fable (Random House)
F IN U	Faulkner in the University (Univ. of Virginia Press)
GDM	Go Down, Moses (Penguin)
H	The Hamlet (Vintage)
ID	Intruder in the Dust (Signet)
KG	Knight's Gambit (Signet)
LA	Light in August (Modern Library)
M	The Mansion (Random House)
MOS	Mosquitoes (Dell)
NOS	New Orleans Sketches (Grove Press)
P	Pylon (Signet)
R	The Reivers (Random House)
RFN	Requiem for a Nun (Signet)
S	Sanctuary (Signet)
SAR	Sartoris (Signet)
SP	Soldier's Pay (Signet)
SF	The Sound and the Fury (Modern Library)
T	The Town (Vintage)
TD	Three Decades of Criticism (Michigan State Univ. Press)
U	The Unvanquished (Signet)
WP	The Wild Palms and Old Man (Signet)

Contents

Genealogical Charts

Crowell's Handbook of

FAULKNER

The History of Yoknapatawpha County

YOKNAPATAWPHA COUNTY is closely modeled on Lafayette County, Mississippi. Both the real and fictional counties are roughly bounded on the northeast by the Tallahatchie River; in the fictional county the Yocana River to the south is named the Yoknapatawpha. Jefferson, the seat of the imaginary county, corresponds in location and many other aspects to Oxford, the seat of Lafayette County and for many years Faulkner's home town. In Faulkner's saga the city of Oxford is located some forty miles in an unspecified direction from Jefferson, and plays a small part as the seat of the University of Mississippi.

In the discussion that follows, the fictional county, its inhabitants, and the events that take place are treated as if they were real. No attempt has been made to distinguish between purely imaginary incidents and those based on fact, or to suggest parallels between the histories of the real and imaginary counties. The only primary sources available on Yoknapatawpha County are Faulkner's novels, and there are occasional inconsistencies and gaps.

Yoknapatawpha County, William Faulkner's "mythical kingdom," is situated in northern Mississippi, roughly bounded by the Tallahatchie River on the north and the Yoknapatawpha River on the south, and bisected north and south by John Sartoris' railroad. The face of the land varies from low-lying, fertile and heavily timbered river bottoms to sandy pine hills in the northeast section known as Beat Four. Jefferson, the county seat, is surrounded by gently rolling farmland and is located approximately at the geographical center of the county. Like many Southern towns of the same period, it is built around a columned and porticoed courthouse set in an octagonal park in the center of the Square; at one end of the Square is a monument of a Confederate soldier, shielding his eyes from the sun in the classic searcher's pose and staring boldly south—whether for some lost Yankee regiment heading north for home or for some departing Confederates no one knows. The buildings around the Square are two-storied, most of them with a second-storey gallery reached by an outside staircase. The only other town of any significance is the hamlet of Frenchman's Bend at the southeastern corner of the county. Memphis, the closest large city, is seventy-five miles northwest of Jefferson, and Oxford, the location of the state university, is forty miles away. The county's 2,400 square miles are populated by about 15,000 persons, over half of them Negroes.

The name Yoknapatawpha is derived from that of the Yocana River, sometimes referred to as the Yocanapatafa (or Yocanapatapha) in old records; according to Faulkner, the Chickasaw words *yocana* and *petopha* means "water runs slow through flat land." In the old days, the northern part of the county near the Tallahatchie river bottom was a heavily timbered land rife with wildlife—possums, coons, rabbits, squirrels, wild turkeys, deer, and even bears. Then the land was inhabited by the Chickasaw Indians, whose nation was ruled by a great chieftain referred to as David Colbert; the Yoknapatawpha Chickasaws had their own local chief whose title, "the Man," was passed on from father to son. However, perhaps because the history of the Chickasaws was told to the white settlers of the county many years later, long after "the People," as the Indians called themselves, had been driven to a reservation in Oklahoma, the various stories about the Indians are not always consistent with one another. The most famous—or notorious—of the chiefs was Ikkemotubbe (sometimes spelled Ikkemoutubbe). He "had been born merely a subchief, a Mingo, one of three children of the mother's side of the family. He made a journey— he was a young man then and New Orleans was a European city—from north Mississippi to New Orleans by keel boat, where he . . . passed as the chief, the Man, the hereditary owner of that land which belonged to the male side of the family." (317 cs) In French-speaking New Orleans he was called *du homme* (or *l'Homme* or *de l'Homme*), from which came Doom, the name he was later called by the People. All the stories agree that Doom returned from New Orleans with, among other things, a wicker basket full of puppies and a small gold box filled with white powder, which, when administered to a puppy, would quickly kill it. Soon afterwards, his uncle, the Man, and the Man's son both died suddenly, and the Man's brother refused to accept the chieftainship which was his hereditary right; Doom, as the next in line of succession, became the Man. Beyond this point, however, the legend of Doom has variants. In "A Justice" Sam Fathers tells young Quentin Compson how Doom came back from New Orleans and succeeded to the chieftainship. After becoming the Man, Doom took some of the People to drag out a steamboat that had died in the Tallahatchie River twelve miles away and bring it back to the Plantation, where Doom could use the boat as his house. One of the People, Craw-ford (sometimes called Crawfish-ford) stayed at home complaining of a bad back in order to be near one of the black women Doom had brought with him from New Orleans. The woman, although married to a black man, later gave birth to a copper-colored son; Doom settled the quarrel between Craw-ford and the black man and named the child Had-Two-Fathers—the full name of Sam Fathers. In "The Old People," however, Sam Fathers says that he is the son of Doom and a quadroon slave; in this variant of the legend Doom married the pregnant slave to a black man and named the baby Had-Two-

Fathers. In both versions Doom sells the mother and child to a neighboring white man—in the former story to Lucius Quintus Carothers McCaslin, in the latter to Quentin McLachan Compson II.

The order of succession of the Chickasaw chiefs is not consistent, due to variants of the legend. In "Red Leaves" Doom is the father of Issetibbeha, who succeeds him as the Man, and the grandfather of Moketubbe. In this variant Issetibbeha became the Man at nineteen. During his chieftainship there arose the problem of what to do with the Negro slaves acquired during his father's lifetime; the question was finally solved by having the Negroes clear the land and plant grain, which the Indians sold. From the sale of grain and slaves Issetibbeha acquired the money to travel to France; he returned with

> a gilt bed, a pair of girandoles by whose light it was said that Pompadour arranged her hair while Louis smirked at his mirrored face across her powdered shoulder, and a pair of slippers with red heels. They were too small for him, since he had not worn shoes at all until he reached New Orleans on his way abroad. (320 cs)

Issetibbeha's son Moketubbe, a fat, squat, indolent boy, developed a fondness for the high-heeled slippers that amounted almost to fetishism. The influence of the white man, direct or otherwise, had by this time subtly corrupted the Indians: they had come to own slaves, to sell their produce for money, and to buy and cherish useless ornaments. Moketubbe, the last of their chiefs, who succeeded to the chieftainship after Issetibbeha's death, was nothing more than a sweating mound of flesh, too lazy even to want to take his traditional place in the manhunt to capture the escaped slave who, as Issetibbeha's body servant, was required to be buried with him.

In "The Old People" a version of the legend is given that appears to be more reliable in view of later facts. Here Doom is the son of the sister of old Issetibbeha, the ruling Man. When Doom returned after his seven-year visit to New Orleans, he found that Issetibbeha had died and been succeeded by his son, Moketubbe. The day after Doom's return, Moketubbe's eight-year-old son died suddenly and Moketubbe himself abdicated, having been shown by Doom how quickly Doom's white powder would dispatch a puppy. Doom became the Man in 1807. The early settlers of the county are reported to have bought or bartered land from Ikkemotubbe (Doom) between 1810 and 1835—the years during which Doom would have been the Man had he succeeded to the chieftainship in 1807.

During the 1830s the Indians were dispossessed and began to move to Oklahoma. About twenty-five years earlier, the first white men had arrived in Jefferson, then only a Chickasaw trading post in the wilderness. The earliest settlers were Alexander Holston, who accompanied Dr. Samuel Habersham and the latter's eight-year-old motherless son, and Louis

Grenier, a Huguenot "younger son" who acquired a vast plantation in the southeastern part of the county and became the first cotton planter. Holston became the "first publican, establishing the tavern still known as the Holston House," and Dr. Habersham "became the settlement itself . . . for a time, before it was named the settlement was known as Doctor Habersham's then Habersham's, then simply Habersham." (182, RFN) After Holston's death the county remembered his name in the tavern he had owned. When Grenier died, his mansion and his estate fell into ruin and even his name was forgotten; but his property gave the name to the hamlet of Frenchman's Bend, and his house was known as the Old Frenchman place long after Grenier himself had passed from public memory.

Another early settler was Lucius Quintus Carothers McCaslin, who was born in Carolina in 1772 and who arrived in the county in 1813. He brought with him a wife and three children—the twins, Theophilus (Uncle Buck) and Amodeus (Uncle Buddy), and a daughter. McCaslin acquired land from Ikkemotubbe in the northeastern part of the county, seventeen miles from what was to become Jefferson, and began to build a great house which was never completely finished. He had brought some slaves with him from Carolina, but made a special trip to New Orleans and came home with a female slave named Eunice who bore him a daughter, Tomey, in 1810. Some twenty years later Tomey bore her master—and father—a son, Terrel, known as Tomey's Turl. Again from Ikkemotubbe (in exchange for a horse) McCaslin acquired a quadroon slave and her son, the infant Sam Fathers, who was to grow to manhood and live to old age on the McCaslin plantation in the anomalous position of carpenter and hunter, not black and not slave and yet not white and not free. He lived to be the last descendant of Ikkemotubbe remaining in the county and was to become the mentor and guide of young Isaac McCaslin, old McCaslin's only white grandson to bear his name.

A few years later, in 1811, Jason Lycurgus Compson I came down the Natchez Trace toward the Chickasaw agency that was to become Jefferson, owning little besides a pair of pistols and the fine little racing mare he rode. Within a year he was half-owner of the store and trading post; within another year he had traded the mare to Ikkemotubbe, or Doom, for a "square mile of what was to be the most valuable land in the future town of Jefferson." (185, RFN) He built his house and his slave quarters and his stables, and the property, which came to be known as Compson's Mile or Compson's Domain, housed his successors: Quentin MacLachan Compson II, his son, who was, even if for a short time, a governor of Mississippi; Quentin's son, Jason II, a brigadier general in the Civil War, who put the first mortgage on the property in 1866; and his son in turn, Jason III, a lawyer, who sold part of the property in 1909 to pay for his son Quentin III's tuition at Harvard. Of Jason's four children—Quentin III, Candace,

Jason IV, and Benjy—only Jason remained long enough to see the final dissolution of the property and house and even the name, which would die with him, that had been illustrious in the county for almost one hundred years.

After Jason I came Dr. Peabody, old Dr. Habersham's successor, a preacher named Whitfield, and a new post trader named Ratcliffe. There was also a man named Pettigrew, who, though his surname was later forgotten, contributed his first name at the christening of the new town:

> 'We're going to have a town,' Peabody said. 'We already got a church—that's Whitfield's cabin. And we're going to build a school too soon as we get around to it. But we're going to build the courthouse today. . . . Then we'll have a town. We've already even named her.'
>
> Now Pettigrew stood up, very slowly. They looked at one another. After a moment Pettigrew said, 'So?'
>
> 'Ratcliffe says your name's Jefferson,' Peabody said.
>
> 'That's right,'' Pettigrew said. 'Thomas Jefferson Pettigrew. I'm from old Ferginny.'
>
> [Peabody said] 'We decided to name her Jefferson.' Now Pettigrew didn't seem to breathe even. He just stood there, small, frail, less than boy-size, childless and bachelor, incorrigibly kinless and tieless. (193, RFN)

Soon after Jefferson was named, in the early 1830s, a mysterious stranger named Thomas Sutpen arrived in town, causing some local stir because of his silence regarding his antecedents and the wagonload of twenty wild French-speaking Negroes and the dapper little French architect who accompanied him. Sutpen, the son of a West Virginia poor white, had conceived a "grand design" of becoming a member of the ruling aristocracy, and, in pursuance of his dream, had first married the daughter of a Haitian sugar-plantation owner. When he discovered—too late—that his wife had Negro blood and would thus prevent him from ever taking his desired place in Southern society, he divorced her and left Haiti, taking with him only the slaves and his French architect. Sutpen arrived in Mississippi and bartered or bought from Ikkemotubbe a hundred square miles of fertile bottom land near the Tallahatchie. He spent two years clearing the land and building his plantation house, which was to be, for a time, the grandest in the county. When his house was finished and furnished, Sutpen bargained with Goodhue Coldfield, a Jefferson merchant, for the hand of Ellen, his oldest daughter. She became Sutpen's wife and the mother of two children, Henry and Judith, who, in Sutpen's dream, were to provide him with grandchildren to carry on his name and inhabit his house after his own demise. But Charles Bon, Sutpen's son by his first marriage, met and became an intimate friend of young Henry Sutpen; Henry brought Charles home, where, largely through the machinations of Ellen Sutpen,

Charles became engaged to Judith. Henry later discovered that Charles was his half-brother and part Negro, and, horrified at the idea of miscegenation even more than incest, shot Charles at the gate of Sutpen's Hundred to prevent the marriage. Sutpen returned from the Civil War, where he had replaced Colonel Sartoris as head of his regiment, to find his daughter "confirmed in spinsterhood" and his son a vanished fugitive. He tried to obtain a male heir to carry on his name by seducing the granddaughter of Wash Jones, his poor-white handyman, but the girl gave birth to a daughter; Jones killed Sutpen, the girl, her infant, and himself.

A few years after Sutpen arrived there was another newcomer, a man named John Sartoris, who came from Carolina with slaves and money. He bought land and built his house four miles north of Jefferson; in 1861 he would "stand in the first Confederate uniform the town had ever seen, while in the Square below the Richmond mustering officer enrolled . . . the regiment which Sartoris as its colonel would take to Virginia." (203, RFN) Intertwined with the saga of the Sartorises, the family most representative of all that was heroic and romantic in the ante-bellum South, is the beginning of the history of the Snopeses, a numerous clan of mean and avaricious poor whites who swooped down on the county like buzzards in the early years of the twentieth century. Ab Snopes, the first of the line, made his appearance during the Civil War as a horse and mule thief operating on both Yankee and Confederate troops. Although he began by aiding Colonel Sartoris' mother-in-law, Rosa Millard, in "requisitioning" animals from both armies, he was at least partially responsible for her death at the hands of a band of lawless poor whites. There were other names linked with that of the Sartoris family through violence, such as the Burdens of New Hampshire, fiery abolitionists who had come to Jefferson during Reconstruction. Two Burdens, grandfather and grandson, were shot in the Square on Election Day by Colonel Sartoris, encouraged by Drusilla Hawk as they were on their way to their wedding. Later Sartoris entered a partnership with Ben Redmond in order to build a railroad that would bisect the county. The two men quarreled, the partnership was dissolved, and Redmond finally shot and killed Sartoris after the latter had run against him—and won—in the election to the state legislature. After Sartoris' death the honorary title of Colonel was bestowed on his son Bayard, who became president of the bank in Jefferson. Bayard's son John (whose history is not recorded) married and fathered twin sons named John and Bayard; John was killed in the First World War, and Bayard was responsible both for the death of his grandfather in an automobile accident and for his own death soon after, when, in Ohio, he tested an airplane that he knew to be unsafe.

Shortly after the end of the Civil War, a young man named Lucius Priest arrived in Mississippi from Carolina. A distant kinsman of old

Lucius Quintus Carothers McCaslin, Priest sought out the Yoknapatawpha County branch of his family and found Sarah Edmonds, the great-grand-daughter of old McCaslin. The two branches of the family were joined when he and Sarah married in 1869. Lucius came to be a solid and respected townsman; by the turn of the century he was the president of the Bank of Jefferson, the town's first bank, and was known as Boss Priest. His son Maury married Alison Lessup, the daughter of Boss Priest's old friend and schoolmate; Maury and Alison had three children, Lucius, Maury, Jr., and Alexander.

Besides the McCaslins, Compsons, Sutpens, and Sartorises, there were other families of somewhat less distinction and importance. The Beauchamps, brother and sister, intermarried with Yoknapatawpha County people even though they lived in a neighboring county. Miss Sophonsiba Beauchamp married Uncle Buck McCaslin. The name Beauchamp itself was later borne by the Negro part of the McCaslin family, stemming from Tennie Beauchamp, the slave won from Hubert Beauchamp by Uncle Buddy in a poker game and married to old McCaslin's Negro son, Tomey's Turl. The Coldfields, though their name died with the spinster Miss Rosa Coldfield in 1910, were once respected and relatively prosperous in the early days in Jefferson. The Stevenses were a pioneer family whose line bore its finest fruit after the Civil War in the person of Gavin Stevens, county attorney, Phi Beta Kappa at Harvard and Ph.D. from Heidelberg. There were the Benbows, whose family included a county judge, a lawyer (the judge's son Horace), and a girl, Narcissa, who married into the Sartoris family and bore a male heir just before her husband, the last male Sartoris, met his rash and untimely end. The De Spains boasted a major in the Civil War, a president of the bank in Jefferson, and Jefferson's most stately mansion.

In the pine hills of the district to the north, known as Beat Four, and in Frenchman's Bend, twenty miles southeast of Jefferson, there sprang up a very different breed of people from the pre-Civil War aristocrats—self-made or otherwise—of Jefferson and its environs. The inhabitants of Frenchman's Bend had come

> from the northeast, through the Tennessee mountains by stages marked by the bearing and raising of a generation of children. They came from the Atlantic seaboard and before that, from England and the Scottish and Welsh Marches. . . . They took up land and built one- and two-room cabins and never painted them, and married one another and produced children . . . and their descendants still planted cotton in the bottom land and corn along the edge of the hills and in the secret coves in the hills made whiskey of the corn and sold what they did not drink . . . there was not one Negro landowner in the entire section. Strange Negroes would absolutely refuse to pass through it after dark. (5, H)

At about the turn of the twentieth century the old Frenchman place was owned by sixty-year-old Will (Uncle Billy) Varner, who, aside from being the biggest landowner, owned the store, cotton gin and grist mill, and blacksmith shop, and came close to running—if not actually owning—the town itself. The store was managed by Varner's thirty-year-old bachelor son, Jody, and it was to Jody that Ab Snopes applied to rent a farm for the season. This event marked the beginning of the influx of Snopeses into the county. Hearing that Ab Snopes had set fire to Major De Spain's barn some years previously and fearing a similar fate for Varner property, Jody installed Ab's son Flem as a clerk in Varner's store as a kind of peace offering—or perhaps a bribe. Soon Flem began importing and installing various cousins in the county: Eck Snopes, who became the blacksmith; I. O. Snopes, who was for a time the schoolteacher; Ike Snopes, an idiot and Flem's ward; Mink Snopes, another tenant farmer; and others. Eck married the daughter of the family at whose house he boarded, promptly fathered a son, named Admiral Dewey, and produced another, older son from a previous marriage—Wallstreet Panic. The Snopeses multiplied, to the discomfiture of various members of the local citizenry—Jack Houston, Henry Armstid, Vernon Tull, and others.

In less than five years Flem had risen from a clerkship at Varner's store to become an owner of cattle and a barn, a party to various quick and profitable sales, and a petty usurer—turning his hand, in short, to any reasonably lawful money-getting enterprise. As a kind of climax to his career in Frenchman's Bend, he married Eula, the beautiful and much sought-after daughter of Will Varner. The marriage, though one of convenience (Eula was pregnant by another man and Flem was impotent), brought Flem the deed to the Old Frenchman Place and a considerable sum of money—both wedding presents, or perhaps bribes, of his new father-in-law—as well as social position as a relative of the most important man in town. Following his wedding and a lengthy Texas honeymoon, Flem moved his family—Eula and her daughter, Linda, who bore the name of Snopes legally if not otherwise—to Jefferson, where Flem became superintendent of the town power plant. Again, as he had done in Frenchman's Bend, Flem quickly moved up to bigger and better positions, and imported more Snopes cousins.

Shortly after the turn of the century—about the time that Flem Snopes arrived in Jefferson—it was beginning to be apparent that the old aristocracy was fighting a losing battle for survival. Their decline was partially due to the difficulty of maintaining plantations without slave labor and to the trying days of Reconstruction. More important, though, was the inability of the once-great planters to come to terms with the post-bellum world. They persisted in trying to live by the economic and moral standards they had known before the war, and they raised their children and grandchildren to believe in these standards, thus rendering them, too, unable to cope with the realities of the twentieth century. It was as if a kind of internal decay, begun in the old aristocracy after the war, was gradually destroying both its strength and its moral fiber. By 1920 not a single member of the greatest prewar families was left who was able to assume a position of leadership in the county.

Thomas Sutpen's family, perhaps the most outrageously unfortunate, had come to an end, as far as most of Jefferson knew, with Sutpen's death in 1869; yet three of Sutpen's descendants, and one of his relatives by marriage, survived forty years more. In 1909 Miss Rosa Coldfield, Sutpen's sister-in-law, discovered Sutpen's son Henry ill and hiding in the old plantation house, cared for by his Negro half-sister, Clytie. Miss Rosa summoned an ambulance in an attempt to take Henry to the Jefferson hospital, but Clytie, thinking that the authorities had come to take Henry to prison for the murder of Charles Bon over fifty years before, set fire to the house over her own and Henry's heads. All that was left were the smoking ashes of the once-great house and an idiot Negro named Jim Bond, the great-grandson of Sutpen, who disappeared and was never heard of again.

By 1910 the Compson fortunes had also declined severely. Of the four children of Jason III, Benjy was an idiot, Candace (Caddy) a promiscuous girl who was hastily married to provide a father for the child she carried, Quentin a suicide, and Jason IV a petty, rapacious man whose mind and temperament were more like those of the Snopeses than of the Compsons. Caddy brought her daughter Quentin (named for Caddy's dead brother) back to Jefferson to be raised by the family, and she herself disappeared. Quentin also disappeared, running off with a traveling carnival man at seventeen, and the name of Compson came to an end in Jason IV, a childless bachelor, who sold the property to Flem Snopes during the 1940s.

Although the McCaslin family, particularly as represented by Uncle Buck and Uncle Buddy, had laid no claim to aristocracy, it too—or at least the white branch of it—was beginning to die out. The only male McCaslin to bear the name was Isaac, who, at the end of the First World War, was a childless widower. The McCaslin property, however, was owned by the Edmondses, the descendants of old McCaslin's daughter. Isaac had refused to accept his share, and the property had gone to his cousin McCaslin (Cass) Edmonds, the great-grandson of old Carothers McCaslin, and was passed on to Edmonds' son and grandson in turn. The Edmondses leased it to tenant farmers and set apart a section for Lucas Beauchamp, the Negro grandson of the first McCaslin. The South, and in particular the Old South, still considered descent on the female side to be of lesser strength and importance than lineal descent on the male side—the side which, after all, bore the family name. Thus, although the descendants of McCaslin's Negro son Turl and his wife Tennie Beauchamp bore the family name of Beauchamp, they were in one sense more legitimate heirs of the first Mc-

Caslin than were the white descendants of McCaslin's daughter. Furthermore, because Turl's mother was also the daughter of McCaslin, Turl's descendants were two generations closer to McCaslin. Thus Lucas Beauchamp, who was born in 1874, was McCaslin's grandson, while Zack Edmonds, who was born in 1873, was McCaslin's great-great-grandson. The Negro side of the family, which outnumbered the white members three to one, was again joined with the white side in the illicit union of Roth Edmonds and the great-granddaughter of Turl in 1940. Since Roth did not marry the girl, the child remained nameless, and the name of Edmonds came to an end with Roth.

In 1920 only one male Sartoris remained alive: Benbow Sartoris, the infant son of Narcissa Benbow and the late John Sartoris III. Colonel Bayard Sartoris, who died in 1919, had been succeeded as bank president by Manfred de Spain, a descendant of Major de Spain. However, through the machinations of Flem Snopes, De Spain was later driven from town as the result of a scandal over Flem's wife, Eula, and Flem moved into the bank presidency and the De Spain mansion.

There were, however, a few descendants of Jefferson's first settlers who came into prominence in the twentieth century. Among them were V. K. Ratliff, a descendant of the original Ratcliffe of Jefferson's early history, who became a sewing-machine salesman in four counties and a more reliable purveyor of information and local gossip than any newspaper. Gavin Stevens returned from Heidelberg and began to assist his father, Judge Lemuel Stevens, before setting up his own law office and finally becoming county attorney. His second cousin, young Gowan Stevens, was growing up and would soon boast his University of Virginia education and his ability (more boast than fact) to hold his liquor like a man. Gavin's sister, Margaret, married Charles Mallison and bore a son, Chick, who grew up to play his part in the unfolding saga of the county.

The 1930s saw the influx of a number of strangers in Jefferson, and the town became the scene of some violence and at least one tragicomic episode, the burial of Addie Bundren. The Bundrens were poor-white farmers who lived just south of the Yoknapatawpha River, but Addie Bundren had originally come from Jefferson, and her people were buried there. She had made her husband, Anse, promise to bury her with her kinsfolk when she died, and, in accordance with his promise (and a few ulterior desires of his own), Anse and the rest of the family—Cash, Darl, Jewel, Dewey Dell, and Vardaman—began the trip with Addie's body, despite the July heat and the flood-swollen river. After a nine-day journey the family and its putrescent burden arrived in Jefferson, where Addie was finally buried, and where Anse promptly acquired a new wife.

Also during the thirties Lena Grove arrived in Jefferson, having walked from Alabama, far gone in pregnancy and in search of Lucas Burch, the lover who had deserted her. She could not find her truant lover, who, under the name of Joe Brown, was sharing a cabin with another newcomer to the town, Joe Christmas, on the property of Joanna Burden, the spinster descendant of the Northern abolitionists killed by Colonel John Sartoris. Joe and Lucas peddled illicit liquor, among other things, and were regarded— as was Miss Burden—with suspicion by the townsfolk. Joe, who appeared to be white but maintained that he had Negro blood, murdered Miss Burden after she attempted to convert him and threatened him with a pistol. He promptly became the object of a manhunt by the outraged townfolk, who forgot their suspicion of the Northern woman and accepted her as the symbol of Southern womanhood violated and murdered by a "nigger." Leading the manhunt was a young and belligerent deputy, Percy Grimm, who was descended from a Snopes girl, and who cornered, castrated, and finally killed Joe.

The thirties was a violent era for the county, as well as for Jefferson. During that time an amoral and vicious creature known as Popeye began to do business with Lee Goodwin, a moonshiner living in the old Frenchman place. There Popeye murdered a simple-minded white man and raped Temple Drake, an irresponsible and provocative college girl from Jackson, who had been brought to Goodwin's place by her drunken escort, Gowan Stevens. In an attempt to pin the murder on Goodwin, Popeye took the unresisting Temple, the only witness, to a brothel in Memphis where he could keep an eye on her. Despite the efforts of Horace Benbow to clear Goodwin, he was tried, convicted, and lynched by the angry townspeople. Temple later married a somewhat reformed and matured Gowan Stevens, all the while maintaining the fiction that she was forcibly detained in the brothel, an innocent victim of a pervert and murderer.

The forties, somewhat quieter than the years between the two wars, saw greater triumphs of Snopesism and of the "progress" associated with, if not actually related to, Snopes avarice: mechanization and standardization, the substitution of mechanical and commercial values for human ones. Jefferson was teeming with Snopeses; Flem Snopes, who had bought the Compson property and had it subdivided, moved into the De Spain mansion and became president of the Merchants and Farmers Bank. Ironically, it was another Snopes—Mink—who, feeling he had been wronged by his cousin forty years before, was responsible for Flem's ultimely end.

A different incident served to spotlight the barrier between Negro and white that had existed since the days of slavery and had grown worse since Reconstruction. Lucas Beauchamp, old Carothers McCaslin's Negro grandson, had long irritated the townsfolk by his independence and his refusal to accept the attitude of servility adopted by the Negroes. When he was accused of murdering one of the Gowries, a fierce hill clan of poor whites living in Beat Four, no one but a boy, Chick Mallison, and an old lady,

Miss Eunice Habersham, even thought to question Lucas' guilt, let alone
try to prove him innocent.

Thus, over a period of more than a hundred years, a pattern of life in
Yoknapatawpha County emerges, a whole small society is seen in terms of
struggle and aspiration and development. The vitality and even perhaps the
grandeur of pre-Civil War days is contrasted with the impotence and
sterility of the present, but it must be remembered that the wrongs committed by the old aristocrats have been, almost literally, visited upon those
that came after them. Before the coming of the white man, the Indians had
considered the land to be the private property of no one, to be enjoyed in
common by all. The settlers brought with them two crucial concepts—that
of private property and that of slavery. It is to the outgrowths of these two
concepts that almost all the evils of their society can be traced. Ante-bellum
life, built on slavery and property, contained within it the seeds of its own
ruin. Unfortunately, the positive aspects of that life—courage, gallantry,
and graciousness—were also destroyed, and a residue of evils remained and
persisted into the present—artificial social distinctions, greed, and a regard
for the appearance, but not the fact, of respectability.

Both the economy and the morality of the Old South were built upon
the concepts of private property and slavery, the juncture of which resulted
in the formation of a society and a ruling aristocracy. The saga of Yoknapatawpha County suggests that a society built upon a precept that ignores
the common humanity of mankind and establishes a morality and an economy that place social and economic codes above human values is doomed
to fail. Thus Sutpen, who rejected his part-Negro wife and son in order
to conform to a social code that abhorred miscegenation, failed to fulfill his
dream of becoming a founder of a great family. Thus Quentin Compson,
who placed the abstract idea of honor above the reality of his sister as a
human being, was driven to suicide. The end of slavery spelled the end of
the plantation economy, but the economy that replaced it was represented
by men like Jason Compson and Flem Snopes, whose values were mercenary rather than humanistic, whose morality consisted in adhering to the
letter but not the spirit of the law, and to whom other men were tools to
be manipulated for profit.

A Note on Faulkner's Style

FAULKNER'S STYLE, initially the bane and despair of critics, and more recently the subject of several excellent but fairly tentative essays and articles, is without doubt as important an element in the novelist's craft as are the themes that are found, in various guises, throughout his work. Indeed, the style is almost in itself a theme, a motif, emphasizing by means of technique alone the contradictory and essentially irresolvable conflicts present in the subject matter. The problems of achieving a unity of form (the way in which an idea is presented) and content (the idea itself) are more often found in the literary analysis of poetry than of the novel, at least in its more traditional forms. To speak of such a unity in Faulkner's work immediately suggests the experimental nature of much of Faulkner's writing and points to certain stylistic effects that have much in common with the aims of poetic expression.

The province of poetry, in the main, is emotional rather than intellectual. Any such generalization necessarily distorts the facts to a degree. Nevertheless, it may be said that poetry tends to be successful *as poetry* in inverse ratio to its easy reducibility to a logical statement of fact. It is not that poetry is *ipso facto* unclear, but that, in seeking to apprehend the profound realities of human existence, it tends toward paradox, toward the logically inexplicable, toward a union of opposites that creates a metaphysical tension and contains in this fusion a truth that is perhaps essentially inexpressible. The emotional impact of a poem is at least as much formal as it is contextual, that is, the arrangement of words contributes as much as, if not more than, the precise meanings of those words. The literal and logical meaning of a poem operates on only one level—and that perhaps the most superficial one. The essence of a poem, its total effect and most profound meaning, lies in a variety of interacting modalities: primarily, the tension between form and content that gives the sense of being contained only under immense pressure, because the fusion of words generates a power that the formal structure can scarcely handle. A good poem maintains a precarious balance in which the emotional content constantly threatens to escape the formal bounds that have created it and give it identity.

In appealing to emotional—or perhaps visceral—understanding more than to purely intellectual apprehension, the poem demands the participation of the reader, a kind of commitment to the poetic experience that transcends the mere identification of the reader with a character in a novel.

At its best, the poem does not simply capture a mood or an experience, but creates in a different and more permanent form the ever-shifting and never totally apprehensible flux of life itself.

These characteristics of poetry apply equally to the bulk of Faulkner's work. In an age when the novel has generally tended toward a hard spareness of style and a meticulous rendering of objective detail, Faulkner has persistently maintained his own voice, indifferent to critical jibes at his unstylish verbosity, his romantic rhetoric, his lush obscurity, and his long, involuted sentences. There is little question that much of the early, strongly unfavorable criticism of Faulkner stemmed from the simple fact that his work is not easy to read. Critics of the 1930s, used to the pruned prose of the Hemingway school or the obvious sociological bent of the then blooming proletarian realists, bogged down ingloriously in his marathon sentences and pronounced him a "bad writer." Others saw no obvious sociological message in his writing, and therefore informed the public that he wrote of perversion, idiocy, and depravity for their own sake. It seems difficult, at this point, to take these accusations seriously, or even to understand how they could have been made. Faulkner is undoubtedly difficult to read—the most difficult of contemporary American writers. If he is obscure, however, it is never for the sake of obscurity itself; if his writing is occasionally over-rich, it is rarely so as a result of his intoxication with his own virtuosity. Faulkner started out as a poet in the formal sense. In turning to fiction, he took with him the impetus toward poetic expression that had first moved him to write, and found a technique in which the aims of poetry were largely retained in fictional form.

Conrad Aiken, writing in 1939, was the first to perceive the basic purpose behind what is usually considered Faulkner's obscurity: it is an "elaborate method of deliberately withheld meaning . . . a calculated system of screens and obtrusions, of confusions and ambiguous interpolations and delays, with one express purpose . . . to keep the form—and the idea—fluid and unfinished, still in motion, as it were, and unknown, until the dropping into place of the very last syllable." (138 TD) This sense of formal motion is as crucial to an understanding of Faulkner's technique as the identification of life with motion and change is basic to his subject matter. In writing of the hunt, for instance (particularly in the stories in Go Down, Moses), he uses the content of the story to underline the theme that all life, as long as it remains vital, is a kind of pursuit. In much of his writing, whether it deals with the metaphor of the hunt or not, the style conveys this same sense of the fluidity and ever-shifting motion of living experience.

The idea of motion as a technical recreation of the fluidity of life can be said to be the basic determinant of Faulkner's style. The techniques through which this sense of motion is achieved in form are seen at their most elaborate and most successful in *Absalom, Absalom!*, although they are present in varying degrees in the majority of his novels.

The traditional novel ordinarily operates on a linear basis in which characters are introduced, conflicts set up, and resolution achieved, frequently with due regard to chronology. In contrast to this Faulkner's novels can best be seen in terms of overlapping circles, with a point of entry that is not, strictly speaking, a beginning, but simply a point in time in which the novelist has chosen to intercept his characters. Faulkner has not merely disordered the chronology of his plot. The chronology may be reconstructed after the fact, but piecing together the events can convey only the facts of the story, not its essence as a recreation of life that Faulkner has given it. The circularity of narration, particularly in *Absalom, Absalom!*, has a very definite purpose: to immerse the reader in the living flow of the narrators' consciousness of Sutpen and, by extension, to capture for a moment out of time a living image of the mind of the South as reflected in the characters of Sutpen, Miss Rosa Coldfield, Mr. Compson, and Quentin.

In an interesting study of Faulkner's rhetoric Walter J. Slatoff * has suggested that Faulkner has deliberately left his works in a state of suspension and irresolution; this is reflected stylistically in his use of paradox, oxymoron, the juxtaposition of mutually exclusive conditions such as sound and silence, stillness and frantic motion, and so forth. Mr. Slatoff finds the lack of resolution at the end of the novels intended "to leave the reader with a high degree of emotional and intellectual tension" (190 TD) analogous to the tension conveyed by the union of contradictory ideas in the oxymoron. Stylistically, of course, Faulkner's use of paradox and polarity is related to the technique of deliberately withheld meaning, of keeping the form in motion. Contextually, it underlines Faulkner's unwillingness to commit himself to final answers, to offer anything more positive than the ambiguous final statement of the Runner in *A Fable*, or the vague injunction to "believe" of Nancy in *Requiem for a Nun*, or even the eloquent but essentially unspecific statement of his own faith in man's capacity to endure in the Nobel Prize address. This, however, is not to say that Faulkner is either pessimistic or uncommitted. Rather, it seems to indicate his profound awareness of the impossibility of ever completely resolving, at least more than temporarily, the dualities of existence.

---

* Cf. his essay "The Edge of Order: The Pattern of Faulkner's Rhetoric" in *Three Decades of Criticism*, and his full-length study *Quest for Failure* (Cornell University Press, 1960).

The Novels

SARTORIS [1929]

Characters [living]

COLONEL BAYARD SARTORIS, president of a bank, aged sixty-nine
VIRGINIA [MISS JENNY] SARTORIS DUPRE, Colonel Bayard's aunt, aged eighty
BAYARD SARTORIS, Colonel Bayard's grandson, aged twenty-six
NARCISSA BENBOW, later Bayard's wife
HORACE BENBOW, Narcissa's brother
WILL FALLS, a friend of the late Colonel John Sartoris, aged ninety-three
BYRON SNOPES, a bank clerk

Characters [dead]

COLONEL JOHN SARTORIS [1823–76], Colonel Bayard's father
BAYARD SARTORIS [1838–62], Colonel John's brother
JOHNNY SARTORIS [1893–1918], Colonel John's great-grandson and twin
brother of the youngest (living) Bayard

Faulkner's third novel, *Sartoris* was his first book to deal with Yoknapatawpha County and its people, the "postage stamp" of land so like that in which Faulkner spent his life. In *Sartoris* are found characters and themes—some only suggested, some almost completely drawn—of later Yoknapatawpha County stories, the raw material for the building of an entire fictional world. Structurally, however, it is one of Faulkner's weakest novels. The elements of the story are placed in propinquity to one another but never fully integrated; the lives of the characters are intertwined more by circumstances than by any necessity springing from character itself. As a result, the book is episodic, loosely tied together by the linking of temporal events and by the contrast between the remembered past glory of the Sartoris family and the actual present. Although the action takes place in 1919–20, the broad framework of the story embraces eighty years (from the Civil War to the 1920s) of the history of the Sartoris family.

The action begins in Jefferson in 1919, as Colonel Bayard and the elderly pauper Will Falls evoke the ghost of Colonel John Sartoris, dead fifty years. The family history, which is sketchily revealed through the reminiscences of the characters as the story progresses, is summarized below.

HISTORY OF THE SARTORIS FAMILY

John Sartoris arrived in Jefferson in the early 1830s, bought property four miles from town, and built his house. There, in 1850, his son Bayard was born. His mother-in-law, Mrs. Rosa Millard, came to live with him and raise the child, whose mother had died in giving birth. In 1861 Sartoris organized a regiment and, as its colonel, led it to Virginia; the following year, however, the regiment deposed him and elected Thomas Sutpen colonel. Sartoris, resentful of his men's defection, returned to Mississippi and organized a unit of irregulars. Just before the second battle of Manassas his rash and fiery young brother Bayard was killed in an attempt to raid a Yankee commissary tent for a tin of anchovies. Mrs. Rosa Millard was killed by the leader of a lawless band of local poor whites in 1864. Colonel Sartoris returned home at the end of the war with his dead wife's cousin, Drusilla Hawk, who had run away from home to fight for the Confederacy, and whom Sartoris soon married. He rebuilt his house, which had been burned by the Yankees, and led the county in resisting government Reconstruction policies by killing a pair of Northerners who were attempting to ensure the Negro right to vote and run for office. In 1869 his youngest sister, the widowed Virginia (Miss Jenny) DuPre, came from Carolina to live with him. His railroad, which connected with the railroad in Memphis and bisected the county north and south, was completed in 1873. He ran for the state legislature against his former railroad partner, Ben Redmond, now his rival and declared enemy, defeated him, and shortly afterwards was killed by him. Bayard, a young man of twenty-four, faced his father's killer unarmed the next day, thus repudiating the family code of violence and vengeance. Bayard married and begot a son, John; the latter married and fathered twin sons, John and Bayard, before his death in 1901. The twins, inseparable from childhood, were mischievous and harebrained, and had to be sent to separate colleges because of their pranks. At the outbreak of the First World War they joined the R.A.F. John was killed in 1918 when he rashly attacked a group of more powerful German planes.

PRESENT ACTION OF THE NOVEL

Bayard comes home from the war in the spring of 1919, still grief-stricken over his brother's death. Shortly after his arrival in Jefferson, he buys a powerful car, which he drives around the county with complete disregard for the safety either of himself or of others. Colonel Bayard, his grandfather, insists on riding with young Bayard wherever he goes, hoping by this tactic to force him to drive more slowly. Bayard, however, is seemingly bent on his own destruction. Forcibly borrowing a half-wild stallion, he rides it through the streets of Jefferson until the animal pitches him on his head on the concrete. Patched up by the doctor and told to go home, Bayard, with V. K. Suratt and another man, drives out to Frenchman's Bend where Suratt has a cache of whiskey. They pick up three Negro musicians and proceed to serenade every unmarried girl in town, including Narcissa Benbow. Bayard, finally nabbed by the sheriff, spends the night in jail.

In June Bayard begins to work on the plantation and, lulled by the rhythms of the earth, becomes for a time placid and almost normal. After sowing time is over, however, he takes to racing his car again, turns it over in a creek bed and breaks several ribs. During his convalescence, Narcissa Benbow comes to read to him and manages to extract from him a promise to behave himself in the future. After a short, strange courtship, he and Narcissa are married, and by early autumn Narcissa is with child. Bayard begins to go possum-hunting with the Negroes, but Narcissa is unable to share his interest. Again pursued by his old despair, he draws further away from her and goes hunting almost daily. Finally, he runs his car over a cliff while his grandfather is riding with him, and the old man, though otherwise unhurt, dies of a heart attack. Afraid to go home and face his family, Bayard takes refuge at the MacCallum place in the northeast part of the county, where he stays for several days, finding some measure of respite in his flight from himself in the MacCallums' quiet acceptance of him. The day before Christmas he heads north again, spending Christmas Eve in a barn and the following day with the Negro owner's poverty-stricken family. That evening he boards a train and disappears for several months, sending Miss Jenny an occasional postcard and two requests for money. Late in the spring he finds himself testing airplanes in Ohio and is killed flying a plane he knows to be unsafe. On the day of his death his son is born. The child is called John by Miss Jenny but christened Benbow by Narcissa.

Loosely linked to the Sartoris story are two subplots, one dealing with Narcissa's brother Horace Benbow and Belle Mitchell, the other with Narcissa and Byron Snopes, a clerk in the Sartoris bank. Horace, also just home from the war, becomes entangled with Belle Mitchell, a married woman with a young daughter, and consequently estranged from Narcissa, who despises Belle as having a "backstairs nature." Narcissa, meanwhile, has been the object of anonymous and obscene letters from Byron Snopes. Though advised by Miss Jenny to give them to the proper authorities so that their writer can be tracked down, Narcissa hides the letters. Just before her wedding, Snopes breaks into her room and steals the letters, then robs the bank and flees to Mexico.

The action of *Sartoris* is contained within the time between Bayard's return from the war and his death a year later; however, the book is not so much about any one Sartoris as it is about the *mythos* of the entire family, the legend, history, and tradition associated with the name. The very name Sartoris has in it not only a "glamorous fatality" but an obligation to its owner to live up to its traditions, to embody the ideas and ideals— courage, honor, foolhardiness, and glorious, violent death—of previous Sartorises. The opening of the novel emphasizes the extent to which the family is dominated by the past glory of its first representative in Jefferson, Colonel John Sartoris. Dead and freed "of time and flesh" he is a "far more palpable presence" than either his son, Colonel Bayard, or his old friend, Will Falls. The dead Colonel Sartoris is lifted in legend above the limitations and failings of life, and the legend of the past overshadows the more pallid actuality of the present.

The repetition of the names John and Bayard serve to emphasize the influence of dead Sartorises upon living ones. The first Bayard, called by Faulkner more of a nuisance than a black sheep, met his death at the hands of a frightened cook while gallantly abducting a can of anchovies from the Yankees—yet this "hare-brained prank" became the stuff out of which a legend of devil-may-care bravery and high spirits was woven for the edification of future Sartorises. Three generations later, Johnny Sartoris appears as a kind of reincarnation of the Civil War Bayard, complete with dangerous pranks and early death in war.

The twentieth-century Bayard is less an individual than a representative Sartoris who is unable to reconcile his tradition with the world in which he lives—his sense of having to act like a Sartoris with whatever little apprehension of individuality he has. The most obvious characteristic of Bayard is his overwhelming death wish, and this in turn is related to his inability to love, his irresponsibility, his total selfishness, and his isolation. His desire for death probably stems largely from his grief at his twin's death and guilt for his own failure to prevent that death, as well as guilt for simply being alive while Johnny is dead. More important, however, is his conviction, instilled from birth, that he is obliged to live and die according to the Sartoris tradition. Subconsciously unwilling to be forced into the Sartoris pattern, Bayard abjures all responsibility and sets about doing away with the life that he is unable to accept. His destruction is both a punishment of the Sartorises for demanding that he conform to the family pattern, and, ironically, a characteristic Sartoris impulsive and violent end.

Interwoven with the story of Bayard's search for death are the remembered scenes of past times now become legend—the first Bayard's exploits with Jeb Stuart, Colonel John Sartoris' coolheaded escape from the pursuing Yankees and his accidental and almost singlehanded capture of a Yankee camp—and the contrasting activities of characters in the periphery of Bayard's existence. Bayard's own character is more clearly defined by the implied comparison with both Horace Benbow, son of a Jefferson family of lawyers and judges, and Buddy MacCallum, youngest son of a hill man in the northeast part of the county. Like Bayard, Horace and Buddy have just returned from the war and are faced, in their own spheres, with the difficulty of readjusting to life in rural Mississippi. Buddy goes back to an uncomplex and wholesome existence close to the land. Horace, though he finds life more complicated and human relationships more painful, is able to discover something of value in the small, almost perfect vases he makes with the glass-blowing set he brought back from Venice. Though he becomes a lawyer only out of loyalty to the family tradition, he gives in to the tradition gracefully and does his rather inadequate best. Unlike Bayard, he is reconciled to living in the mold cast for him by others, and is a man who loves words and thoughts, rather than action. Though Horace when he acts at all is conscious of the absurdity of the part he is playing, he still attempts to give direction to his life, whereas Bayard's actions are only noisily and childishly destructive.

Also contrasted to Bayard is Narcissa Benbow. It seems that she loves as well as hates him becauses he is able to disturb the otherwise unbroken calm of her existence. It is possible that Bayard marries her in the hope that her serenity will somehow be transferred to him. But Narcissa's beautiful tranquillity is a result of her total self-absorption, and she and Bayard remain spiritually as isolated as ever. Narcissa is, in many ways, the absolute antithesis of Bayard: whereas he is frantically fleeing from himself, she is immersed in herself. She strives to appear to be what others believe her to be—gentle, demure, above all "respectable," almost inviolate. Yet she secretly keeps the anonymous letters, perhaps partially because she cannot, as she says, bear to have people know that a man thought such things about her, but also for the secret pleasure she gains from having them.

Although Colonel John Sartoris embodies the swashbuckling and the glory of the Sartoris tradition, it is Miss Jenny who represents all that is most genuinely valuable. Strong, sensible, and eminently capable, she is able to reflect the best qualities of bygone days without living in the past or letting the past dominate the present. Yet Sartoris values, like the Sartorises themselves, are dying out in the modern world. No young woman in Jefferson in 1919—certainly not Narcissa or Belle—shows any sign of developing into a woman of Miss Jenny's stature. Faulkner seems to be suggesting that the traditions of the Old South, although maintained in theory after the Civil War and Reconstruction, were almost completely moribund by the end of the First World War, and were being replaced by the new morality of a mechanized civilization, one based on shrewdness rather than honor and gall rather than courage. This is suggested, but not delineated, in *Sartoris* by the presence of the Snopeses, a multitudinous family of vicious, cunning, animallike "red-necks" whose infiltration of Frenchman's Bend and Jefferson is related in *The Hamlet*, *The Town*, and *The Mansion*. Sartoris decline is accompanied by a rise in Snopes fortunes, so that, in 1919, Colonel Bayard Sartoris and Flem Snopes are president and vice-president of the same bank. But if the modern world is out of joint, it is at least partially because Sartoris values, though "better" than Snopes values, have somehow failed.

It is frequently assumed that the Sartoris tradition represents all that was good of ante-bellum society, that the past actions of the dead Sartorises overshadow those of the living because the deeds of the dead were morally good insofar as they were in accord with the accepted code of Southern society, whereas the acts of the living (particularly of young Bayard) stem from no coherent moral code whatsoever. To a limited degree, this assumption is true; certainly the younger characters—Bayard, Narcissa, Horace, and even to a degree Buddy MacCallum—are all more or less rootless. The traditions of their forebears are almost useless to them in the postwar world, and they themselves are completely incapable of formulating new traditions through which they can cope with their experience. As a result, each clings to a part of his past—Bayard to Sartoris violence, Narcissa to the appearance of virtue, and Horace to a blind belief in goodness—which has been falsified and emptied of significance in being separated from the tradition out of which it grew.

However, this is not to say that the morality of the Old South, the Sartoris tradition, is necessarily the best of all possible traditions. In the first place, it is death-oriented, looking to the past rather than the present or the future. Secondly, it is static; rather than evolving with time and change, fitting itself to the ever-renewing present and being remolded by the best of each generation, it became fixed at the end of the Civil War. Being static, it must, in order to survive, shape its inheritors to its lineaments, morally—and frequently physically—destroying them as individuals. Thus, regardless of the fact that the Sartoris tradition upheld honor, dignity, courage, and loyalty to one's own, in fact it offered nothing but death to every Sartoris bound by it. Only one, Colonel Bayard, refused to be shaped by it (Faulkner tells this story in "An Odor of Verbena" in *The Unvanquished*). It is significant, in view of this, that Colonel Bayard's death was considered by Miss Jenny to be a flouting of them all, that he had "committed lese majesty toward his ancestors and the lusty glamor of the family doom by dying . . . practically from the 'inside out.' " (297)

THE SOUND AND
THE FURY [1929]

Characters

JASON COMPSON III, *father of the four Compson children*
CAROLINE BASCOMB COMPSON, *his wife*
MAURY BASCOMB, *her brother*
CANDACE [CADDY] COMPSON [1891–   ], *eldest daughter of Jason and Caroline*
QUENTIN COMPSON [1889–1910], *eldest son of Jason and Caroline*
JASON COMPSON IV [1893–   ], *second son of Jason and Caroline*
BENJY COMPSON [1895–1935?], *an idiot, youngest son of Jason and Caroline*
QUENTIN COMPSON [1911–   ], *daughter of Caddy*

DILSEY, *the Compson's Negro cook*
FRONY, *Dilsey's daughter*
LUSTER, *Frony's son and Benjy's nurse boy*
T.P., *a Negro boy, an earlier nurse boy of Benjy's*
VERSH, *a Negro, Benjy's first nurse boy*
SHREVE MC CANNON, *Quentin's roommate at Harvard*
GERALD BLAND, *another Harvard student*
DALTON AMES, *the seducer of Caddy and the father of her daughter, Quentin*
SYDNEY HERBERT HEAD, *Caddy's first husband, an Indiana banker*
DAMUDDY, *the Compson children's grandmother, is often referred to but never appears as a character*

The Sound and the Fury, the major document of the Compson family, has no plot in the sense of sustained development of action following in a cause and effect manner. In four sections it deals with certain happenings within the family over a period of about thirty years. The first section, which takes place on Holy Saturday, 1928, focuses on the sense impressions of Benjy, an idiot of thirty-three. In the second, Quentin, Benjy's elder brother, lives through a day at Harvard, June 2, 1910. The third is seen through the eyes of Jason, two years Benjy's senior, on Good Friday, 1928. The fourth and final section, narrated objectively by the author, presents the household as it exists on Easter Sunday, 1928, but focuses on Dilsey and Jason.

The Compson family, which could claim a one-time governor of Mississippi (Quentin II) and a Civil War brigadier general (Jason II) among its ancestors, had, by the beginning of the twentieth century, fallen into decay. Jason Compson III, the father of the four central characters in the novel, was trained as a lawyer but gradually let his practice fall off and slipped gently into dipsomania. A basically uncritical, detached man, he now spends his time sitting in his old office or on the porch of the Compson house reading the Latin poets and making up satiric Latin verses about the local townsfolk. His wife, nee Caroline Bascomb, a neurotic, complaining woman, strives to maintain pretensions of gentility despite the decline of the family fortunes. She has very little love for any of her children except Jason IV, whom she considers her only "true" son, since in personality he is a Bascomb rather than a Compson. Her alcoholic and irresponsible brother Maury sponges off the entire household.

Past events of importance in the narrative include the following.

1898: The death of Damuddy.

1900: The recognition of Benjy's idiocy and the changing of his name from Maury (for Maury Bascomb, his uncle) to Benjamin.

1909: The selling of Benjy's pasture to the golf club to provide money to send Quentin to Harvard.

1910: Caddy's seduction by Dalton Ames.

1910: Caddy's marriage to Sydney Herbert Head (April 25).

1910: Quentin's suicide in Cambridge (June 2).

1911: Caddy's brief return to Jefferson to leave her infant daughter, named Quentin for Caddy's dead brother, to be raised by the Compson family.

1912: Jason III's death.

1913: Benjy's castration, insisted on by Jason, after Benjy had frightened a group of schoolgirls.

SECTION I: APRIL 7, 1928

This section is a recreation of experience as perceived by Benjy, an idiot, and is written in a stream-of-consciousness technique. Benjy reports both what he sees and what he remembers, without comment and without understanding its significance. Present events evoke memories by association, in no logical sequence; they enter his consciousness and are recorded as if they were occurring at the moment. Time, for Benjy, does not exist. For this reason, his section of the novel is sometimes difficult to follow. Some of the time shifts in Benjy's consciousness are indicated by passages in italics; these sometimes constitute a whole episode, at other times only introduce a part of a longer scene.

Present Events in Section I

It is the day before Easter and Benjy's thirty-third birthday; a traveling carnival is in town. Benjy's Negro nurse boy, Luster, takes him out by the fence of the golf links while Luster hunts for a quarter given to him the night before by his mother; without the quarter Luster cannot go to the carnival. The golf course takes up much of the old Compson pasture which Benjy loved and which Mr. Compson sold in 1909 to pay for Quentin's year at Harvard. Luster and Benjy wander down to the creek branch, where Luster meets and talks with a group of unnamed Negro friends. Luster and Benjy then go back to the house, where Benjy spies Quentin (Caddy's daughter) sitting in the porch swing with a carnival man who wears a red tie. Luster takes Benjy back to the pasture, where Luster tries to sell a golfer a golf ball for a quarter. The man takes the ball without paying him. Then Luster takes away Benjy's jimson weed and upsets the bottles of flowers in Benjy's "graveyard." They go into the house and Dilsey, Luster's grandmother, gives Benjy his birthday cake. In the kitchen, Benjy, who is fascinated by fire, puts his hand in the fire and burns himself. Supper is prepared. Luster begs Jason for a quarter, which Jason refuses. During dinner Jason and Quentin quarrel. Luster puts Benjy to bed and they watch Quentin climbing down the pear tree by her window.

Alterations Between Past and Present

As Luster and Benjy go through the fence to the golf course, Benjy snags himself on a nail and remembers a similar experience in the past: "*Caddy uncaught me and we crawled through.*" (24) About a dozen lines following are also in italics, indicating that Benjy's mind is reliving a past experience. The incidents of the following page and a half (not italicized) are a second memory recalled by the first, as the first was recalled by present occurrence. It ends with:

Keep your hands in your pockets, Caddy said. Or they'll get froze.

From this scene to Benjy's memory of another time associated with cold is an easy transition:

"It's cold out there." Versh said. "You don't want to go out doors."

The idea of cold forms the link, in Benjy's mind, between the two memories. The reader is given an additional clue to the time by the reference to Versh, Benjy's first nurse boy.

The next italicized segment indicates present time. Luster interrupts Benjy's memories by speaking to him, but Benjy soon slips back into his memory, and the two pages that follow continue Benjy's memories of the cold winter day, Versh, and Caddy as a child coming home from school.

As Versh is associated with the period from 1898, another nurse boy, named T.P., is associated with the time after 1910. When Luster (in italics) mentions the carriage house, Benjy recalls the period shortly after the death of Mr. Compson in 1912 when the family, with Benjy, took the carriage and drove once a week to the cemetery with flowers for the grave. Luster takes Benjy into the barn; it again reminds him of the winter day when Caddy had unsnagged him from the fence, and he continues his recollection of that day.

The reader should pay careful attention to the key words (such as "cold," "barn," later "flowers," and many others) that form the links between Benjy's memories or between present and past. Benjy's age and the approximate time of the events he remembers is always indicated by various references: the name of Benjy's then-current nurse boy, an incident (such as Damuddy's death or Caddy's wedding), or the age of another character (in one of Benjy's memories, Luster is an infant and Quentin a little girl; in another, Caddy is fourteen).

Benjy loves three things: Caddy, the pasture sold to the golf course, and fire. Caddy—that is, the Caddy of his childhood, who "smells like trees" and whose image remains clear and unchanging in his mind—is the stable center of Benjy's world. When she was present, he resisted the slightest external alteration in her, objecting with a wail when she wore perfume and no longer smelled like trees. Now that she is gone, he experiences a vague feeling of loss and cries at the mention of her name, but her memory is as real to him as her presence formerly was. Benjy's world is ordered, static, and timeless; any external event that threatens this order is greeted with an outraged howl, as when Luster drives to the left instead of the accustomed right of the Confederate monument in the town square of Jefferson.

SECTION II: JUNE 2, 1910

Since Benjy remembers only what he sees and hears, we must assume that his section of the novel, however incoherent, is factually accurate. Quentin's section, on the other hand, is told in the words and through the perceptions of a highly articulate, morbidly sensitive young man. It is sometimes not clear what he remembers and what he imagines. Like Benjy, Quentin is most concerned with Caddy—specifically, with her loss of virginity. Unlike Benjy, for whom time does not exist, Quentin is obsessed with time, as is evident by his constant references to clocks. By breaking his watch he tries to destroy time, but the watch, though mangled and smeared with his blood, refuses to stop ticking. Quentin is concerned with time on the day of his narrative primarily because he is planning to commit suicide in order to escape from time forever. As in Benjy's section, shifts in time are indicated by italics. Many of the long memory passages are easily recognizable by their lack of any punctuation at all.

Present events in Section II

Quentin awakens in his dormitory room at Harvard. He breaks the watch his father had given him, cuts himself on the broken crystal, packs his trunk, bathes and shaves, and is (deliberately) late for class. He goes out, has breakfast, takes his broken watch to a jeweler, but does not leave it; fascinated by the unwound clocks in the window, he asks the jeweler if any of them tell the right time. He then goes to a hardware store and buys a pair of flatirons. He boards a streetcar and gets off near the river, where he watches the water, on which a fellow student named Gerald Bland is sculling. He meets an old Negro porter named Deacon and gives him a letter to be delivered to his roommate, Shreve, the following day. He goes to the post office, meets Shreve, and gets on another trolley; getting off, he walks along the road until he comes to a bridge, where he meets and talks with three boys who are fishing. Then he goes to a bakery and buys some buns and meets a little Italian girl, who follows him; he tries to take her home, but she either will not or cannot tell him where she lives. He looks vainly for Anse, the local constable, to turn the child over to him. Finally Anse and the girl's brother, Julio, find Quentin and accuse him of kidnapping the child. Quentin is saved from the hysterical Julio by the appearance of a car containing two girls, Shreve, Gerald, Mrs. Bland, and Spoade, another student. With the Blands' party, Quentin goes on a picnic, where, apparently for no reason, he attacks Gerald and is badly beaten. He leaves the picnic, walks back along the river and gets a trolley, then returns to his room. He takes off his clothes, bloody from his fight with Gerald, sponges out the stains with gasoline, dresses, and goes out again.

These are the literal, physical "facts" of Quentin's day—seemingly trivial, unrelated to any particular focal point, and lacking in meaning. Their meaning becomes clear in the context of Quentin's thoughts which, from the beginning, are concerned with three things: time—which will not stop—sisters, and virginity. Quentin's disjointed thoughts are like pieces of a jigsaw puzzle that begin to fall into place as his day continues. Gradually his reveries supply more facts, giving coherence to details that had previously seemed meaningless. We learn, for instance, that Dalton Ames, whose name Quentin frequently repeats, was Caddy's seducer; that Quentin had once tried to avenge Caddy's honor by fighting with Ames, but failed miserably and fainted; that in his unprovoked attack on Gerald, Quentin, obsessed with his memories, was reliving this fight with Ames; that Caddy had met Sydney Herbert Head (whom she married and whom Quentin, with reason, detests) while vacationing with her mother at French Lick, Indiana; and that Quentin has tried to convince his father that he had committed incest with Caddy. Quentin commits suicide shortly after his narrative ends; the many references to water, the notes he leaves, and the flatirons he buys (he is particularly concerned with their weight) clearly indicate that he is planning to drown himself.

Not only is Quentin's world, like Benjy's, centered on Caddy, but he is equally incapable of adjusting to external realities. Attempting to preserve the moral code of the Old South, in which the honor of a family was equated with the chastity of its women, Quentin makes Caddy the repository of the Compson family honor. Although much is frequently made by critics of Quentin's incestuous desires toward his sister, according to the text he "loved not his sister's body but some concept of Compson honor precariously and (he knew well) only temporarily supported by the minute fragile membrane of her maidenhead. . . . [he] loved not the idea of the incest which he could not commit, but some presbyterian concept of its eternal punishment. . . . But [he] loved death above all, [he] loved only death." (9) Because he can neither accept a new code nor reject the moral code that invests value in a concept or a tradition rather than in human beings, Quentin chooses to kill himself so that Caddy's dishonor will die with his memory of it. Unable to reconcile reality with his rigid demands of what it should be, he removes himself irrevocably from the area of the conflict.

SECTION III: APRIL 6, 1928

In the first two sections Jason has been characterized, even as a child, as interested not in ideas, like Quentin, but in things—and particularly in their monetary value. In Benjy's section, the child Jason rejects Quentin's earlier gift of a bow and arrow on the grounds that it is now broken; since the object is now useless, the idea of the gift no longer exists. Similarly, Jason was often the treasurer in one or another childish enterprise, and is frequently described as keeping his fists in his pockets. As an adult, he is totally money-oriented, trusting no one and putting his faith only in money and the things it can buy. As Quentin blamed his own condition upon Caddy's failure to live up to his demands on her, so Jason blames Caddy for cheating him, Jason, of his promised career. Jason had hoped to become a banker through the influence of Caddy's first husband—a hope that came to nothing when the man divorced her within a year after their wedding. Since Caddy's illegitimate daughter, Quentin, was probably the primary reason for the divorce, Jason has transferred his antipathy toward the absent Caddy to her present daughter, the embodied cause of his deprivation.

Quentin, growing up like Caddy in a loveless environment in which her relatives, for selfish reasons, demand a certain type of behavior from her, shows every sign of following in her mother's wayward footsteps. Jason tries to force her to maintain not the family honor that preoccupied his dead brother, but the appearance of respectability because he, Jason, has a position to uphold in the community.

Present events in Section III

Jason's section of the book, which takes place on Good Friday, is highly logical and therefore much easier to follow than the preceding two; the references to past events are quite clear in context. As the section opens, Jason drives Quentin to school and threatens her if she should cut her classes again. He then drives on into Jefferson to the farm-supply store where he works and finds waiting for him a letter from Caddy enclosing the monthly check for Quentin's support—from which Jason has been systematically stealing for seventeen years. There is also a letter from Caddy for Quentin with a fifty-dollar money order; Jason opens the letter and, when Quentin later demands it, he tells her the money order is for ten dollars and makes her endorse it without seeing the face of it. Later in the afternoon he sees Quentin with a man wearing a red tie—a carnival pitchman. Furious at her for cutting school and for what he considers her loose behavior, he follows the pair until he is intercepted by a boy bearing a telegram saying that Jason's account on the cotton market, which had been falling all morning, has been closed out. An hour later, Jason again sees Quentin with the man in the red tie, this time riding in a car, and Jason again pursues but does not catch them. Finally he goes home, having acquired two unwanted passes to the carnival. In the kitchen, Luster is moaning his lack of a quarter to see the show; Jason shows him the passes, but burns them rather than give them to the boy. During dinner Jason and Quentin quarrel, and Quentin leaves the table. Later in the evening Mrs. Compson locks Quentin's door, as is her custom, in order to prevent her from going out at night.

Jason's inner world is ruled by the letter—if not the spirit—of the law, by money, and by rules of conduct aimed at preserving an appearance of respectability. "Everybody in this town knows what you are," he tells Quentin. "I don't care what you do, myself. . . . But I've got a position in this town, and I'm not going to have any member of my family going on like a nigger wench." (297) On Caddy's final visit to Jefferson in 1912 to attend—in disguise—her father's funeral, she had given Jason one hundred dollars to let her see her daughter "just for a minute." Jason kept his word to the letter: he drove past the spot where Caddy was waiting and held the baby Quentin up to the window of the buggy. When Caddy did not keep her part of the "bargain" by taking a train out of town immediately after,

Jason became indignant: "Didn't I do everything you said? I said see her a minute, didn't I. Well, didn't you?" (223)

Jason's relationships with other people are economic rather than emotional; he distrusts anything he cannot control. His arrangement with Lorraine, his peroxided mistress from Memphis, is lasting and satisfactory solely because no vestige of emotion ever enters into it. "You's a cold man, Jason, if man you is," Dilsey says, apropos of Jason's angry refusal to let Caddy sees her daughter. "I thank de Lawd I got mo heart dan dat, eben ef hit is black." "At least I'm man enough to keep that flour barrel full," Jason replies. (225)

SECTION IV: APRIL 8, 1928

The last section of the novel is narrated by the author in the third person and takes place entirely in the present. In it the personality of Dilsey, dimly seen in Benjy's section, is brought into sharp focus. She is, in many senses, the mainstay of the family, though they do not realize it. She has offered Quentin the only love the girl has ever known, and loves and cares for Benjy, whom no one cares about now that Caddy is gone. She puts up uncomplainingly with Mrs. Compson's whining, and she is not above criticism of Jason's sharp treatment of Quentin. On Easter morning, Dilsey rises early, but finds that Luster has overslept and that the woodbox in the kitchen is empty and the stove cold. While Mrs. Compson complains from the head of the stairs, Dilsey goes about her work, gets Mrs. Compson back to bed, sets the unwilling Luster to work, feeds Benjy, and prepares breakfast for the family. When Quentin does not appear for breakfast, Jason sends Dilsey up to get her, but Mrs. Compson has not yet unlocked Quentin's door and the girl does not answer. Jason snatches the ring of keys from his mother, but when he opens the door he finds the room empty and Quentin gone. Suspecting what has happened and almost frantic, he locks himself in his own room and takes his money box from its hiding place under the closet floor. The lock is broken and the money missing. Mrs. Compson, not knowing about the money, has immediately come to the conclusion that Quentin, like her uncle, has committed suicide. When Dilsey protests that Quentin has no reason to commit suicide, Mrs. Compson replies:

"What reason did Quentin [her son] have? Under God's heaven what reason did he have? It cant be simply to flout and hurt me. Whoever God is, He would not permit that. I'm a lady. You might not believe that from my offspring, but I am." (315)

Jason calls the sheriff and leaves immediately; while he is out on his futile chase after the girl and the money, Dilsey, Luster, Frony, and Benjy go to the Easter service at the Negro church. After they return, Benjy cries and will not be hushed. Fearing that he will disturb Mrs. Compson, Dilsey lets Luster drive him out to the cemetery. As they reach the Confederate statue in the town square, Luster spies a group of his Negro friends and turns the horse to the left of the monument instead of the accustomed right; Benjy immediately begins to roar in agony and Jason, just back from his fruitless search, comes running. He strikes Luster out of the way and turns the horse around to the right side of the statue, forbidding Luster ever to take Benjy out again.

> Tomorrow, and tomorrow, and tomorrow,
> Creeps in this petty pace from day to day
> To the last syllable of recorded time,
> And all our yesterdays have lighted fools
> The way to dusty death. Out, out, brief candle!
> Life's but a walking shadow, a poor player
> That struts and frets his hour upon the stage
> And then is heard no more; it is a tale
> Told by an idiot, full of sound and fury,
> Signifying nothing.
>   SHAKESPEARE, Macbeth, Act V, scene 5, lines 19–28

The "sound" and the "fury," of course, can refer specifically to Benjy's section, literally "a tale told by an idiot." Situations he does not like bring forth from the idiot either crying or an outraged, inarticulate bellow:

> Then Ben wailed again, hopeless and prolonged. It was nothing. Just sound. It might have been all time and injustice and sorrow become vocal for an instant by a conjunction of planets. (303–4)

Benjy is incapable of communication, except for his wordless whimpering and bellowing—"just sound." Like an animal, he can indicate a desire to go out or come in, or to be fed, and he can express distress, though not the cause of it; but he cannot communicate verbally with anyone. Yet, despite his total lack of mental ability, he is the most intuitive of the Compsons. It is frequently mentioned that he can "smell death." He knows, without knowing how he knows, that Caddy loves him, just as he knows that his mother, despite her conventional gestures of affection, dislikes him. Not understanding what those around him say, he reacts to the way he senses that they feel.

However, it is not only the "tale told by an idiot" that signifies nothing; recalling the entire quotation, life itself may be the idiot's tale. More likely, it is the telling of the tale of life that is meaningless—the words, the verbalizations and falsifications of experience. It is interesting to note that, of the sections narrated by the Compsons, Benjy's is the most factually accurate, since he reports only what he sees and hears, without first filtering it through his imagination and without misrepresenting it because of his point of view. (He is as incapable of misinterpreting experience as he is of interpreting it in the first place.) This fact, of course, contributes to the difficulty many readers have in understanding his section. There are none of the familiar landmarks ordinarily found in a narrator's mind, no point of reference from which the action can be viewed; it is all there, in one continuous stream of Benjy's thought, in which past and present are un-differentiated, in which events are presented objectively and without ap-parent logic. Thus we know only that Benjy cries when he sees Quentin and the carnival man in the porch swing; he does not say why he cries, and we must infer (as we will learn later) that he remembers Caddy and an-other man in the same swing.

Quentin, a highly articulate young man, is scarcely more "reasonable" than Benjy; but whereas Benjy, unable to speak, is thus freed from the tyranny of words, Quentin is trapped by words which, by themselves, have no meaning—chastity, honor, sin. He is deeply disturbed that both Caddy and her father refuse to take her seduction very seriously, for thus Caddy's dishonor and the resultant dishonor (in Quentin's mind) of the family become trivial. If Quentin could make of Caddy's "fall" something mo-mentous, he could also make the family dishonor the result of a moral catastrophe—a sin—and therefore significant.

At the same time Quentin, a modern man, is unable to believe in the fact of sin, unable to find any act that is particularly terrible or worthy of the name of sin and damnation. He finds life—the "loud world"—chaotic and unbearable, for it intrudes upon his inner world of ideal and abstrac-tion, the static and changeless world of his mind which, unfortunately for him, can remain intact only so long as Caddy accedes to his unrealistic demands on her. Trapped by words and paralyzed by his own egotism, Quentin tries to substitute words—which he has invested with a power and a meaning far above the act for which the word stands—for the acts he cannot bring himself to commit. He is thus unable to do anything, to stalk out and kill Caddy's seducer (as Julio tries to kill him for the supposed "theft" of the little girl), as the outraged brother would have done accord-ing to the code of the Old South, for he knows that the act of vengeance can never counterbalance his purely abstract concept of dishonor. He needs to convince the world—by words, not by the act—that he has committed incest with Caddy, so that the world, in horror, would make outcasts of them, and they would be safely removed from reality and change. He tells his father that it was he, not Ames, who seduced Caddy:

> and i you dont believe i am serious
> and he i think you are too serious to give me any cause for alarm you

couldnt have felt driven to the expedient of telling me if you had committed incest otherwise

and i i wasnt lying i wasnt lying

and he you wanted to sublimate a piece of natural human folly into
a horror and then exorcise it with truth

and i it was to isolate her out of the loud world so that it would be as
though it had never been

and he did you try to make her do it

and i i was afraid to i was afraid she might and then it wouldnt have
done any good but if i could tell you we did it would have been so and
then the others wouldnt be so and then the world would roar away

and he . . . you are contemplating an apotheosis in which a temporary
state of mind will become symmetrical above the flesh and aware both of
itself and of the flesh it will not quite discard . . . you cannot bear to think
that someday it will no longer hurt you like this.* (195–6)

Quentin searches blindly for a sin that will prove the reality of virtue,
a dishonor that will validate the idea of honor. However, he is concerned
not with the fact of virtue and honor, but with the idea of them; and his
search is verbal rather than active, turned inward upon himself rather than
outward toward others. He is as incapable of love as he is of incest, for both
involve action, and love involves both communication and the acceptance
of another person as a human being, not as a symbol. Thus, dissimilar as are
Quentin and Jason in other ways, each in his own form of egocentricity
regards other human beings as objects, and each attempts to use these
"objects" for his own ends.

All three of the narrators find the external world "full of sound and
fury," and all three attempt to create some sort of order and coherence out
of it; all have a need for absolutely stable centers of their respective uni-
verses. Benjy makes Caddy, who loves him, the center of his world; since
for him time does not exist, her unchanging image remains even when she
is no longer present. Quentin, who prefers abstraction to reality, makes his
ideal Caddy the center of his world; when the ideal collapses in the conflict
with reality, Quentin is left with chaos. Jason—logical, cold, and methodical
—finds reality more adaptable to his needs than do his brothers, for the
values of the external world are centered in just such things as Jason values;
logic, law, the appearance of respectability, and money.

Only Dilsey, with her inner serenity, her faith, and her understanding,
has an undistorted view of reality, and she alone, of all the characters, can
perceive and respond to the needs of others. Quentin, an idealist, has taken
a part of life and rejected the rest, in the same way that Jason rejects all
that has no material value. Dilsey can accept the whole, and because of

* I have set this passage in paragraphs to facilitate reading it out of context. It appears
in the novel as one unbroken paragraph.

this she can see and respond to Ben's and Caddy's and her daughter Quentin's need for affection, and can recognize Jason's blindness and Mrs. Compson's whining selfishness. Because she is emotionally whole, she can minister to the weaknesses of the rest of the family, as they cannot. To Dilsey, the world is filled not with "sound and fury," but with compassion, sorrow, and love. The materialistic Jason may survive for a while in a materialistic world, but it is the qualities that belong to Dilsey that will endure long after Jason is gone.

AS I LAY DYING [1930]

Characters

ANSE BUNDREN
ADDIE BUNDREN, *his wife*
CASH, *their eldest son, a carpenter, aged about thirty*
DARL, *their second son, aged twenty-eight*
JEWEL, *Addie's son by Whitfield, aged eighteen*
DEWEY DELL, *Addie's and Anse's daughter, aged seventeen*
VARDAMAN, *their youngest child, aged nine*

WHITFIELD, *a preacher and the father of Jewel*
VERNON TULL, *the Bundrens' nearest neighbor*
CORA TULL, *his wife*
LUCIUS PEABODY, *the doctor*
SAMSON, *a neighbor*
HENRY ARMSTID, *a neighbor*
MOSELEY, *a druggist in Mottson*
MAC GOWAN, *a drugstore clerk in Jefferson*

PLOT

Addie, once a schoolteacher near Frenchman's Bend, married Anse Bundren, a country man with a small farm near the Yoknapatawpha River. After she had borne him two children, she asked him to promise to take her to Jefferson to be buried with her kin when she died—this in revenge for what she considered to be Anse's trickery of her with words about love, which, she comes to realize, he can neither understand nor feel. Believing that the only reason for living was to experience the violation of one's aloneness, and knowing that Anse could never break through their separate cells of individuality, she had an affair with Whitfield, the preacher. After their relationship was over, Addie found that she was pregnant with Jewel, whom Anse accepted as his own child. She then gave Anse another child, Dewey Dell, to "negative" Jewel, and still another, Vardaman, to "replace the child [she] had robbed him of." (467)

Nine years after the youngest child was born, Addie lay dying, while outside the window Cash hammered on her coffin and neighbors came to visit. Darl persuaded Jewel to go with him to pick up a load of lumber, knowing in his preternatural way that Addie would die before they returned and that Jewel, her favorite son, would be absent from her bedside. Just after Addie's death a violent storm broke, the lumber-loaded wagon lost a wheel in a ditch, and what with one thing and another it was three days before the coffin was loaded in the wagon and the family set off on the twenty-odd mile journey to Jefferson and the cemetery. Since their bridge was out because of the storm and high water, they traveled eight miles to Samson's, but found the bridge there out as well. They backtracked to Tull's and crossed at his ford, but the river was so treacherous that the mules were drowned and Cash's leg was badly broken, and the wagon and coffin would have been lost but for Jewel. Across the river, they stopped at Armstid's, and Anse went into Frenchman's Bend to barter for another span of mules, finally throwing in the eight dollars Cash had saved to buy a phonograph and Jewel's beloved horse to conclude the bargain. Since the main road from Frenchman's Bend to Jefferson was washed out, the Bundrens went around by way of Mottson, where they bought some cement to make a cast for Cash's broken leg and Dewey Dell tried unsuccessfully to buy some abortion pills. When they stopped to spend the night at Gillespie's place, halfway between Mottson and Jefferson, Darl set fire to Gillespie's barn in order to destroy Addie's body, a week dead and attracting buzzards, but Jewel rescued the coffin from the fire. Vardaman saw Darl set the fire and told Dewey Dell, who hated Darl because he knew she was pregnant.

Nine days after Addie's death, the family arrived in Jefferson. Anse borrowed some shovels with which to dig the grave, and Addie was at last out of the sight of man. Cash was taken to the doctor and Darl was sent off to the insane asylum in Jackson; the family had either to commit him or be sued by Gillespie, who learned from Dewey Dell that Darl had fired his barn. Dewey Dell tried again to get her abortion medicine and was taken advantage of by an unscrupulous drugstore clerk. Finally, Anse, having taken the money Dewey Dell's sweetheart had given her to pay for the pills, bought a new set of teeth and acquired a wife, a pop-eyed, duck-shaped woman who owned a phonograph.

As I Lay Dying is constructed out of the thoughts and feelings of fifteen characters—the seven Bundrens and eight "outsiders" (both neighbors and strangers)—each of whom narrates one or more short sections describing Addie's death or funeral journey. The neighbors supply primarily objective information and physical details, while the Bundrens, circling in their small orbit around Addie, talk about each other and reveal themselves. The action is seen through Darl's eyes nearly a third of the time; the object of his thoughts is frequently Jewel, the most silent member of the family. As the other narrators speak, impression is added to impression as the same event is given slightly different emphasis in the eyes of each beholder, and broad outlines of personalities are suggested, to be corrected and filled in as the action of the book progresses.

This technique of multiple perspective results in a gradual unfolding of meaning in which an action described by one character is given further significance when the scene is passed through the imagination of another person and another perspective and more bits of information are presented. As the book opens, we see the Bundrens as Addie is dying; their individual past lives—and particularly their emotional relationship with Addie—are at first unknown and only gradually revealed. Indeed, not until Addie speaks, two-thirds of the way through the book, do we understand the reason for the rivalry between Darl and Jewel, or the real reason for the funeral journey, or the character of Addie, the motivating force behind the family. By withholding the meaning, by supplying hints and pieces before we have seen the pattern into which we must fit them, Faulkner withdraws himself from the author's accustomed position as mediator between the reader and the action; the author's voice is almost entirely lacking. We are not told about the characters, but set down in the midst of them and left to find out for ourselves what they are like, while Faulkner—like Joyce's God of Creation—sits back and pares his fingernails. As a result, we are handed no conclusions and given no judgments about the characters except those that they themselves have made.

The tone of the book is partially comic. Anse, with his hunchback, his whining, and his complete ineptitude, is almost a stock comic figure. Moreover, there is frequently a comic discrepancy between the expected response to a situation and the actual one. When Addie dies, Anse says with genuine feeling, "God's will be done. . . . Now I can get them teeth." (375) Cash, enduring immense and largely unnecessary pain, maintains that his leg doesn't hurt—"not to speak of," anyway. The comic action is usually an extreme one, a distortion of what is expected. Pushed to a further extreme, and with the addition of a result that is unpleasant or perhaps repulsive, the comic often becomes grotesque. Vardaman, believing his mother will suffocate in the closed coffin, drills holes in the lid and incidentally bores into her face.

The physical fact of Addie's death and the funeral journey provide the occasion for the action. With the addition of flood-producing rains, July heat, and washed-out bridges and roads, the stage is set, and the unfortunate Bundrens encounter a series of disasters that makes their progress one of alternating—and sometimes mixed—farce and horror. In the course of the novel the Bundrens face death and flood and fire, the most elemental obstacles to man's mastery of his environment, and those over which he has least control. In coping—or trying to cope—with them, each member of the family is subjected to stress that reveals the most basic aspects of his personality.

In one sense, then, the novel deals with the revelation of character through stress. Anse and Dewey Dell, who have the least depth of character and are most nearly stock figures, are least affected by Addie's death and are for all practical purposes unchanged at the end of the novel. Anse has replaced his wife, and one suspects that he will find life with the new Mrs. Bundren indistinguishable from life with Addie. Dewey Dell is still pregnant. To the other members of the family, however, Addie's death is an event of deep significance, her loss something with which each must cope according to his own resources. Thus, on a more important level, the novel does not so much deal with the simple revelation of character through stress as with the search for the self, the attempts of Addie's sons to understand themselves now that she is no longer living.

Vardaman, the youngest, reacts to Addie's death the most directly. Too young to maintain his identity independent of his mother, he must keep her alive in some physical and concrete way that his child's mind can comprehend. To this end, he takes refuge in a primitive type of reasoning that draws logical and satisfying conclusions from the most implausible of premises. When an enormous fish he had caught was whole, his mother was alive; after it was cut in pieces, she was dead: therefore he sees an identity between a whole fish and a living Addie. His mother, dead, no longer inhabits her body; that is not-her, as the cut-up pieces of fish are not-fish. Vardaman never states his too-easily-disproved conviction that his mother is not dead, but makes the more easily proved existence of the fish a crucial element in his logic. Remembering that both he and Tull had seen the fish alive, he sets out for Tull's in the middle of the night to have him verify the fact of the fish's—and thus of his mother's—existence.

When Addie was alive, Darl, whose tenuous emotional balance depends on his being able to define his existence through his recognition by others, had been able to assert himself to some degree as a member of the relatively stable family. When she dies, leaving the family no longer a coherent unit, one of Darl's mirrors of himself is broken. Thus he begins his journey to the mental disintegration that he reveals when, on the train for the state mental hospital, he speaks of himself in the third person: "Our brother Darl in a cage in Jackson where, his grimed hands lying light in the quiet interstices, looking out he foams." (527) Reacting to Addie's emotional rejection of him, Darl forces an awareness of himself on others in an attempt to assert the reality of his self. With extraordinary perception, he is able to divine the secrets of the other members of the family. As Tull says, he looks at you "like he had got into the inside of you." (426) Thus Dewey Dell is forced to recognize Darl because his knowledge intrudes between her and her secret sweetheart Lafe. As a result, she hates Darl and is finally responsible for having him shipped off to Jackson. But hate is as much a response as love or acceptance, and Darl's reality is defined in Dewey Dell's hatred of him. Similarly, Darl divines Jewel's illegitimacy because of Addie's favoritism, and Darl's knowledge hammers at Jewel's being, creating the rivalry and tension between them. Sensing that Jewel lavishes his violent love for his mother on his horse, Darl jibes that Jewel's mother is a horse; but Darl knows that he himself has no mother, and says, "Then I am not. . . . Am I?" When Vardaman replies, "But you are, Darl," he counters, "That's why I am not is. Are is too many for one woman to foal." (409) Separated from these family responses, Darl's self is fragmented—an "are" rather than an "is"—and on the verge of collapse into insanity.

Jewel, almost completely unreflective, is not apparently concerned with his identity; he seemed sure of himself in relation to Addie when she lived, and equally sure of himself when she is dead. As Darl realizes, Jewel "knows he is, because he does not know that he does not know whether he is or not." (396) The child of Addie's passionate experience with Whitfield, Jewel is most like Addie in his directness and strength, though apparently without her ability to verbalize experience. Her love and faith in him ["He will save me from the water and from the fire. Even though I have laid down my life, he will save me." (460)] gives him the psychic strength to exist independently of her, even to part with his horse—a symbol of his mother which in some ways, like Vardaman's fish, became equated with her—in order that her coffin could be taken to Jefferson. Like Jewel, Cash was accepted by Addie, and the love between them, though unspoken, was strong; as a result, Cash is secure in himself and can accept Addie's death. Less intense than Jewel, Cash is almost too well balanced. Having no need to assert himself, he allows the other members of the family to intrude themselves upon him, and stoically suffers unnecessary pain rather than make the family aware of him by complaining.

One of the basic premises of human relationships in the novel is that the individual is doomed to a cellular existence whose isolation can be broken by contact with another only rarely and, in many cases, not at all. Addie, at first unaware of the intrinsic superficiality of contact even between husband and wife, discovers with a shock, when her aloneness is violated by the birth of Cash, that Anse has never touched her, that he had interposed empty words between them without ever knowing the reality of the things for which the words stand. Darl, the most sensitive of her children, feels his isolation perhaps the most deeply, but uses his perception as a weapon to intrude upon other consciousnesses, as a means—to borrow a phrase from Hawthorne—of violating the sanctity of the heart. This type of violation is intellectual rather than emotional, and thus deadly. Darl learns not to give but to probe, not to touch but to threaten.

Related to the idea of human isolation is the failure of almost all of the characters to live except at second hand, according to a verbal formula. Cora Tull is the most extreme example. Conventional and righteous, as devoid of brains as her chickens—yet withal kind and well-meaning—she is a comic figure, but not one that can be thereby ignored. Her speech is full of the phrases and rhythms of rural Southern religion, her life is largely shaped according to its verbal formulas, and her response to both individuals and situations is automatically dictated by it. She sees life only in terms of words like "sin" and "pride" and "repentance" and "duty" and other pious phrases which are the more appalling because she implicity believes in what she is saying without having the least understanding of it. Addie reveals both her pity and contempt for Cora, whose life is composed only of words, without any significant action, when she speaks of her as "Cora, who could never even cook." (465)

As opposed to Cora, Addie has an intense commitment to the non-verbal reality of experience, and meets life directly and violently. To her, the only reason for living is the "duty to the alive, to the terrible blood, the red bitter flood boiling through the land." (466) The most vital character in the novel, she recognizes the ever-widening and unbridgeable gap between doing and saying, and abjures words as being only shapes to fill a lack. Hence she rejects and ultimately destroys Darl, simply because he was born as a result of Anse's trickery of her with words about love. Thus there is a deadliness—though of a different kind than Darl's—in Addie, as well as a fierce commitment to the necessity of violence to "shape and coerce the terrible blood to the forlorn echo of the dead word high in the air." (466) Indeed, in one sense Addie is life in so far as she is an earth-mother, a symbol of the earth, of fecundity, and of the violence and blood of birth; she is identified with a fish (fertility), and with a horse (sexuality). Like the road that crosses the land, like the acts that cleave to the earth and do not rise up like words, Addie is permanently horizontal, wearing her wedding dress as a symbol of her perpetual bridehood, the repeatedly ravished and ever-virgin Mother. And, in her capacity as earth-mother and giver of life, she is also, and of necessity, connected with death, for the Mother is also the Destroyer, the earth that is the womb of life is also the grave in which the corpse is buried. Similarly, though death is present throughout the story and though death motivates the action, it is life—and the various ways of living, or failing to live, it—which is the subject of the book.

SANCTUARY [1931]

Characters

HORACE BENBOW, *a lawyer, aged 43*
BELLE MITCHELL BENBOW, *his wife*
LITTLE BELLE, *his stepdaughter, aged about 18*
NARCISSA BENBOW SARTORIS, *his widowed sister, aged 36*

TEMPLE DRAKE, *a college girl, aged 17*
LEE GOODWIN, *a bootlegger*
RUBY GOODWIN, *his common-law wife*
POPEYE, *a Memphis gangster*
MISS REBA, *madam of a Memphis brothel*
RED, *a young hoodlum*
GOWAN STEVENS, *Temple Drake's escort, aged about 21*
TOMMY, *a feeble-minded man*

PLOT

As the novel opens, Horace Benbow, having left his wife after ten years of marriage, is on his way from Kinston to his old home in Jefferson. He stops at the spring near the Old Frenchman Place and is accosted by Popeye, a gangster temporarily staying with the bootlegger Lee Goodwin. Four days after this incident Temple Drake is brought to the Old Frenchman Place by her drunken escort Gowan Stevens, who wrecks his car and, unable to face Temple, later abandons her there. Although she is frightened by the men on the place, her behavior toward them is provocative, and she refuses to heed Ruby Goodwin's urgent warnings to leave the place before dark. Finally, protected by Ruby, she spends the night in the barn. The following morning she hides from Goodwin in the corncrib while the feeble-minded Tommy keeps watch outside, having promised he will let none of the men in. Meanwhile Popeye enters the crib from a trap door in the loft overhead. He opens the door and shoots Tommy, and then, since he is impotent, rapes the frightened but unresisting Temple with a corncob. He then takes her, still completely unresisting, with him to Memphis, where he establishes her in Miss Reba's brothel and provides her with a lover in order to enjoy her, as it were, by proxy. He later murders Red, the lover, for trying to see Temple alone.

Meanwhile, Lee Goodwin is arrested for the murder of Tommy, and

Horace Benbow undertakes to defend him and look after Ruby and her infant son. The local townsfolk, however, persecute Ruby because of her relationship with the supposed murderer, and finally make it impossible for her to get a room anywhere in Jefferson. Goodwin refuses to admit even Popeye's presence at his place at the time of the murder, fearing that Popeye will kill him if he does. Horace manages to locate Temple at the Memphis brothel and tries to persuade her to testify at Goodwin's trial. She refuses, but later appears as a surprise witness for the prosecution and falsely testifies that it was Goodwin who killed Tommy and raped her. Goodwin is convicted and shortly afterwards taken from jail and burned to death by a mob. Horace, defeated in his attempt to see justice done, returns to Kinston and his wife. Temple is taken off to Europe by her father, and Popeye is arrested and executed on a charge of murdering a man in Alabama—a crime he could not possibly have committed, since it occurred on the night that he was in Memphis killing Red, Temple's lover.

The first of Faulkner's novels to have any kind of commercial success, Sanctuary has been unfortunately branded with Faulkner's own comment that it was a cheap idea, conceived solely to make money. Initially, it may have been so; the first draft was written in three weeks in the early summer of 1929 and sent off to the publisher, who feared to print anything so scandalous and shelved the manuscript for over a year. In November, 1930, a year and a half later, Faulkner received the galley proofs of the first version, and realized that he could not shame the work he had already done by allowing Sanctuary to be published in its present form. Accordingly, he revised and rewrote extensively, and the Sanctuary that appeared in 1931 was a considerably different book from the "cheap" and "horrific" tale he had written two years earlier. Certainly not one of his best books, Sanctuary is nevertheless an honest piece of writing, and contains themes that are an important part of the total body of Faulkner's work.

Sanctuary suffers from three major weaknesses. Its characters tend to be two-dimensional and sometimes nearly allegorical figures: Popeye is a figure of pure evil; Temple is wanton, weak, and utterly without conscience or any sense of responsibility; Gowan Stevens is a drunken cavalier; Horace Benbow is the good but inept man who is unable to match the forces of evil in the world; Tommy is the innocent undeservedly destroyed by evil; and so forth. There is little actual conflict, even between the allegorical good and evil, because Horace is too weak and ambiguous a character to have any effect on evil. The conflict dies on the vine, its outcome certain almost before it has begun. Because of this failure of conflict, the book fails to have any significant resolution. The characters who die achieve no understanding before their deaths, those who go on living remain apparently unchanged by their experiences.

Faulkner seems to be suggesting that in the modern world the presence of evil no longer implies the existence of good. The evil in *Sanctuary* is a result of amorality, not immorality; there is no sin in a positive or religious sense, which implies the possibility of salvation, but only in a negative sense, as the complete absence of a capacity for or awareness of virtue. Viewed in conjunction with *Requiem for a Nun* (1951), *Sanctuary* can be seen as the beginning of a search for meaning in the world, or for redemption, presenting the aspects of sin as *Requiem for a Nun* presents the possibility—as well as the necessity—of suffering, in the nearly blind hope that beyond suffering will be found salvation. By itself, however, *Sanctuary* seems to be only a record of the complete failure in the modern world of even the smallest hope of redemption or meaning. If *Sanctuary* is, as many critics have noted, Faulkner's equivalent of T. S. Eliot's *The Waste Land*, it is a wasteland in which the thunder does not presage rain, and in which the protagonist finds not even fragments to shore against his ruins.

There are three moral environments in *Sanctuary*. The Old Frenchman Place might be seen allegorically as nature beyond the law, uncultivated and growing into a rank jungle. Here (before Popeye's arrival, at least) the illegal but basically good and "natural" relationship of Lee and Ruby can exist in peace; here a child has been born and lives, although feebly; here is the naif, Tommy, and a helpless old man, blind and deaf, cared for by Goodwin; and here Goodwin distills into alcohol the earth's corn—certainly a symbol of fertility and increase, even though distorted and used for "unnatural" purposes. The Memphis underworld, Popeye's natural habitat, is the antithesis of this, being civilization beyond the law. Like Popeye, it is antinatural, sterile, mechanical, exploiting for its own profit the natural lusts of men, not so much hostile to life as utterly indifferent to it. The third allegorical environment is the town of Jefferson, which tries, within the framework of social law and order, to have the best of both worlds, the natural and the mechanical. However, if the Old Frenchman Place and Miss Reba's are amoral, Jefferson is pseudo-moral. It verbally upholds the standards of respectability, the sacredness of womanhood, and the idea of justice; but in so doing it mistakes conventional action for moral action, and is either unable or unwilling to look beneath the surface of apparent reality and recognize the existence of good and evil in every person and every action.

Each of the characters reflects his moral environment. Tommy is incapable of either moral or immoral action, yet he is temperamentally—naturally—good-natured and kind. Ruby and Lee, whatever their past and present failings, have potentialities for good. Popeye is the quintessence of evil in the most negative sense possible, that of a total absence of virtue. Horace, a respectable man from respectable Jefferson, is held in bondage, somewhat against his will, to respectability. Temple, from a similar environment, courts an appearance of respectability both before and after her complete immersion in depravity. Narcissa, respectability personified, admittedly cares nothing for truth, but only for the appearance of virtue and righteous action.

The title "sanctuary" is ironic. Temple, whose very name underlines the irony, is herself a violated, even desecrated vessel to whom desecration has no meaning. Her sanctuary is, fittingly perhaps, a Memphis brothel. Lee and Ruby Goodwin had apparently found a kind of sanctuary in the abandoned Old Frenchman Place—a sanctuary for illegal bootlegging on the one hand, but on the other a place in which Ruby sought to maintain some kind of positive relationship with a man to whom she had chosen to be faithful. When this haven was destroyed with Tommy's murder, there was no sanctuary for Goodwin in legal justice, nor for Ruby in morally upright Jefferson; again, ironically, it was the ladies of the church who forced Ruby and her child to take refuge in the cabin of a supposed witch outside of town. After Goodwin's immolation, Horace was driven by failure back to the depressing sanctuary of an empty life with the wife he had left just before he began his unsuccessful attempt to uphold justice.

As there is no true sanctuary, no consecrated place, in the novel, there is no true justice. Goodwin is convicted of a murder of which he was innocent, and burned by a mob before he could be legally executed. Tommy, the most innocent of all the characters, is coldly and needlessly murdered. Temple, who deserved a far worse fate than Ruby for her part in the drama, is taken to Europe by her father. Even Popeye is executed for a murder of which he is innocent. However, if there is only ironic justice, there is no true innocence, either. Tommy, the only exception, is innocent insofar as he is incapable of distinguishing between good and evil. All the rest are guilty in one way or another. The inhabitants of the Old Frenchman Place and the Memphis underworld have committed various crimes from murder to prostitution. The inhabitants of Jefferson fail to accept moral responsibility—a less heinous crime in the eyes of the law, but one equally destructive of human potential. Narcissa, the moral leader of those righteous women who define as sin any deviation from the conventional rules of decent conduct, persistently refuses to concern herself with the truth or justice of the Goodwin affair. "I dont see that it makes any difference who did it," she retorts to Horace. "The question is, are you going to stay mixed up with it?" (104) Horace, despite all his good intentions, lacks the courage of his convictions and bows to Narcissa's refusal to let Ruby take refuge in the Benbow family home. There can be no justice in Jefferson as long as women such as Narcissa rule their men—and the town—and as long as men like Horace fail by their own example to challenge conventional morality when it conflicts with their human values.

In varying degrees all of the characters suffer from an inability to assimilate their experiences—in other words, to grow or to mature. Essentially, they suffer from a failure to live, finding their own sanctuary from reality within figurative glass cases through which experience cannot penetrate. Thus Temple, the most glaring example of this failure, clings to the tokens of her respectability ("My father's a judge") while flaunting herself before the men at Goodwin's place. After her voluntary sojourn in the depths of vice she returns unchanged to Jefferson to play the part of the victim, of Southern Womanhood violated and constrained against her will. Though she obviously desires to flirt with evil, she has no wish to experience it, or anything else, in the full sense of responding to it and being changed by it. When attacked by Popeye, she cries in horror, "Something is happening to me!" She cannot ignore what has been done to her person, but she feels herself the victim, the passive object, in a situation in which she has unwittingly found herself. By regarding even this violent collision with experience as a purely physical event, Temple is able to avoid any feeling of responsibility for her own part in the affair; she disavows her own provocative acts to such a degree that, for all practical purposes, she might as well not have committed them. Thus she absolves herself of any possibility of guilt for what has happened.

Horace is the only character who shows even the smallest degree of insight into his—and the human—condition, but that insight is insufficient to save him. By leaving his wife and the meaningless life he had lived with her for ten years, he was attempting to assert the possibility of a meaningful existence. Yet he is still bound by his dependent relationship to his sister. Though he recognizes the indifference to truth behind Narcissa's front of pious respectability, he still cannot evade her, and respectability's, hold on him. His fantasies on looking at Little Belle's picture clearly indicate his sexual response toward her, but he cannot reconcile the voluptuary aspects of womanhood with his and Jefferson's conception of Pure Womanhood, chaste and undefiled. His unwillingness to come to terms with his quasi-incestuous passion for his stepdaughter is a parallel to his failure to carry out his beliefs in action—to defy Narcissa and the other wagging, righteous tongues by continuing to shelter Ruby in his own house. Horace may have reached the point at which he can recognize the failure of conventional morality, but he is not yet capable of ending his own emotional subservience to respectability, and therefore incapable of taking Jefferson to task for its similar failure.

The novel ends on a deeply ironic note; law has triumphed but not justice. The inhabitants of the natural, lawless world of the Old Frenchman Place are either dead or dispersed, and Popeye, the leader of the Memphis underworld, has been executed for a crime he did not commit. The evil which Popeye represents has gone, but so have the Goodwins' potentialities for good. Jefferson, for all its contact with the two worlds beyond the law, remains essentially as it was before, without having suffered either any great harm or any particular benefit. Like the people who inhabit it, Jefferson continues to be respectable and law-abiding, a sanctuary of empty conventionality.

LIGHT IN AUGUST   [1932]

Characters

JOE CHRISTMAS, *aged about 36*
GAIL HIGHTOWER, a *former minister, aged about 50*
JOANNA BURDEN, a *spinster, aged about 44*
LENA GROVE, *aged 20*
BYRON BUNCH, *aged about 35*
LUCAS BURCH [*alias Joe Brown*]
MR. AND MRS. SIMON MC EACHERN, *foster parents of Joe Christmas*
EUPHEUS [DOC] HINES, *Joe's grandfather*
MRS. HINES, *Joe's grandmother*
PERCY GRIMM

PLOT

Lena Grove, far advanced in pregnancy, has set out from her home in Alabama in search of her lover, Lucas Burch, who left her some months back with the promise that he would soon send for her. She has been on the road nearly four weeks, and has been told Lucas is working in a planing mill in Jefferson. She arrives on Saturday, the day that Joanna Burden's house burns down and Joanna herself is found murdered. At the mill, Lena finds Byron Bunch, who unwittingly reveals that her lover is using the name of Joe Brown and is a former employee of the mill. After leaving Lena safe at his boarding house, Byron goes to see Hightower, an unfrocked minister who has been living in isolation for twenty-five years. He tells him of Lena's predicament and of the day's events: the sheriff having given notice that a one-thousand-dollar reward was offered for the capture of Joanna's killer, Brown has come forward with the information that Joe Christmas had been having an affair with Joanna for three years, that he had killed her, and that he had Negro blood.

Chapters 5–12 are devoted to Joe Christmas: his childhood, young manhood, and finally the last three years he lived with Joanna, ending with the night of her death. Raised in an orphanage until he was five, he had no knowledge of his parents or their backgrounds, but through the suggestions of the janitor (later revealed to be Doc Hines, his grandfather), came to believe that he had Negro blood. Hiding in the dietitian's room one day he overheard, without understanding, the dietitian making love with an interne. The woman discovered him and, frightened that he would tell on her, told the matron that the child was a Negro. Rather than have him placed in a Negro orphanage, the matron arranged to have him adopted, and Joe went to live with the McEacherns. A harsh disciplinarian and a rigid Calvinist, Mr. McEachern tried to teach Joe to "fear God and abhor idleness and vanity." Mrs. McEachern, a soft, weak woman, tried to gain Joe's affection through kindness, which Joe resented and distrusted. When he was seventeen he began sneaking out at night to see Bobbie Allen, a waitress and prostitute. McEachern found them at a dance and called Bobbie a harlot, whereupon Joe bludgeoned him with a chair and, having possibly killed him, ran away from home.

After nearly fifteen years of drifting, Joe found himself in Jefferson, where he encountered Joanna Burden, a forty-year-old spinster and a descendant of New Hampshire abolitionists. During the three years of his affair with her he lived in a cabin on her property, being joined during the last year by Lucas Burch (alias Joe Brown), who helped him distribute bootleg whiskey. Finally Joanna began to think she was pregnant, and then realized that she had reached the menopause. She then tried to change Joe, who she believed to be a Negro, from a sexual partner into a "respectable" Negro, and wanted to send him to a Negro college to be a lawyer. Joe refused, and finally killed her when—after she had insisted that he pray with her—she drew a pistol with the intent of killing them both. Joe fled, and Brown, apparently drunk, discovered the body the next morning and set fire to the house, possibly in an ill-considered attempt to destroy the evidence of the killing.

During the week that follows the murder, Byron—having told Lena that Brown is "away on business for the sheriff"—takes her out to live in Brown's cabin to await the birth of her baby. Christmas, having eluded pursuit for nearly a week, turns up on Friday in nearby Mottstown, where he walks the streets until someone recognizes him and calls the sheriff. Attracted by the crowd that gathers and by the sound of Christmas' name being called, Doc Hines, a religious fanatic and racist, breaks through the crowd and confronts Christmas, whom he strikes until he is pulled away. Over thirty years before, Hines, Christmas' grandfather, had caught his daughter running away with a Mexican circus-hand; he killed the man, who he believed to be part Negro, and later, when his daughter was giving birth, refused to let a doctor attend her. The girl died, and some months later Hines took the child to the Memphis orphanage, where he worked as a janitor. Now, at Christmas' capture, Hines is convinced that God's will is working itself out and that "Satan's spawn" will be destroyed. Mrs. Hines, wanting to see her grandson again, takes Hines with her to Jefferson, where they are taken by Byron to see Hightower. After Mrs. Hines tells her story, Byron pleads with Hightower to give Christmas an alibi by saying that

Christmas was with him on the night of Joanna's death. Hightower refuses violently.

The next day, Monday, Lena's child is born, delivered by Hightower since Byron could not get a doctor in time. Byron arranges for Lucas Burch to be brought out to the cabin, but Lucas, unexpectedly confronted with Lena and her child, flees. Byron encounters Lucas at the railroad grade, fights him, and is badly beaten. Lucas hops a train and disappears, and Byron, walking back into town, learns that Christmas has been killed by a mob. As reconstructed by Gavin Stevens, the district attorney, Mrs. Hines had somehow persuaded Christmas to make a break for it, and to seek refuge at Hightower's house. Christmas was pursued by a group of men led by Percy Grimm, a fanatical young deputy, who cornered him in High-tower's kitchen. Hightower tried to stop Grimm, desperately claiming that Christmas was with him the night of the murder, but Grimm pushed Hightower aside, ran into the kitchen and shot and castrated Christmas.

The book closes, as it opens, with the travels of Lena Grove. With Byron, whom she allows to accompany her but whom she placidly keeps at a respectable distance, she continues on her serene search for the vanished Lucas.

The longest and least experimental of Faulkner's major novels, *Light in August* is circular in content, beginning and ending with the journey of Lena Grove in search of her lover, and focusing in the midsection of the book on the circular road traveled for thirty years by Joe Christmas in search of his identity. For ten days the orbits of their lives overlap, and, though they never meet, their actions—Lena's giving birth and Joe's death —draw others into crucial involvement with both of them. The formal structure, the telling of the story, is somewhat loose and episodic. Faulkner interrupts the progress in the present to narrate four long chapters dealing with Joe's childhood and young manhood; later he stops the action in order to relate the history of Mr. and Mrs. Hines, still later, that of Percy Grimm. However, the contextual integrity of the book is maintained by the short space of time in which the present action occurs and by the tight drawing-in of all the characters to the active center provided by Lena and Joe.

Besides functioning as the means by which Byron, and, through him, Hightower, are precipitated into the circle of Joe's life, Lena serves as a contrast to Joe, lightening the grimness of the novel with her placid and sometimes almost comic acceptance of herself and her situation, almost literally shedding light and peace in a town darkened by murder and violence. She is a symbol of life and animal fecundity set against the destructiveness and barrenness of Joe and those in his background. This juxtaposition of light and dark, animal innocence and tormented consciousness, placidity and outrage, forms the thematic core of the novel and is reiterated constantly, not only between the two opposing characters but within individual characters themselves, and is echoed in the style and imagery of the book.

Joe's entire life is seen in terms of splitting, rejection, and separation; from his early childhood, guided by Hines, he learns to feel himself different, set apart. But he can never know whether he is Negro or not, and he is unable to accept the opposing aspects of life, here symbolized as black and white and living in him. From his experience with the dietitian, who tries to bribe him when he expects punishment, he learns to fear women for their unpredictability. Related to this, and more important, he hates the female in her close relation to nature; thus, when the adolescent Joe learns of menstruation, he is repulsed and horrified, and sacrifices a sheep in an obscure attempt to come to terms with this hated knowledge. Paradoxically, the bloody sacrifice of the animal is a recognition of—perhaps an attempt to placate—the irrational, chthonic forces of nature that Joe so greatly fears. Joe's search for himself is, like his life, circular and doomed to failure, for his every act of self-definition carries with it a complementary rejection of part of himself and part of life. He is compelled to assert himself as a white man—he taunts other whites into calling him "nigger" so that he can fight them—but he is unable to escape his belief that he is Negro. Similarly, he rejects his white blood for a time and lives entirely among Negroes, "trying to expel from himself the white blood and the white thinking and being" while at the same time his whole being is writhing and straining "with physical outrage and spiritual denial." (197) It is not only that society demands that he be either Negro or white, and act accordingly; Joe himself is unable to accept himself as both, and he becomes the antagonist in both the Negro and white worlds.

Hopelessly in conflict with himself, both searching for and trying to escape from himself, Joe demands an order and fixity in his environment that can give some balance to his inner strife. Thus he finds in the authoritarian, rigidly delineated Calvinism of McEachern a kind of security, and uses it as a framework for his own existence; with the stern implacability of McEachern himself young Joe refuses to learn his catechism, thereby asserting himself as an individual against his fosterfather. It is not only ironic that Joe uses the spiritual rigidity of Calvinism to successfully reject religion, and that in refusing to learn his catechism he wears the rapt expression of a monk or resembles a Catholic choirboy. By this conjunction of opposing images Faulkner again reiterates the dual nature of all experience, the equal impossibility of separating a given aspect of life from its opposite, or ever wholly reconciling the two. Joe, as the symbolic embodiment of this polarity of experience, swings from extreme to extreme, from whiteness to Negrohood, from rigid impassivity to raging violence. The boy who asserts himself by accepting his whippings with a beatific expression on his face is also the man who attempts to destroy the normal order of the external world through compulsive, seemingly capricious acts of violence—as if hoping, by this destruction, to force the world to recognize him for what he chooses to be.

Joe is seen most clearly in his confrontation with Joanna Burden, to whom he is both a contrast and a complement. As Joe is self-exiled from humanity because of his inability to accept himself, Joanna is isolated from the community because of her family background and her belief that she is burdened by God with guilt toward the black race. In their strange, almost perverted relationship Joe is a white man by day, a Negro by night; Joanna is alternately a Puritan philanthropically engaged in Negro uplift and education and a completely corrupted nymphomaniac reveling in the excesses of the flesh. In this expression of the contradictory sides of their personalities, each seems to find some relative stability. However, when Joanna, reaching the menopause, begins to channel her sexuality back into more normally acceptable areas, the conflict begins again. No longer desiring Joe as a lover, she tries to change him from a Negro embodiment of brutal, animal sexuality and raise him to her white woman's level by educating him and making him a respectable Negro. To her, Joe is not an individual, a man, but an object, a means by which she can expiate part of her guilt toward the black race. Paradoxically, she must incur a concrete sexual guilt in order to be able to expiate the purely abstract guilt she has inherited. Thus, her response to Joe is not to a person, but to an abstraction, to the idea of Negro which for her Joe represents. It is the Negro, not Joe, who must be lifted up, who must repent and be saved. In one sense, her relationship with Joe is a ritualistic acting-out of her obsessions both with the Negro and with history. When she realizes that Joe will not commit himself to Negrohood and to her Puritanism—when he refuses what she must view as the means of salvation for both of them—she plans to kill both him and herself. Significantly, her weapon is an old Civil War pistol, a relic, as she herself is a relic, of her family's past.

A gradual process of transformation is forced upon Joe from without, first from Joanna and then, after her death, from the townsfolk. Asserting by violence his right to make himself what he chooses to be, he forces an awareness of himself on the community, which, like Joanna, reacts to him not as a person but as a Negro. Once Brown, frightened and greedy, has revealed that Joe is part Negro, the town forgets all considerations of Joe's possible innocence, of Brown's own dubious reputation, even of the obvious fact that Joe looks like a white man and that the town has only Brown's word to the contrary. In the popular imagination, Joe becomes an embodiment of all the evil, brutality, and fearsomeness that the idea of Negro evokes in the Southern white mind, while his victim, Joanna, the despised

Northerner and "nigger-lover," is elevated to the familiar role of Southern Womanhood raped and murdered by The Negro. Automatic and long-inbred social responses have taken over, relieving the community of the need to think and to take individual responsibility for their actions. The wheels have been put in motion and will not stop until the "nigger murderer" has been ritually pursued, captured, and crucified.

Ironically, it is during the week following the murder, when Joe is hiding in the woods and almost completely out of contact with humanity, losing track even of the day of the week, that he first feels any ties with humanity. Now that his appearance evokes fear in both whites and Negroes, he feels drawn toward them. He politely thanks the frightened woman of whom he asked the day of the week, and thinks with a kind of chagrin of the Negro family who fed him: " 'And they were afraid. Of their brother afraid.' " (293) Reduced to the barest essentials of life, with little food and no shelter, he comes for the first time to some sort of realization of what he has done and to a passive acceptance of its consequences:

> . . . he is entering it again, the street which ran for thirty years. . . . It has made a circle and he is still inside of it. . . . 'And yet I have been farther in these seven days than in all the thirty years,' he thinks. 'But I have never got outside that circle. I have never broken out of the ring of what I have already done and cannot ever undo,' he thinks quietly. . . .(296–7)

Joe's murder of Joanna and his death are the active agents that force Hightower out of his isolation and contribute to his climactic realization of his failure and responsibility. Like Joe's, Hightower's search for identity was directed away from humanity; but whereas Joe used violence against the world in order to assert his existence, Hightower escaped from the world into the phantom past, identifying himself with the strong, lusty image of his grandfather, dead twenty years before Hightower's birth. Believing that the shame of losing his church and being nearly driven from town were the price of his immunity from the present and from involvement with the living, he had retired from the world to be a ghost among ghosts for twenty-five years. When Byron comes to tell him about Lena and her search for her lover, Hightower senses Byron's incipient involvement with her, and he fears that this will draw him, unwilling, into the living present of the events born of Joe's murder of Joanna. Learning that Christmas is part Negro, Hightower realizes the tragic enormity of what is about to happen: "Is it certain, proved, that he has Negro blood? Think, Byron; what it will mean when the people—if they catch . . . Poor man. Poor mankind." (87)

Later, when he hears from the grocer that Christmas' trail has been found, he is almost overcome. Feeling the whirlwind of circumstances growing larger and sucking him toward its center, and knowing the inevitable result, he cries in anguish: "I wont. I wont. I have bought my immunity. . . . I *will* not!" (271–2) He will not accept the necessity of his involvement, he will not enter the world and abjure his ghosthood.

Yet, though unwilling, he is drawn to the edge of the abyss, on the further side of which is life, as he listens to Mrs. Hines. Byron listens to them, thinking: "It's right funny. You'd think they had done got swapped somewhere. Like it was him that had a nigger grandson waiting to be hung." (339) Alarmed to find himself participating emotionally in the lives of others, Hightower violently, almost hysterically, refuses to try to save Christmas by giving him an alibi for the night of the murder.

> "It's not because I cant, dont dare to," he says; "it's because I wont! I wont! do you hear?" Byron does not move . . . thinking *It aint me he is shouting at. It's like he knows there is something nearer him than me to convince of that.* (342)

But the following morning, dragged out of sleep by Byron, he goes to Lena and delivers her baby. As he helps to bring life into the world, so he himself emerges into life, into an awareness and appreciation of the world of nature which Lena represents. Yet this is only half of what he must undertake if he is to be reborn into an awareness of himself, to give meaning to an otherwise meaningless life. The remaining act which will signify his commitment to the living is the confrontation with death. The final link in the chain of circumstances that force Hightower into life is completed, with the fatality and inevitability of some intricate design, when Joe, pursued by Percy Grimm, tries to hide in Hightower's house. Though struck down by Joe, Hightower makes a desperate and fruitless attempt to save him crying to the men: "Listen to me. He was here that night. He was with me the night of the murder. I swear to God—" (406)

Hightower's final reverie, a mixture of memory and the terror of realization, is a superb drama of consciousness reaching a climax of awareness that is almost unbearably intense, followed by a release equal in its dramatic reality to the purgation of pity and terror in the resolution of tragic action. Hightower, reliving in memory his history and his life, is drawn inevitably toward the realization he has so long refused to face, and even now tries to sidestep, arguing with himself that after all he has paid for his ghosthood, even with the price of his own life; he tries to convince himself that "it is any man's privilege to destroy himself, so long as he does not injure anyone else, so long as he lives to and of himself—" (429) But he cannot—as no man can—live only for himself. The price of his ghosthood was not only his own life, but his wife's as well. He realizes that he had come to Jefferson not to serve God but to idolize the memory of his grandfather, that in so doing he had betrayed his responsibility to his parishioners, and that he had resigned his pulpit and accepted the town's persecution not for a martyr's reasons, but to ensure his escape from the world. He sees now that he had been the instrument of his wife's despair and death, and knows that

> . . . for fifty years I have not even been clay: I have been a single instant of darkness in which a horse galloped and a gun crashed. And if I am my dead grandfather on the instant of his death, then my wife, his grandson's wife . . . [then I am] the debaucher and murderer of my grandson's wife, since I could neither let my grandson live or die. . . . (430)

Although there is no assurance that Hightower will now actively seek involvement with the living, or that he will no longer wait for the ghost-visited moments at twilight, his recognition of what he has been is a triumphantly positive achievement in which he gains stature as a kind of tragic figure rising from the shadows of an empty life.

Byron is in many senses a comic version of Hightower; like the elder man, Byron shuns real contact with life, existing so inconspicuously that few know of his existence, living so that "the chance to be hurt could not [find] him." (366) Through Lena, Byron becomes actively involved in the life of another, and comically, almost ludicrously, commits himself to her. In the process, he loses his quiet ineffectualness and learns to act, to walk with pride, and to accept the possibility of being hurt. Most important, he emerges from a shadowy world of vague reality into a realization of ultimate actuality:

> It was like me, and her, and all the other folks that I had to get mixed up in it, were just a lot of words that never even stood for anything, were not even us, while all the time what was us was going on and going on without even missing the lack of words. (352)

In short, he begins to be alive. As a comic figure, his realization is properly less dramatic than Hightower's, and in the end (as should the hero of any comedy) he gets his girl—or, at least, he gets permission to follow her. The account of their travels, as retailed by the furniture dealer, provides an almost bawdy comic relief after Joe's immolation and Hightower's tragic apotheosis.

Light in August posits two radically different ways of living, of dealing with experience: the pagan, primitive outlook of Lena Grove, and the basically Calvinistic world view of the civilized community. Essentially, it is a contrast between the extremes of animal unawareness of sin and human consciousness of man's fallen estate. Lena is possessed of a prelapsarian innocence; she obviously does not consider herself a fallen woman in any sense of the word, nor can she imagine others doing so; naïve and trusting, she has as little guile as she has awareness of sin. In contrast to her tranquillity is the atmosphere of Calvinism brooding over the center of the novel. Masculine, authoritarian, and rigid, it is based on the concept of an implacable God of wrath, of man's inherent sinfulness, of guilt and of the inevitability of punishment. Justice in this Calvinistic world is without pity or compassion; in it Christ appears rarely, if at all, as a merciful mediator between man and a just and terrible God.

Lena is an embodiment of a far older type of religion—that of the mother goddess of early Greek culture. That Faulkner intended this implied comparison between ancient pagan and modern Christian religion is apparent from his comments on the meaning of the title:

> In August in Mississippi there's a few days . . . when . . . there's a lambence, a luminous quality to the light, as though it came not from just today but from back in the old classic times. It might have fauns and satyrs and the gods . . . from Olympus in it somewhere . . . it [the title] reminded me of that time, of a luminosity older than our Christian civilization. Maybe the connection was with Lena Grove, who had something of that pagan quality of being able to assume everything. . . . (199, F IN U)

Thus Lena (whose name is a diminutive of the Greek name Helena, meaning a torch or a light one), reflecting the radiance of an older time, moves placidly through the novel, while the somber shadows of the present accompany the figure of Joe Christmas.

Much has been made of Joe as a negative Christ-figure, an impotent savior who can only suffer but not redeem. Certainly there is a tendency on the part of critics to find suspicious symbolism in the fact that Joe does not know of his parentage, that he was left on the orphanage doorstep on Christmas Eve, and that he was betrayed by a friend for money. There is a difference, however, between direct symbolism and a parallelism of symbol and fact. Joe is not so much a symbol of an impotent Christ as he is a fictional character whose experience is made more dramatic, more emotionally charged for the reader, by being associated—even negatively—with Christian symbolism. Joe never assumes purely religious symbology, but reacts—and is reacted to—within a broader context in which the forms of religious belief and expression have become sternly regulated, as a result of which stringent moral imperatives dictate an individual's thought and action. "And so why should not their religion drive them to the crucifixion of themselves and one another?" Hightower asks himself. "Since to pity him [Christmas] would be to admit selfdoubt and to hope for and need pity themselves." (321–2) The Calvinistic characters—McEachern, Hines, Grimm, and Joanna Burden—all, in their fanatic vision, see life solely in terms of black and white, good and evil, God and Satan; by basing their actions on this rigid structure they are spared both the necessity of choice and the possibility of responding to others as human beings.

Common to many of Faulkner's novels is the theme of human isolation, of the difficulty or impossibility of establishing anything but superficial contact between individuals. This is usually seen as the result of a failure to apprehend reality except in terms of formulated phrases, such as those of a religion, or some other pattern to which, like the occupants of Procrustes' bed, reality is made to fit. In *Light in August* this dual theme—the failure of contact and the forcing of life into a preestablished pattern—is given additional depth by the literal, physical isolation of the main characters from the community, which is a complement to their spiritual and emotional aloneness. However, the characters still must accept part of their self-definition from the community, which in turn redefines itself in terms of its exclusion of them. In asserting itself to be white, Southern, and Protestant, Jefferson puts itself in opposition to Joe, the Negro, to Joanna, the Northerner, and to Hightower, the apostate. Thus, in a negative sense the community and the isolated individual are still interdependent. Moreover, both the individual and the community see life in terms of patterned responses and suffer from a rigidity of outlook and a corresponding failure to act either ethically or responsibly. Both the community and the individual are guilty—the community of living by and reacting to dead formulas, the individual of attempting to separate himself from the community, which in the final analysis is equivalent to a rejection of humanity. As Hightower comes to realize, no man is able to destroy himself without, even unintentionally, destroying others; and no act is free of reverberations in the lives of others. The community—or humanity—and the individual are inextricably linked.

ABSALOM, ABSALOM! [1936]

Characters

THOMAS SUTPEN
ELLEN COLDFIELD SUTPEN, *his second wife*
HENRY SUTPEN, *their son*
JUDITH SUTPEN, *their daughter*
ROSA COLDFIELD, *Ellen's younger sister*
GOODHUE COLDFIELD, *their father*
GENERAL JASON COMPSON II, *Sutpen's only friend*
WASH JONES, *Sutpen's poor-white handyman*
MILLY JONES, *Wash's granddaughter*
CLYTIE [CLYTEMNESTRA], *Sutpen's daughter by a Negro slave*
CHARLES BON, *Sutpen's son by his first wife*
CHARLES ETIENNE SAINT-VALERY BON, *Charles's son by an octoroon*
JIM BOND, *the idiot son of Etienne Bon and a Negro woman*

Narrators

ROSA COLDFIELD, *who tells her story to Quentin*
JASON COMPSON III, *who tells the story he heard from his father, General
    Compson, to Quentin, his son*
QUENTIN COMPSON, *who tells what he heard from Miss Rosa and his father,
    as well as what he, himself, recalls*
SHREVE MC CANNON, *Quentin's Harvard roommate*

PLOT

The son of a poor-white Virginia mountaineer, Thomas Sutpen was
nearly out of boyhood when his family moved east to the Tidewater and
for the first time he saw white men of great wealth and property who
owned Negro slaves. Having grown up thinking that one man was essentially the same as another, that possessions or a bit of money were a sign
of luck rather than superiority, young Sutpen could not imagine that the
wealthy planters would consider him or his family inferior. However, when
delivering a message to a plantation house, he was told by a liveried Negro
to go around to the back, and his naïve view of life was destroyed. He
concluded that "they"—men who judged other men's worth by what they
owned rather than what they were—could only be fought with their own

weapons: money, slaves, and possessions. In order to assert his right to be recognized as a human being by other men, he determined to become a member of the class that had snubbed him, and adopted the aristocratic Southern social code as his guiding principle. Sutpen ran away to the West Indies to make his fortune and married the daughter of a Haitian sugar planter. Soon after the birth of their son, however, Sutpen discovered that his wife had Negro blood. Knowing that this "grand design" to become a wealthy Southern planter and found a dynasty could never be fulfilled if his wife and offspring had a taint of black blood, he divorced her and left Haiti, forced to start over again in his attempt to achieve his dream.

In 1833 Sutpen, with no apparent past and almost no possessions, arrived in Jefferson, Mississippi. He acquired a hundred square miles of fertile bottom land near the Tallahatchie River from Ikkemotubbe, the Chickasaw chief, paid with his last gold coin to have his deed to the property recorded in the town patent office, and disappeared. Returning a month later with a wagonload of wild French-speaking Negroes and a French architect, he began to build his house. After two years the house was completed and Sutpen lived alone for another three years in the unfurnished and windowless mansion, borrowing seed from General Compson to plant his first crops. Five years after his arrival he furnished the house and married Ellen Coldfield, the daughter of Goodhue Coldfield, the most piously respectable man in town. Ellen bore him two children, Henry and Judith.

In 1859 Henry Sutpen entered the University of Mississippi, forty miles away in Oxford. There he met and became a close friend of Charles Bon, some ten years Henry's senior, not knowing that Bon was the unacknowledged son of Sutpen's first marriage. The two young men spent Christmas at Sutpen's Hundred, and Ellen at once projected a betrothal between Charles and Judith. When, on the following Christmas, Charles again accompanied Henry to the plantation, Sutpen told Henry that the marriage between Judith and Charles could not take place. Henry, unwilling to believe the reasons for his father's decision, renounced his birthright and left for New Orleans with Charles. At the outbreak of the Civil War the following spring, the young men returned to Mississippi and joined a regiment formed at the university. Sutpen himself went to the war as second in command in Colonel Sartoris' 23rd Mississippi Infantry, of which he was elected colonel the following year. Charles and Henry stayed together all during the war, and came back to Sutpen's Hundred when the war was nearing its close. Then, in order to prevent him from going through with the forbidden marriage to Judith, Henry shot Charles at the plantation gate and disappeared.

When Sutpen returned from the war a few months later, he found his design to found a dynasty in ruins: his wife had been dead for three years, his son was a fugitive, and his daughter was confirmed in spinsterhood. In order to beget a male heir to replace Henry, Sutpen became engaged to his sister-in-law, Rosa Coldfield, who, in spite of her hatred for him, would have married him had he not insulted her by suggesting that "they try it first and if it was a boy and lived, they would be married." Sutpen then seduced the fifteen-year-old granddaughter of Wash Jones, his poor-white handyman, but the girl gave birth to a daughter. Because of Sutpen's total lack of concern for the girl and her child, Jones killed him; later that day Jones killed the girl and her infant and brought about his own death by threatening the posse that had come to arrest him for Sutpen's murder.

After Sutpen's death Judith went on living in the plantation house with Clytie, her mulatto half-sister. In 1871 she sent Clytie to New Orleans to bring back the orphaned Charles Etienne Saint-Valery Bon, Charles's son by his octoroon mistress. Judith and Clytie raised the boy, who was white in appearance, to think of himself as a Negro. As a result, he rejected his white blood entirely and married an apelike and very black Negro woman, who bore him an idiot son named Jim Bond. In 1884 Etienne caught yellow fever; Judith came down with the disease while nursing him, and both died.

In 1909 Miss Rosa Coldfield, Sutpen's sister-in-law and one-time betrothed, discovered that someone besides Clytie and Jim Bond was living in the dilapidated plantation house. Accompanied by Quentin Compson, she drove out to Sutpen's Hundred, where she found Henry Sutpen in hiding, ill and cared for by Clytie. Three months later Miss Rosa brought an ambulance to take Henry to the hospital but Clytie, thinking Henry was being taken for the killing of Charles over fifty years before, set fire to the house over her own and Henry's heads. The idiot Negro Jim Bond, howling in the ashes of the ruined house, was left as Sutpen's only descendant.

THE NARRATORS

Miss Rosa Coldfield, the first narrator, is both closest to Sutpen and least able to view him objectively. Summoning Quentin Compson to hear her story (Chapter 1), she evokes a vision of Sutpen as a demon mounted on horseback and fresh from hell, followed by his "wild niggers" and his captive French architect. She pictures Sutpen as a villain without pity or honor, a man whom she had learned to regard as an ogre before she first met him. Yet, though in many ways Sutpen had been the center of her bleak life, Miss Rosa knows little about him except hearsay, and had seen him scarcely a hundred times before she went to live at Sutpen's Hundred after Charles's death. Thus her information is limited to what she had heard of him as a child and her own brief personal experience with him; her account is further distorted by her thwarted personality. Embittered and lonely from childhood, Miss Rosa regards Sutpen as the cause of her family's misfortunes, a demon that must be destroyed, even though the destruction of her own family is involved in his. Having nothing around which to build her life but her hatred of Sutpen, Miss Rosa could forgive him anything but dying, for it had left her with nothing in his place.

Mr. Compson, the second narrator, gives a more objective picture of Sutpen's life because it has not involved him emotionally, and because he is by temperament a detached, somewhat cynical man. His version of Sutpen's life, which he had heard from his father, General Compson, casts a completely different light on Sutpen; no longer a demon or a brigand, he is seen on his arrival in Jefferson as only recently recovered from a long illness, gaunt, owning nothing save a pair of pistols and the horse he rode, unwilling to mix with the men in the Holston House bar because he did not have the money to pay for his share and would not accept what he could not return in kind.

Quentin Compson sees Sutpen as a representative of the South, particularly of the failings of Southern life and morality which he can recognize but from which he cannot separate himself. He sees in the Henry-Charles-Judith relationship a parallel to his relationship with his own sister, Caddy, and her lovers(see *The Sound and the Fury*). Quentin and his roommate Shreve so thoroughly project themselves into their characterizations of Sutpen's sons that at one point they seem to become Charles and Henry.

Shreve McCannon, Quentin's Harvard roommate, is the least involved of all the narrators, and thus is able to see Sutpen the most clearly. Having been told Miss Rosa's, Compson's, and Quentin's versions of the story, he summarizes and reconstructs with ironic detachment what he imagines to have been Charles's background. With Quentin, he creates a dramatization of the events just prior to Henry's murder of Charles.

CHAPTER OUTLINE

Chapters 1–5: a Sunday afternoon in Jefferson, Mississippi, September, 1909.

1. Miss Rosa Coldfield, having summoned Quentin Compson to listen to her story, tells him about Sutpen from the time he arrived in Jefferson in 1833 until about 1850. In the beginning of the chapter an omniscient narrator describes the setting—Miss Rosa's "office," her verbal evocation of Sutpen the demon, and Quentin's thoughts as he listens. The bulk of the chapter, however, is given over to Miss Rosa's narration.

2. It is the evening of the same day, and Quentin sits on the porch with his father, waiting until it is time for him to take Miss Rosa on her mysterious errand out to Sutpen's Hundred. The chapter begins in the

present but quickly blends into "that Sunday morning in 1833" when Sutpen arrived. Although the first part of the chapter is narrated by the author, it is clearly Mr. Compson's version of the tale that is being rehearsed. Compson himself takes over the telling of it at the point at which Sutpen leaves town for the second time.

3. The chapter begins with Quentin's question: Why, if Sutpen jilted Miss Rosa, should she want to tell anybody about it? Mr. Compson then begins his account of Miss Rosa, from her birth in 1845 to the death of Charles in 1865.

4. Quentin is still waiting for it to be dark enough for him to start for Miss Rosa's. Mr. Compson has just gone inside to get the letter written by Charles to Judith, and given by Judith to Quentin's grandmother. Mr. Compson then tells the story of Henry and Charles, beginning in 1860 and ending with Charles's murder.

5. Narrated in its entirety by Miss Rosa (save for the last page), this chapter begins at the point at which the two preceding chapters ended—the death of Charles—and ends with Sutpen's death. At the end of the chapter Miss Rosa tells Quentin why she wants him to accompany her out to Sutpen's Hundred.

Chapters 6–9: a cold night in Cambridge, Massachusetts, January, 1910.

6. Shreve McCannon, Quentin's roommate, has just come in; Quentin has been reading a letter from his father saying that Miss Rosa is dead. Shreve had asked him to tell him about the South, and Quentin remembers the beginning of his trip out to Sutpen's Hundred with Miss Rosa; Shreve interrupts and summarizes what he has by now been told of Miss Rosa and Sutpen. Quentin thinks of the death of Sutpen, and Shreve again interrupts, asking about the visit made by Quentin and his father to the graveyard at Sutpen's Hundred, where Mr. Compson had told Quentin of Bon's son, Charles Etienne, and how he was raised by Judith and Clytie, married a black woman, and begot an idiot son. The chapter ends as Quentin tells Shreve that someone besides Clytie and the idiot was living at Sutpen's Hundred the night he and Miss Rosa went out.

7. Quentin tells Shreve what he learned of Sutpen's life as a result of his visit to the plantation to find out who was hiding there.

8. Shreve gives his interpretation of Charles's early life and of his relationship to Henry and Judith; Quentin and Shreve together create a kind of mental dramatization of the events leading up to Henry's murder of Charles.

9. The room is freezing, and the boys get into bed. Quentin relives the night he and Miss Rosa found Henry hiding at Sutpen's Hundred. Shreve, having been told about the South, now wonders why Quentin hates it so much; but Quentin frantically denies that he hates it at all.

STRUCTURE

Absalom, Absalom! is composed of pieces—fragments of Sutpen's story —almost like the pieces of a pattern or a puzzle to be fitted together. Gradually, the fragments are pulled into place, the overlapping pieces of the narrative woven together, and the resultant picture of Sutpen and his family is one that is somehow greater than the sum of its individual parts. We are not so much *told* about Sutpen as forced to live through the narrators' knowledge, either real or imaginary, of Sutpen's life, to undergo the narrators' experiences in relation to the Sutpen saga. We are first given a glimpse of a stranger about whom perhaps half a dozen facts are known—his arrival in Jefferson, his marriage, his war career, his son's disappearance, and his death; then each narrator tries, with varying degrees of success, to fill in the gaps between the facts and to reconstruct Sutpen's life and personality.

Both structurally and contextually, Absalom, Absalom! is a novel dealing with the nature of truth, and with the inability of any single person to perceive more than a fragment of it. In the first place, the nature of the perceiver determines to a large degree the nature of the thing perceived; Miss Rosa sees a fragment of the reality of Sutpen, which might be a partial or provisional truth, but to her this fragment is the total man, Sutpen the demon the total truth. Against Miss Rosa's vision is played the counterpoint of Mr. Compson's story, in which Sutpen emerges as a man of more ordinary stature and with no more than an ordinary capacity for evil. Though more reasonable and more in accord with such facts as are known of Sutpen, Mr. Compson's vision is still determined by his own personality and perspective; his view of Henry as a raw provincial youth seduced by the cosmopolitan glamor and world-weary sophistication of Bon is the attitude of an aging ironist toward the too-serious preoccupations of youth (compare his remarks to Quentin in The Sound and the Fury on the subject of virginity, with which Quentin is obsessed, and of Quentin's agony over his sister). Shreve combines pieces of Miss Rosa's demonizing and Mr. Compson's objectivity and mild satire with his own flippancy and his emotional and temporal distance from the story to create a third version, as if he were playing the two counterpointed voices in a different key. He provides a variation to the tale with his story of the vengeful mother and greedy lawyer bringing up Charles to be the instrument of Sutpen's destruction. Quentin and Shreve create a new picture of Sutpen's sons by dramatizing Henry's attempt to rationalize away his hereditary fear of incest and positing his more socially oriented horror of miscegenation as his reason for killing Charles to prevent the marriage to Judith. To Miss Rosa, Charles was the unseen and idealized knight to whom she could transfer her thwarted girlhood's need to love; to Compson, he was a young fatalist, a decadent too old in the ways of the world to be reasonably expected to turn up at a new college in the wilds of Mississippi and yet inexplicably there, the sybaritic seducer of both Henry and Judith. Quentin and Shreve give Charles his final shape and articulation, seeing him and Henry as themselves, seeing their own individual concerns reflected in Charles's and Henry's overintense relationship and problematical agonizings.

Even if any one person were able from some godlike perspective to apprehend simultaneously all the implications and apparent contradictions and motivations involved in an act—let alone in an entire lifetime—and thus see the total reality, the composite truth, of the act, he would, because of the nature of language, be unable to communicate this truth to another. Miss Rosa repeatedly (Chapter 5) says of Charles: "But I didn't love him," trying to explain the truth of the word *love*, the reality of her emotions toward him. She immerses her listener in words, trying to capture by tone, sound, and repetition more than by syntactical sense the evanescence of feeling, the nonverbal reality of experience. But the complete reality—the truth—of an experience cannot be conveyed by words without losing something in translation, for words are only arbitrary counters for emotions or ideas or sensations that are too fluid, too individual, too complex to be contained within fixed limits of meaning. Attempting to recreate the reality of Sutpen, none of the narrators are satisfied with their attempts to describe him or account for his actions; as a result, they constantly qualify, repeat, and rephrase their statements, constantly search for a different word, a different way of putting it, that will somehow convey the fullness, the total reality, of their perception.

In broadest terms, Sutpen is a representative of the Old South: exaggerated, perhaps, because his rise and fall had to be compassed in a period of thirty years, not over several generations, more ruthless and less cultured than men of his generation who were members of already established families (Sartoris, Compson), because he did not think he could afford pity and he knew he did not have the time for culture. His faults were the faults of the Old South as a whole, magnified—like Sutpen himself, somewhat larger than life—but not therefore distorted. His downfall, the "mistake" he could not locate or begin to understand, was the result of his most fundamental failing: his inability to recognize, though the same choice was offered him again and again, the superiority of human values over social ones. In every instance—his repudiation of his part-Negro wife and son, his refusal to acknowledge Charles, and his rejection of Milly when she bore him a daughter—Sutpen adhered to the Southern social code that abhorred miscegenation and decreed the necessity of sons to perpetuate the line, completely denying his human obligation to wife and son, mistress and daughter. His morality, based only on logic and rationality, denied the validity, perhaps even the existence, of emotional obligation, and led him to view human relationships as accounts in a ledger, capable of being cleared as one clears a legal debt.

Given more awareness, Sutpen might have been a truly tragic figure in the Greek fashion, for he had the stature; his physical accomplishments were those of a man of heroic courage and determination. His besetting ambition and pride resemble the hubris that prefigures tragedy, and his tragic flaw was perhaps the inhuman singlemindedness that prevented him from seeing life in terms of anything other than the fulfillment of his design. However, unlike Oedipus, he died morally blind, aware that he had failed but totally unaware of the reasons for his failure, let alone the fact that his failure could be laid only at his own doorstep. Sutpen falls short of being a tragic hero, for he never attains the moment of truth, the realization of how and why he has failed; as he is something of a giant he is also something of a child. It is as if his moral development and his understanding were frozen on that afternoon the "monkey-nigger" told the poorwhite boy to go around to the back door; only the boy's body and strength and courage continued to grow, while his understanding remained that of the boy despoiled of his innocence. Yet there is a certain pitiableness in his attempts to deal honestly with others, in his total lack of understanding that human values cannot be equated with dollars-and-cents values, that morality is not entirely a product of logic and reason.

According to his own lights, Sutpen acted justly and justifiably. This inability to understand the nature of his mistake is doubly ironic: what had begun as a design to assert his right to be recognized as a human being became a rigid pattern which forced Sutpen to choose to repudiate the human claims of his wife and son; the very recognition he so desperately wanted himself he failed to give to those who stood in relation to him as he had to the Tidewater aristocrats. Charles is repeatedly shown in the position of Sutpen's "boy-symbol," the forlorn child whom Sutpen had vowed would never be turned away from the door again; and Wash Jones (Sutpen is referred to as the apotheosis of Jones) is presented as what Sutpen might himself have been, had he not been fired with ambition to be recognized as the equal of the plantation owner. With the blindness both of a man obsessed and of an unthinking child, Sutpen rejected Charles; as a result, Charles was killed, Henry forced to flee, and Sutpen cheated of the possibility of grandchildren. Still obsessed and unthinking, he insulted Jones; the latter, wounded by the man he had idolized far more than Sutpen had been wounded by the scorn of the "monkey-nigger" forty-five years before, killed Sutpen because he, too, being human, had to do something in order to live with himself, even for the few hours before Major de Spain came to take him to jail. In both instances, Sutpen was confronted by a man wanting recognition as a *human being*; in both instances, Sutpen denied that recognition because it could not be included as a part of his design.

The major characters of *Absalom, Absalom!* suffer from a failure to organize their experience into some coherent and viable whole, a tendency to substitute a rigid world order for a living one. Sutpen once saw life in terms of his boyhood belief that men were equal; when this vision was shattered, he was forced to put something in place of it, some system— religious, social, or personal—according to which he could see himself in some sort of ordered relation to the world. Thus he projected his grand design, his plan to become a wealthy planter. Once conceived, however, his design was unchangeable, and he spent the rest of his life trying to force life to conform to it. The static inflexibility of the design put it in opposition to life, which will not fit a pattern that does not allow for time and change.

Whereas Sutpen saw everything in terms of the fulfillment of his design, Miss Rosa saw everything in terms of her hatred for Sutpen; her demonizing served much the same purpose for her that Sutpen's design did for him: it gave perspective to her world, and arranged what would otherwise be unrelated events into a reasonable order. If Sutpen is a demon, then Miss Rosa's life can have some meaning, some purpose, even if the only reason for Miss Rosa's embittered spinsterhood and the destruction of her family is their instrumentality in the destruction of Sutpen. Thus, as she saw it, Ellen and the children were sacrificed to him; Miss Rosa herself, though saved from the embraces of the demon, was actually only preserved for the "later, colder sacrifice" of living in lonely bitterness. And, just as Miss Rosa's conception of Sutpen is rigid—no matter what he did, she saw it as the act of a demon—so Miss Rosa herself is rigid: bitter, implacable, unforgiving. Unwilling to change with the changing times, she refused to relinquish the lost cause of the war, and lived completely in the past. Physically, she is described as stiff and unbending:

> sitting so bolt upright in the straight hard chair that was so tall for her that her legs hung straight and rigid as if she had iron shinbones and ankles, clear of the floor with that air of impotent and static rage like children's feet. . . .(7)

Perhaps she lives as long as she does only out of some grotesque need to see the final holocaust of Sutpen's design, to have her vision of the demon vindicated, to know that once again she was right.

As we know from *The Sound and the Fury,* Quentin had ordered his world around his sister Caddy, and tried to retain his ideal and unchangeable vision of her in the face of her flagrant departure from what he wished her to be. His love for her was not love for a living and therefore changing being, but for an abstraction, an ideal shape into which a living being cannot be molded. At the time that Quentin is telling the story to Shreve, he is suffering from his inability either to accept his sister's promiscuity or to avenge the family's smudged honor by killing her seducer. Thus Quentin is fascinated by the vision of Henry facing his sister after he had killed Charles, telling her "now you can't marry him, because he's dead; I killed him." This scene parallels, in Quentin's mind, his own attempt and inglorious failure to fight Dalton Ames, Caddy's seducer; the successful Henry, having prevented the forbidden marriage which threatened the honor of his family, is superimposed in Quentin's mind over the picture of himself fainting on the field of battle and being jeeringly dismissed by the man he had come to kill. In addition, Quentin identifies himself with both Henry and Charles: with Henry, of course, who loves his sister and is driven to kill her would-be husband, and with Charles, who plays the role of the sister's lover and is therefore the man—the part of himself— whom he must kill to prevent dishonor. Thus, when Quentin stops before the picture of Henry confronting Judith over the body of their half-brother and her would-be lover, he is seeing himself both as failing to kill Ames, the seducer, and as successfully killing himself, the would-be lover who wanted to erase petty dishonor by overshadowing it with the sin of incest.

    Absalom, Absalom! is full of echoes, of past scenes and figures reappearing for a moment in the posture of the present, of suggestions that, as Quentin says, "nothing ever happens once and is finished." Faulkner's constant preoccupation with time, with the immanence of the past in the present, floods the novel: parts of Sutpen have been reborn in Henry and Charles, and parts of all three in Quentin. The sins of the fathers are visited upon the children because the children, too, ironically and in their innocence, display the same blindness, choose again the design, the tradition, that negates or destroys life. Henry, in choosing to kill Charles rather than permit the social sin of miscegenation, chooses, as his father did, the social value above the human value; having unthinkingly accepted the Southern code, Henry could more easily kill his beloved brother than countenance a violation of the Southern morality. Quentin shows himself to be, spiritually at least, a son of Sutpen when he and Shreve emphasize that it is the threat of miscegenation, not incest, which drives Henry to kill Charles; and Shreve's irony awakens in Quentin's mind echoes of his father, so that Shreve becomes a kind of latter-day Compson, Northern style. The past does not seem simply to influence the present as much as it simultaneously exists in and with the present, so that Quentin can no more be free of the Southern past then he can be free of his own past acts. Its history and traditions are perpetuated in him, and, as he loves the South as a part of himself, he also hates it for the guilt, both sectional and personal, that it has forced him to assume. The guilt that Sutpen, and the ante-bellum South as a whole, incurred without ever recognizing it has been passed on to be expiated only, if at all, by later generations.

THE UNVANQUISHED [1938]*

Characters

COLONEL JOHN SARTORIS
MRS. ROSA [GRANNY] MILLARD, *his mother-in-law*
BAYARD SARTORIS, *Colonel Sartoris' son*
DRUSILLA HAWK, *niece of Rosa Millard and Colonel Sartoris' second wife*
AB SNOPES, *a poor-white horse and mule trader*
BEN REDMOND, *former business partner of Colonel Sartoris*
RINGO, *Bayard's Negro companion*
LOOSH, *a former slave who left with the Yankees*

1. "AMBUSCADE" [summer, 1862]
Vicksburg and Corinth have just fallen, opening Mississippi to the Union army, and Colonel John Sartoris comes home unexpectedly. At his direction the Negroes build a stock pen in the swamp and bury the family silver, and then Sartoris leaves again. Having heard from the Negroes that General Sherman is coming, Bayard and Ringo, twelve years old, watch the road for the arrival of the Yankees. Spying one, they shoot at him, and then discover that there is a whole regiment with him. Bayard's grandmother, Rosa Millard, hides the boys under her skirts while the Yankees search the house, and steadfastly denies that there are any children on the place.

2. "RETREAT" [1863]
Having been told by Colonel Sartoris to leave the plantation and go to Memphis, Mrs. Millard has the Negroes dig up the chest of silver and takes it with her. When the family is on the road, a small band of Yankees meets them and steals the mules. Bayard and Ringo "borrow" a horse from a nearby deserted stable and give the Yankees chase. The boys are found the following morning by Colonel Sartoris, and the three accidentally capture a Yankee camp. (A different version of this incident is given in *Sartoris*.) They return home, where they meet Mrs. Millard and the Negroes, bury the trunk again, and work on the stock pen in the swamp. The next

* The Unvanquished *was published in book form in 1938. The first six stories appeared in* The Saturday Evening Post *and* Scribner's Magazine *between 1934 and 1936; the final story "An Odor of Verbena," was written especially for inclusion in the collection.*

day the Yankees come to the plantation looking for Colonel Sartoris, who, through a clever ruse, manages to escape. The Yankees then set the house on fire, and Loosh, one of the Negroes, tells them where the silver was buried.

3. "RAID" [summer, 1863]
     Mrs. Millard, Bayard, and Ringo leave Jefferson on a trip to Mrs. Millard's sister at Hawkhurst, Alabama. While on the road, they are passed by a massive group of Negroes bound in a kind of hysterical trance for "Jordan." At Hawkhurst, as at Sartoris, the house has been burned and the white people live in a Negro cabin; the railroad, the Atlanta-Chattanooga line, has been torn up by the Yankees. With Drusilla Hawk, the Sartorises try to stop an army of Negroes from crossing the river on a bridge the Yankees are about to blow up, but they are swept by the tide of Negroes into the river. Their horses drown, but they are fetched up on the other side, where Mrs. Millard demands to be brought to the Yankee Colonel Dick. The Colonel, overburdened with the spoils of war, gives them ten chests of silver to replace the one the Yankees had stolen the year before, many mules and Negroes, and a paper requisitioning still more mules, silver, and Negroes from other Yankee regiments.

4. "RIPOSTE IN TERTIO" [1864]
     Having acquired some printed letterheads, Mrs. Millard begins to forge official letters requisitioning mules from Yankee regiments, and, with the aid of Ab Snopes, sells the animals back to other regiments. She gives the profits and some of the mules to the poor people of the county, and keeps an account of what each has received and how he has put it to use. In an attempt to make a profit before all Yankees have withdrawn from the county, Snopes tells the last regiment about the existence of the mules in the swamp stock pen. Afterwards, hoping to make up the money lost when the Yankees took back their mules, Mrs. Millard lets Snopes talk her into trying to get four thoroughbred horses from Grumby, the leader of a band of Confederate raiders. Though Bayard and Ringo try to stop her, she goes to Grumby's lair, where she is murdered.

5. "VENDEE" [1864–5]
     After Mrs. Millard's funeral, Uncle Buck McCaslin, though in his sixties and suffering from rheumatism, joins Bayard and Ringo in their hunt for her killer. When they have been out over a month they meet a stranger who appears to be friendly but shoots Uncle Buck as he rides away. When his wounded arm threatens to become infected, Uncle Buck leaves the boys and returns home. Some time afterward Bayard and Ringo meet up with Grumby and, after a fight, kill him. They nail his carcass—all but the right

hand—to the door of the old cotton compress where he had killed Mrs. Millard, and take the hand home with them to be fastened on to the headboard of her grave.

6. "SKIRMISH AT SARTORIS" [1865]

Drusilla Hawk, who had run away from home to fight with Colonel Sartoris' troop, comes home with him after the war, but continues to work and dress like a man. The ladies in Jefferson come to offer Drusilla their "sympathy and help." Finally Mrs. Hawk arrives from Alabama, forces Drusilla into a dress, and demands that Colonel Sartoris marry her daughter. In Jefferson, meanwhile, a pair of Northerners—the Burdens, grandfather and grandson—are trying to guarantee the Negroes their voting rights, and make Cash Benbow, formerly the Benbow's Negro coachman, a candidate for U. S. marshal. On Election Day Colonel Sartoris stops the election, shoots the Burdens, nominates Drusilla voting commissioner, and says that the election will be carried on at the Sartoris plantation. There only white men vote and all vote "no" for the Negro candidate. In the excitement, Drusilla and Sartoris, to the utter consternation of Mrs. Hawk, forget to get married.

7. "AN ODOR OF VERBENA" [1874]

Bayard, studying law at the University of Mississippi, is called home with the news that his father has been shot dead by his former business partner, Ben Redmond. Bayard knows that the principle in which he has come to believe—that he cannot, like his father, go through life killing men—will be tested. During his ride home he remembers how Colonel Sartoris bought out Redmond's interest in the railroad and taunted Redmond. Sartoris' friends urged Bayard to ask his father to stop his senseless and dangerous prodding of his rival. Sartoris then ran for the legislature against Redmond and won; yet, knowing Redmond's enmity, he told Bayard that he was tired of killing men and would meet Redmond unarmed. As Bayard reaches home he is met by a group of men who were in Colonel Sartoris' troop during the war, and who assume that he has come home to avenge his father's death. Drusilla, like the voracious priestess of some warlike god, urges Bayard with passionate intensity on a mission of holy vengeance. Only Miss Jenny, his father's sister, counsels against bloodshed. The following morning Bayard goes into town unarmed to face Redmond. The latter fires but aims to miss, and immediately afterwards leaves Jefferson for good.

The most easily readable of Faulkner's books, The Unvanquished presents a romanticized and almost entirely uncritical picture of Southern aristocracy. The Sartorises are depicted with affection and admiration, and the action is surrounded by an aura of gallantry, sentimentality, and humor.

Though the first six stories take place either during or shortly after the Civil War and the Sartorises have frequent collisions with the Yankees, the episodes tend to be anecdotal, and nowhere is there more than a suggestion of the grimness of war or of despair over a cause obviously lost. Only the addition of the last story, "An Odor of Verbena," gives the collection perspective and a measure of significance.

Written almost ten years after *Sartoris*, which dealt with the family as it existed in 1919, "An Odor of Verbena" casts the first critical light on the romantic haze surrounding the figure of Colonel John Sartoris and the family tradition he established. If in *Sartoris* he is a symbol of the glory and honor of the men of the Old South, he is seen here in human rather than heroic perspective—intolerant, domineering, and not above needlessly baiting his beaten rival. The revelation of his weaknesses, however, is not intended to shatter the image of him as a great man, but to temper it with truth, so that the Sartoris myth—and the myth of the Old South, with which it is persistently identified—can be seen for what it is; a mixture of nobility and arrogance, honor and intolerance, courage and braggadocio, in short, a mixture of good and evil.

As a boy, Bayard had unquestioningly accepted violence and vengeance as necessary and even desirable, shooting at the Yankees with great high spirits and little regard for the consequences, and tracking down Granny Millard's killer with an utter seriousness which made the manhunt almost a ritualistic discharge of an obligation toward the dead. When at twenty-four, however, he is confronted with what Southern society and his upbringing consider a similar obligation to vengeance, he faces it not as a Sartoris or a Southerner, but as a mature individual for whom violence cannot be an answer, and finds in it a test of himself:

> At least this will be my chance to find out if I am what I think I am or if I just hope; if I am going to do what I have taught myself is right or if I am just going to wish I were.

Thus Bayard is caught in a conflict suggestive of Greek tragedy: the Southern code demands vengeance for a father's murder, but Bayard's personal morality, based on the commandment *Thou shalt not kill*, rejects vengeance. That Faulkner intended Greek echoes in the story is obvious from the description of George Wyatt and the other men as a "chorus," and from his treatment of Drusilla, who plays the part of the priestess of some ancient cult of blood and vengeance. Her presentation of the pistols to Bayard is a ritual gesture, as is the amphoralike posture—arms reaching for the flowers behind her ears—she repeatedly assumes. Both Drusilla, the priestess, and Wyatt, the leader of the chorus, respond in an almost preternatural manner to Bayard's unwillingness to conform to the quasi-religious and social standards they represent. Drusilla snatches back in horror the hand Bayard has kissed, realizing that he is refusing the sanction to kill which she in her priestess capacity has offered to grant to him. Wyatt, momentarily enraged when he senses that Bayard is not going to kill, demands of him whether or not he is a Sartoris, and threatens to kill Redmond himself if Bayard refuses to accept the obligation of vengeance.

The verbena that Drusilla wears and leaves behind as a token for Bayard is also significant, for verbenae were the sacred boughs of laurel, myrtle, or olive carried by priests or heralds and of which garlands were made to crown participants in certain Roman rites. Thus this flower, which is said to have the only scent that can be smelled above horses and courage, has associations with laurel, given by the ancients to heroes and poets, with myrtle, sacred to Venus, and with olive, a symbol of peace. Drusilla, perhaps realizing that Bayard's courage not to kill is of a higher order than her own physical courage, but still unable to accept this realization, swears she will never wear verbena again, but leaves a sprig on Bayard's pillow as a token of his right to it.

"An Odor of Verbena" casts light on two aspects of the Sartoris tradition. First, whereas the Colonel's tradition is usually said to represent (on the basis of Sartoris) the best aspects of the Old South, here the Colonel himself recognizes, at the end of his life, the need for some "moral housecleaning," and Bayard passionately rejects the validity of his father's dream of rebuilding the South, knowing that it must fail because it has little regard for individual human life. Secondly, the Sartoris tradition had become a pattern to which all Sartorises were expected to fit themselves, becoming not individual human beings, but more or less successful imitations of their famous ancestor. In breaking with the tradition Bayard committed a more truly brave and certainly a morally more significant act than the murder of a dozen carpetbaggers or the theft of a gross of anchovies. By shaping and being faithful to his own moral code he became not merely a Sartoris, an extension of his father, but an individual in his own right. Unfortunately, however, the Sartoris mold had already solidified in the imagination of Jefferson, and it was not Bayard's brave deed—his willingness to be thought a coward in standing by his principles—that became the stuff of the Sartoris legend. Two generations later, in Sartoris, the young Sartorises are still being brought up to emulate the violent and glamorous actions of the Colonel, while Bayard, in the background, quietly grows old.

THE SNOPES TRILOGY:

The Hamlet [1940], The Town [1957], and The Mansion [1959]

Principal Characters

FLEM SNOPES [1880?–1946]
WILL [UNCLE BILLY] VARNER, the autocrat of Frenchman's Bend
JODY VARNER, his son
EULA VARNER [1889–1927], his daughter, later Flem's wife
V. K. RATLIFF, a sewing-machine salesman
GAVIN STEVENS [1888?–   ], a lawyer
CHARLES [CHICK] MALLISON [1914?–   ], his nephew
LINDA SNOPES [1908–   ], daughter of Eula Varner and Hoake McCarron

The Snopeses

BYRON SNOPES, a bank robber
CLARENCE EGGLESTONE SNOPES, a Mississippi state senator
DORIS SNOPES, the erstwhile "trainer" of Byron Snopes's vicious children
ECK SNOPES, a blacksmith
IKE SNOPES, an idiot
I. O. SNOPES, a swindler
LUMP SNOPES, a clerk
MINK SNOPES, a murderer
MONTGOMERY WARD SNOPES, a purveyor of pornography
ORESTES SNOPES, a hog-raiser
VIRGIL SNOPES, a sexual athlete
WALLSTREET PANIC SNOPES, a grocer
WATKINS PRODUCTS SNOPES, a carpenter
Four nameless children of Byron Snopes and an Apache squaw

The Country People

HENRY ARMSTID
ODUM BOOKWRIGHT
JACK HOUSTON

MRS. LITTLEJOHN
HOAKE MC CARRON
SOLON QUICK
VERNON TULL

The Townsfolk

MANFRED DE SPAIN, a mayor of Jefferson and president of Colonel Sartoris'
bank, and the lover of Eula Varner Snopes
MELISANDRE BACKUS HARRISS, later Gavin Stevens' wife
GOWAN STEVENS, a young relative of Gavin Stevens
GROVER CLEVELAND WINBUSH, Jefferson's night marshal

The trilogy traces the rise of the Snopes family, symbols of modern commercial avariciousness, from the arrival of Flem Snopes in Frenchman's
Bend in the early 1900s. The Hamlet is devoted to the importation of
Snopeses into Frenchman's Bend and to Flem's rise from the clerkship of
Will Varner's store, through usury and sharp bargaining and a gradual
accretion of financial power, to his marriage to Varner's daughter Eula,
pregnant by another man. In The Town Flem, having outgrown the Bend,
moves with his family to Jefferson, where he contrives to progress from the
ownership of a small back-street restaurant to the superintendency of the
town power plant to the vice-presidency of Colonel Sartoris' bank. The
novel ends with Flem's successful maneuver to oust Manfred de Spain both
from the presidency of the bank and from Mrs. Snopes's bed. Flem becomes bank president and moves into the former De Spain house, the
"mansion" of the last volume. In The Mansion, Flem is a wealthy and
seemingly respectable man, a deacon of the Baptist church. However, the
novel deals primarily with his pretended daughter Linda and with Mink
Snopes, a murderer in Parchman Penitentiary who has sworn to kill him.

The three novels are unified by the tracing of Flem's rise, the presence
of largely the same cast of characters, and the technique, used in The Town
and in part of The Mansion, of multiple narration by Gavin Stevens, V. K.
Ratliff, and Chick Mallison. However, whereas The Hamlet is broadly
comic in tone, the two later books are primarily serious and less dra-
matically immediate (with the exception of the sections dealing with Mink
in The Mansion), and focus less on Flem than on Gavin Stevens, both as
an interpreter and as a character. These differences in tone and approach are
partially explained by the fact that The Hamlet was published almost
twenty years before the two succeeding volumes, and that many of The
Hamlet's episodes were previously written and published as stories in magazines between 1931 and 1936. The Hamlet is almost entirely episodic,

unified by the presence of one Snopes or another in each of the episodes and, more significantly, by the theme of economic man vis-à-vis natural man—of the Snopes's moneygrubbing as opposed to Eula Varner's earthy sensuality or even to Ike Snopes's absurdly romantic love for his cow.

The Town, which is less episodic than simply loose, continues this theme in Flem's acquistion of money and power set against Eula's overwhelming sexual attractiveness. It also reiterates the opposition between social economics and nature, this time in the character of Gavin Stevens. As a lawyer, Stevens is a representative of civilization and lawful commerce; he is also a lover manqué, attracted to the lush femininity of Eula and later to a more diluted form of it in Linda, but unable to come to terms with it.

The Mansion combines the multiple narrative of Stevens, Ratliff, and Chick Mallison with sections of omniscient narrative by the author. It links up with The Hamlet by recounting a longer version of Mink Snopes's murder of Jack Houston and his sense of betrayal by Flem, who made no attempt to help his relative escape the penalty for his crime. Though structurally a far better novel than The Town, The Mansion suffers in the long section on Linda from rather extreme discursiveness and from the repetition of events occurring in the earlier volumes. Furthermore, the shrewd economic manipulations of Flem that gave sharpness to the previous books are almost entirely absent. The Flem of The Mansion pursues respectability as hotly as he had once followed cold cash, and the natural splendor of Eula is unhappily dimmed in Linda and in her unimpassioned relationship with Stevens. The element of natural sexuality seems to be present, if at all, only in the adolescent and occasionally crude remarks of Chick.

The Hamlet

The Hamlet is composed of four sections, each dominated by one of four different but closely related modes: comedy, myth, romance, and what might be called nightmare-comedy, or the grotesque. The tone of the book as a whole, however, is one of carefully controlled comic realism. This results largely from two devices: the contrast between events and the reactions they elicit from their observers [cf. the comic effect achieved when Mrs. Varner, learning that Eula is pregnant, gasps at Will and Jody: "Turning up pregnant and yelling and cursing here in the house when I am trying to take a nap!" (144)] and the detached, wry comments of Ratliff, whose colloquial speech and dispassionate observation transform realism into comedy and often, even further, into irony.

Because of Ratliff's almost constant presence and his first-person narration of the Ab Snopes-Pat Stamper tale, Part I (FLEM) is predominantly comic. In Part II (EULA) comedy is raised to the level of ironic myth through the figure of Eula, an early-flowering, indolent Helen of Troy, whose "entire appearance suggested some symbology out of the old Dionysic times—honey in sunlight and bursting grapes, the writhen bleeding of the crushed fecundated vine beneath the hard rapacious trampling goat-hoof." (95) Though Eula herself is clearly a mythic creature, an anachronistic goddess stolen from old Greece and misplaced in a rural Mississippi village, irony is maintained in her section both through the reactions of her family to her and through her emergency marriage to Flem Snopes—an irony that is underlined by the intensely romanticized rhetoric of the passage describing Eula's departure from the hamlet, now only "a little lost village, nameless, without grace, forsaken, yet which wombed once by blind chance and accident one blind seed of the spendthrift Olympian ejaculation and did not even know it." (149) In Part III (THE LONG SUMMER) a short introductory section, in which Ratliff departs from his normal detachment and attacks the Snopeses with a vicious parody of I. O.'s use of proverbs, establishes the contrast for the major mode of romance. In rich, poetic prose that, though purple, is as carefully controlled as a poem, Faulkner presents the courtly lover, the idiot Ike Snopes, and his coy and maiden mistress—a cow. Again irony is maintained by the implicit contrast between the reader's awareness of the reality of the situation and the highly romanticized description of the lovers, the sublimity of the presentation balanced against the ludicrousness of the objective scene. In the first section of Chapter 2, which concerns Jack Houston and his wife, romance is more closely aligned with reality, both in the more straightforward, almost restrained prose and in the relative appropriateness of the lover's view to the reality of the beloved. In the second section, Mink Snopes is introduced as the last of the triad of lovers, the third phase of love, as it were, in which romance is totally missing and has been replaced by obsession ["It's like drink. It's like dope to me," he thinks (225)]. Mink is married to a former prostitute, a nymphomaniac whose aggressive sexuality has made him feel himself the passive, prone recipient in their relationship. The roles of the lovers have been figuratively, at least, reversed, and romance has turned inward upon itself and become its opposite, no longer courtliness toward the tenderly beloved maiden but passionate hostility toward a "fierce lioness" simultaneously desired and hated. As a result of this reversal, the second section tends away from romance into the grotesque; beginning with Mink's murder of Houston over the matter of a three-dollar pasturage fee (significantly, the account of the murder and the hiding of the corpse are interwoven with the story of Mink and his wife) the element of the grotesque becomes more and more dominant. It culminates in Lump Snopes's attempts to force Mink to go back and steal fifty dollars from Houston's body, and in Mink's outraged belief that everything was "all right" until Houston's body fell apart when he tried to move it to a new hiding-place.

The final section moves again toward comedy with the presence of Ratliff, but there are overtones of pathos for the plight of Mink's wife; for Mink himself, hopelessly awaiting deliverance by Flem; and for the idiot Ike, left with only a wooden effigy of his beloved cow.

Part IV (THE PEASANTS) begins in a kind of nightmare-comedy of grotesquerie with the hobgoblinish spotted horses. Interwoven with the moonlit scene of plunging, harlequin-patterned animals and the half-comic, half-grotesque attempts of the men to capture them is a second mythic vision of Eula standing in the window of the Varner house:

> She did not lean out, she merely stood there, full in the moon, apparently blank-eyed or certainly not looking downward at them—the heavy gold hair, the mask not tragic and perhaps not even doomed: just damned, the strong faint lift of breasts beneath the marblelike fall of the garment; to those below what Brunhilde, what Rhinemaiden on what spurious river-rock of papier-mâché, what Helen returned to what topless and shoddy Argos, waiting for no one. (311)

There is an additional suggestion of the ancient, golden mythic days of Eula's Olympian avatars in the blossoming pear tree in front of Mrs. Littlejohn's lot. Aside from being a fertility symbol, the pear tree is associated with medieval romance (cf. Chaucer, "The Merchant's Tale," in which Damion seduces May, the young wife of old January, in a pear tree. A similar tale is widely known in Europe and Asia, and is referred to by folklorists as the "Pear-Tree Episode") and thus links Part IV to the medieval romance of Part III. The mockingbird (a sexual symbol) that comes to sing in the pear tree is probably the Mississippi counterpart of the nightingale, identified both with the romantic tradition and with sexuality. Playing in counterpoint with these mythic, romantic elements are the mundane, sometimes pathetic and sometimes ludicrous country people: the harried Eck Snopes, trying to keep little Wallstreet Panic from being trampled; the petulant Armstid, determined to buy a horse he cannot afford; his gray overworked wife, incapable of restraining her husband's rashness; the benighted and literally overridden Tulls; and the stolid, sensible Mrs. Littlejohn. Toward the end of the section the blend of grotesque comedy, myth, and romance fades again into comedy and irony as Ratliff takes a dominant part in the conversation and observes Mrs. Armstid's attempts to get her five dollars back from Flem. In the second section, which deals with the Armstids' suit against Flem for the return of the five dollars and the Tulls's against Eck for damages sustained when Eck's spotted horses upset the Tull wagon on the bridge, the comic mode continues, and is carried on to the conclusion of the book.

The Hamlet contains the major themes found in the novels of Faulkner's major period—1929 to 1936—transposed, as it were, into another key.

While the backdrop of the aristocratic Southern past and the tragic agonizing of the deracinated Southerner are absent, the events of *The Hamlet* still, in the final analysis, may be reduced to a concern with the conflict between the accepted standards of a given society and the asocial nature of the human needs and passions of its members. Because the hamlet of Frenchman's Bend is still in its social infancy, the conflict between the commercial and other civilizing aspects of society and the world of nature with its natural passions is seen in its clearest and most elemental state, dramatized by characters whose relative lack of complexity makes them easily assume a stature at least allegorical, and, in some cases, symbolic.

In the beginning of *The Hamlet*, Will Varner rules the village with an iron and autocratic, though not unpaternal, hand. Placidly surveying his domain from his barrel-chair on the ruined gallery of the Old Frenchman Place, he has almost the position of a feudal lord. If he does not own the souls of his serfs, he at least owns everything else in sight; and if he is not averse to giving credit, he does not overlook the fact that there is interest accruing to it. Ironically, his son Jody, in trying to save the Varner barns from the barn burner, Ab Snopes, and simultaneously cheat Ab out of his crop, delivers the Varners into the hands of the Snopeses. Flem becomes a clerk in the Varner store and systematically begins to out-Varner the Varners in acquisitiveness. Meticulously exact in matters of money, he extracts a nickel for a plug of tobacco even from old Will himself, and, unlike Jody, never makes mistakes in change even in his own favor. He adopts Jody's habit of wearing a white shirt, and, when he later moves from the tenant farm to board in the village, he becomes the only man in the community besides Will Varner to wear a tie. Having taken over Jody's former duties in the store, he next succeeds to Jody's role as supervisor of the ginning and weighing of cotton in the fall, then steps into a place beside Will at the old man's yearly settlement of the accounts of his tenants—a position that even Jody had never been allowed to occupy. As Flem had imitated the Varner dress and mannerisms, he now begins to import other Snopeses who appear to be carbon copies of himself. However, if they are hardly less rapacious, they are less shrewd than Flem, and therefore less successful.

The name Snopes itself suggests a variety of unpleasant things: snail, snake, snarl, sneak, sneer, snide, snoop, snot, snout. In addition, the various Snopeses are identified with animals, usually rodents. Mink is named after a vicious member of the weasel family; I. O. is described as having a "rodent's face" (163) or "a talkative weasel's face" (64); Lump has the "bright, alert, amoral eyes of a squirrel or a chipmunk" (146); St. Elmo is "worse than a rat" (323); and Flem is a "bulbous spider," a "dog" or, most frequently, a "frog." Predatory and rapacious, with the vicious characteristics of feral animals but lacking an animal's innocence, the Snopeses are

only half-human. They possess the human qualities of shrewdness, acquisitiveness, and self-interest—human in the sense that they are not shared by animals—but they almost totally lack the humanitarian virtues as Faulkner has elsewhere defined them: "the verities of the human heart . . . courage, honor, pride, compassion, pity." (133, F IN U) All of the Snopeses, and Flem in particular, are economically oriented to a degree that excludes almost all other human interests.

The name Flem is a homonym for phlegm, suggesting both the qualities of coldness and moistness with which it is identified in the early physiological theory of humors, and the viscid, opaque nature of mucus. Accordingly, Flem's character is opaque, almost two-dimensional, like that of a figure cut from cardboard or (like that of Popeye's in *Sanctuary*) from tin. He is seen always from the outside, more in terms of his mannerisms than his actual words, but most of all in terms of his activities—all of which are directed toward the financial aspects of existence. Paralleling this is his complete indifference to and incompetence in affective action. Flem is completely "cold" to any human claims made upon him (cf. his refusal to give credit while working at Varner's store), as well as being sexually impotent—certainly a physical equivalent of his emotional inadequacy.

At the opposite end of the Snopes spectrum from Flem is the idiot Ike, a completely "natural" man in the sense that he is incapable of responding to either the economic or social values of civilization. Significantly, Ike is the only Snopes (with the exception of Eck and Wallstreet Panic, who are not "true" Snopeses) who is not characterized by a similarity to some kind of obnoxious animal. The animality of the other Snopeses is an index of their viciousness and their total failure in humanitarian action; Ike is an animal only insofar as he is motivated by essentially innocent animal instincts. Ike's only inheritance from his Snopes forebears is his idiocy, which, paradoxically, renders him innocent. This innocence in turn makes his love for his cow a natural rather than a perverse passion. It is only in a social context, i.e., when seen and judged by others who are not innocent, that Ike's animal love becomes an act of bestiality.

The contrast between the purely economic man and the totally natural man provides the major theme of the novel. It is exemplified in the episodes dealing with barter—Ab Snopes' horse-trading with Pat Stamper, the auction of the spotted horses, and even Flem's marriage to Eula—and those having to do with love—the pursuit of Eula by the schoolteacher Labove and by McCarron, Ike's love for his cow, Houston's marriage and his despair over his wife's death, and Mink's marriage. Both acquisitiveness and passion are seen in the extreme, almost pure, forms in Flem and Ike. In all the major characters except Ratliff one is dominant almost to the exclusion of the other.

As Olga Vickery has pointed out in her study of Faulkner, the most important difference between economic and sexual activty is that the former is a product of society and custom whereas the latter is inherent in human nature. When carried beyond satisfying the simple needs of existence, economic activity becomes something undertaken for its own sake, and the acquisition of money or property becomes either an end in itself or is combined with a desire to exercise one's shrewdness and ability to outtrade or outsmart another. Ab Snopes attempts to vindicate his honor as a horse-trader by beating Pat Stamper in a deal; Flem outtrades Will Varner, the shrewdest non-Snopes in the country, in the matter of the Old Frenchman Place; Mink attempts to take advantage of Houston and get his scrub yearling wintered free in Houston's pasture. Economic activity becomes something that is inevitably carried out at the expense of another, either in terms of actual money or of pride. Passing beyond the realm of necessity, it becomes a competitive obsession destructive of human relationships and humane values.

Passion, on the other hand, is an innate rather than an acquired characteristic. Significantly, the lovers are committed to love almost in spite of themselves, against their own wishes; love becomes an obsession to which the lover must surrender not only himself but his freedom and, in some cases, his masculinity. Thus, Houston runs from his sweetheart for fifteen years before he is finally and inexorably driven back, only to lose her when she is killed by the stallion he had ostensibly bought for her, but in which he sees the "polygamous and bitless masculinity which he had relinquished" (218) in marriage. The schoolteacher Labove, obsessed with the thirteen-year-old Eula, is unable to tear himself away from the school and the adolescent girl he wants, not as a wife, but just "one time as a man with a gangrened hand or foot thirsts after the axe-stroke which will leave him comparatively whole again." (119) Mink is summoned to the bed of the mill owner's nymphomaniac daughter, and the experience "made a monogamist of him forever, as opium and homicide do of those whom they once accept." (242)

Both obsessive love and obsessive acquisitiveness reduce their subjects to a state of pure concern with one thing. The lover—Labove, Houston, Mink, even Ike—becomes simply the male desiring the beloved, a profoundly and basically human (as well as mammalian) condition. The acquisitive man, however, is reduced—or raised—to a state in which no human claim or interest can compete with the single-minded desire for gain. Thus these two extremes of human endeavor come to symbolize humanity in its most basic aspects and at its furthest remove from concern with other human beings.

Two systems of ethics emerge from these two extremes. At the one end is Ike, whose love for his cow renders normal social morality inoperative as far as he himself is concerned, and to whom the good (assuming him to be capable of ethical judgment) resides solely in the attainment of the beloved; in the same way, Mink overcomes his Southern rural Protestant training that would demand that his beloved be virgin and accepts a nymphomaniac as his wife. At the other extreme stands Flem, the epitome of economic man. His ethics are the ethics of strict legality; not even the devil himself can bribe him, for he asks only what is legally his. Flem's legality is carried out in the letter, not the spirit, of the law, and takes no recognition of extralegal human claims. He refuses to return Mrs. Armstid's five dollars (though this bit of sharp dealing is so clearly untenable morally that even he is forced to offer a nickel's worth of "sweetening for the chap,") because it cannot be legally proved that he did not return her money to the Texan. Flem's "legality" ultimately proves so watertight and so immoral that the justice of the peace presiding at the suits instituted against Flem and Eck Snopes by the Armstids and the Tulls throws up his hands in despair, crying "I cant stand no more! . . . I wont! This court's adjourned! Adjourned!" (338)

The ethics of the majority of characters are largely only spurious attempts to justify their cheating of one another. Jody Varner decides to cheat Ab Snopes out of his crop on the specious grounds that "a man that's got habits that way will just have to suffer the disadvantages of them." (12) I. O. Snopes, by fast talking and remarkable arithmetic, manages to persuade the goodhearted Eck into paying nearly ninety-five per cent of the cost of buying Ike's cow. Lump Snopes urges Mink to go back to Houston's body and relieve the dead man of the money he presumably was carrying, arguing that if they don't get it "that durn Hampton and them deputies" will.

Mink, the only vicious Snopes who is associated with love, is the most nearly human of the tribe (cf. the extended treatment of him in The Mansion). His ethical beliefs, however, are a hopeless confusion of passion and Snopes self-interest, and he judges Houston's life to be the only possible payment for Houston's injury to his pride in the matter of the pasturage fee for the strayed yearling. His jealousy for his rights as a human being are all out of proportion to the nature of the affront he suffers and his vindication of his honor becomes a kind of grotesque version of the ante-bellum Southerner's exaggerated sensitivity in which the abstract idea of honor becomes of greater importance than all other human considerations (cf. Quentin Compson in The Sound and the Fury). Mink—like his relative Ab Snopes, whose sense of his rights as a man compels him to burn the barns of men who have slighted him—acts out of pride as Flem acts out of avarice, with complete indifference toward other human claims. Yet Mink's integrity, though perhaps of dubious moral value, still places him several notches higher than the totally amoral Lump or the hypocritical I. O. Snopes.

Whereas the Snopeses embody the extremes of natural passion and inhuman acquisitiveness, V. K. Ratliff provides the norm of social and economic behavior. He is a shrewd enough trader to enjoy making a modest profit as a traveling sewing-machine salesman, but he is without either avarice or excessive pride, fallible enough to fall for Flem's trick of salting the Old Frenchman Place with buried money, and sufficiently detached to be able to laugh at himself for his mistake. Sympathetic and humane, Ratliff is able to see good even in Ab Snopes, whom he pronounces to be "not naturally mean" but "soured" from his experiences. However, he is no blind optimist seeing good in all men. He is indignant at the salacious Lump Snopes's exploitation of Ike's relationship with his cow, and, with fine irony, coerces the schoolteacher I. O. into thinking of the unsullied name of Snopes and putting an end to the business. Out of pity for Mink's wife, he takes her and her children to stay at his sister's house while Mink is in jail and buys the children new raincoats. Yet he is unwilling to abet the others in their foolishness and refuses to give Henry Armstid the money he lost on the spotted horse: "I never made them Snopeses and I never made the folks that cant wait to bare their backsides to them. I could do more, but I wont. I wont, I tell you." (326) His "I wont" echoes that of the justice of the peace, who also finds the Snopeses and their financial involvements more than he can bear. Because of Ratliff's essential humaneness, it is doubly ironic that his exchange of his share of his Jefferson restaurant for an interest in the Old Frenchman Place starts Flem on his way to Jefferson, where he can carry out his depredations on the larger and wealthier community.

The Town

In about 1909 Flem Snopes, having exhausted the financial soil of Frenchman's Bend, moves into town with his wife, the former Eula Varner, and her baby girl, Linda. Eula, incredibly voluptuous, makes the entire male population of the town gasp at the very sight of her, and soon the community is happily convinced she is the mistress of their romantic young mayor, Manfred de Spain. Gavin Stevens, in his early twenties, becomes thoroughly infatuated with her, and enters a bitter and absurd rivalry with De Spain that culminates with Gavin's chivalrous attack on De Spain for dancing "shamelessly" with Eula at a Christmas Ball. Thereafter, Gavin continues to nurse his adoration for Eula and, though she once offers herself to him out of pity for his unhappiness, he leaves the field of action to De Spain. Flem, with characteristic shrewdness, deliberately refrains from noticing Eula's affair, but nevertheless uses it as a lever to gain himself the job of superintendent of the town power plant—a position that

De Spain creates for him. As Flem moves upward in the social and economic scale, he imports cousins from Frenchman's Bend and elsewhere to
fill the spaces he has vacated, until Jefferson is threatened with being overwhelmed with Snopeses as with a swarm of locusts.

Gavin leaves for two years of study in Heidelberg, charging V. K.
Ratliff with the responsibility of protecting Jefferson from the Snopeses
in his absence. Shortly before Gavin returns, Colonel Bayard Sartoris, the
president of the bank, is killed in an automobile accident; Manfred de
Spain becomes president and Flem Snopes—through the weight of stock
belonging to Will Varner, his father-in-law and a co-founder of the bank—
is named vice-president. Flem soon comes to alter his aims to include respectability as the crown of wealth. He buys a small house, which he
furnishes in a manner becoming to a man of his social and economic position, and in due time becomes a deacon of the Baptist church. Since a vice-
president of a bank cannot afford to have relatives of dubious reputation,
he joins Stevens and Ratliff—covertly, and much to their mystification—in
their mission to protect Jefferson from creeping Snopesism. Apparently
acting in the interests of civic virtue, he eliminates his cousin Montgomery
Ward Snopes from the pornography business by having him sent to Parchman penitentiary on a trumped-up charge of bootlegging. Later, he gets
rid of his cousin I. O. Snopes, an insurance swindler trading in dead mules.
At the conclusion of the book, he packs the noxious half-Apache children
of his cousin Byron Snopes back to Texas, thus ending what Ratliff describes as the last example of "Snopes out-and-out unvarnished behavior in
Jefferson."

Meanwhile Eula's daughter, Linda, is growing up, and soon Gavin no-
tices her and transfers part of his protective adoration from the mother to
the daughter. By the time Linda is in high school, the now-middle-aged
lawyer Stevens is plying her with ice-cream sodas and books of poetry, with
the double excuse of shaping her mind and encouraging her to go away to
college. Flem, however, knows that as soon as Linda is grown and able to
leave home Eula will leave him, taking with her his hopes of gaining control
of Will Varner's money. To retain his hold on Eula, he refuses to let
Linda go away to school until she signs a paper leaving to him any money
she might inherit from her mother. Flem then uses the paper and his
long-hoarded knowledge of Eula's affair to make his father-in-law oust De
Spain from the bank and install Flem as president. Eula, unwilling to run
away with De Spain and leave Linda to cope with the scandal, and equally
unwilling to have De Spain fight Flem for the possession of the bank and
drag out the scandal in the process, kills herself, preferring Linda to know
her mother to be a suicide rather than an adulteress. De Spain leaves town;
Flem steps into the presidency of the bank and moves into the De Spain
mansion, first having it remodeled so that it resembles the mansions of

ante-bellum times. He then makes sure that the town, whatever it may privately believe, publicly supports his position as a grieving husband bereaved of a faithful wife. He enlists the help of Stevens and Linda in the preparation of a monument for Eula's grave:

> A Virtuous Wife Is a Crown to Her Husband
> Her Children Rise and Call Her Blessed.

Having thus made accomplices of the two members of the community that posed the greatest potential threat to his acceptance as a respected and respectable citizen of Jefferson, he can afford to let Linda go away. Immediately after the monument is placed on Eula's grave, Linda departs for New York and Greenwich Village, and Stevens, still grieving, goes on to puzzle over Eula's real motivation in taking her life.

The Town is one of Faulkner's most puzzling and least successful novels. Though his aims in the book seem clear, their achievement is frequently debatable, with the effect that the book as a whole is tentative and uncertain; in one sense, it offers too many tempting and plausible interpretations, none of which can be said with real conviction to spring inevitably from the material of the book itself. Furthermore, action frequently seems only dimly related to character, and characterization itself is hazy. Part of the problem, in all likelihood, stems from the fact that the book is a patchwork both of styles and of content, and that its various parts were written over more than a twenty-year period: "Centaur in Brass," published in the American Mercury in 1932, was included with little revision as the episode of Flem Snopes and the stolen brass; "Mule in the Yard," published in Scribner's Magazine in 1934, appears somewhat revised as the episode in which old Mrs. Hait outwits the swindler I. O. Snopes. These and other episodes involving the Snopeses are good, occasionally brilliant examples of low comedy. The incidents involving non-Snopeses, however—Stevens, Linda, Eula, and De Spain, in their various combinations—are bitterly satirical where humor is present at all and ponderously serious elsewhere.

Technically, The Town has similarities to both Light in August and Absalom, Absalom!: to the former in its use of low comedy at the beginning and end (and in the case of The Town throughout the middle, as well) of a painful, if not in this case tragic, story; to Absalom, Absalom! in its use of three narrators, each of whom sees the action from a different perspective, and only one of whom is more than tangentially involved in the development of the action. Young Charles Mallison is the principal narrator—this in spite of the fact that he is not born until four or five years after the incidents with which his narrative begins, and is only in his middle teens at the end of the book. He is obviously intended to represent the collective voice and opinions of the people of Jefferson; too young to have a defined point of view of his own, he does not color with his own prejudices the gossip and other hand-me-down information that make up his narrative. Whereas Chick himself is rarely involved in the action, his uncle Gavin Stevens, the second narrator, is frequently up to his ears in a kind of passive emotional involvement with the other characters, with the result that his view of events is nearly always distorted. V. K. Ratliff, the peripatetic and ubiquitous observer of Snopes iniquity in Frenchman's Bend, is the most detached and perceptive, and therefore the most reliable, narrator; unfortunately, his narration takes up a very small part of the novel. He is relegated to a minor position, filling in background information on events that happened in *The Hamlet*, and acting as a kind of control-observer interjecting his occasional wry comments when the bemused Stevens persists in missing the point.

This use of multiple narration is clearly intended to suggest the multifaceted nature of truth, to achieve, by its complexity, an approximation of the ever-changing reality of life in motion; unfortunately, it does not quite succeed. The techniques which in *Absalom, Absalom!* resulted in a rich tapestry of impression and meaning create in *The Town* only a blurring of focus. The use of a juxtaposition of comedy and tragedy gives *Light in August* much of its dramatic impact; in *The Town* the low Snopes comedy mixes uneasily with both the satire and the moral earnestness of the other sections of the book. It almost seems as if Faulkner, in pursuing the design of the Snopes trilogy, whipped together *The Town* out of an armload of odd and assorted pieces of fictional devices he had lying around the house. However good some of the individual episodes may be, the book as a whole is formless, undramatic, and without a clear focus.

The moral point of *The Town* is clear enough: the rapacious and inhuman Flem Snopes is able, with very little trouble, to make his way to the top of Jefferson's social and economic ladder because Jefferson, under its veneer of traditional morality and respectability, has already accepted the values—or lack of values—associated with Snopesism. However, though Flem's rise is the ostensible subject of the book, Flem himself is almost completely eclipsed as a center of interest by Eula and her relationship with De Spain and Stevens.

Eula in *The Town* is still occasionally seen as the mythic embodiment of female sexuality and desirability, the rural Helen or Venus, that she was in *The Hamlet*. She can still cast an aura that makes a man feel "a kind of shock of gratitude just for being alive and being male at the same instant with her in space and time." (6) She gains a great deal of intelligence and compassion in *The Town* but, unfortunately, not enough depth of characterization to be able to support the burden the book places upon her.* She is defined only negatively in her encounters with Stevens, her affair with De Spain, and her function as a thematic opposite to Flem; that is to say, she becomes a representative of, shall we say, virtue, not because of her positive actions, but because of the other characters' negative ones. Thus Stevens, acting out of an absurd and overgrown sense of chivalry, first makes an ass of himself over her, defending "with blood the principle that chastity and virtue in women shall be defended whether they exist or not" (76)—not to mention whether the woman wishes to have her honor so defended or not. Later, he acts "honorably" and in the best romantic tradition when, still loving her miserably and from a proper distance, he refuses the offer of herself she makes out of pity for his unhappiness. These incidents, bitterly satirical in tone, point up the ridiculous way in which extreme reliance on tradition can effectively interfere with the development of any kind of mature human relationship.

Though Stevens grows in years in the course of the novel, he does not essentially change his romantic, chivalric outlook. With the best of intentions he sets out to rescue Eula and Linda from the Snopes dragon but, ironically, ends up strengthening Flem's power over Linda by refusing to let her learn that Flem is not her father. As he first regarded Eula as an ideal, unattainable figure, he comes to see Linda as an idealization of all young girlhood; to him, both women are lovely but essentially imaginary creations, rather than flesh-and-blood beings. He follows the same pattern in his behavior with Linda as he had with her mother fifteen years before. He chivalrously fights with young Matt Levitt, De Spain's most recent avatar and Linda's erstwhile suitor. As he had once urged his sister to receive Eula and thus establish her as a woman of blameless reputation, he worries about damaging Linda's reputation by being seen with her. In both instances, Gavin's concern with appearances and with public opinion prevent him from understanding the feelings of the women involved and from acting constructively rather than chivalrously.

Eula's affair with De Spain is made ironic by the fact that De Spain represents everything, socially and financially, that Flem wishes to be. He is of an old, wealthy, aristocratic family, Flem the son of poor-white share-croppers; he is masculine, attractive, and successful with women, while Flem is both sexually impotent and emotionally indifferent to human claims; he is cast in a romantic, if not heroic, role, while Flem is the epit-

---

* Eula's suicide is one of the greatest failures of the novel. Though her character is never sharply presented (we hear her talking, but her voice is always a little disembodied), nothing in it suggests that she is likely to be driven to suicide for any reason —and scarcely to prevent her daughter from thinking of her as an adulteress. Eula, if she is anything, is a woman of honesty and integrity, above both hypocrisy and concern for gossiping tongues.

ome of the antiheroic. However, the apparent disparity between the wealthy and successful lover and the avaricious, inhuman cuckold is simply an ironic comment on their actual similarity. Like Flem, De Spain is economically oriented, and is concerned with the appearance but not particularly with the fact of respectability. He had "tried to barter and haggle . . . to offer the base coinage of [the town] power-plant superintendency and its implied privileges of petty larceny, not only to pay for the gratification of his appetite but to cover his reputation, trying to buy at the same time the right to the wife's bed and the security of his good name from the husband who owned them both." (273) Later, when Flem attempts to drive him from the bank, De Spain is willing to bargain [he would "swap Flem Snopes his bank for Flem Snopes's wife" (331)], but he refuses to let Flem take the bank from him. As a result, Eula is driven to suicide to prevent De Spain from raising a scandal which could possibly destroy Linda.

It is often assumed that Faulkner uses the Snopeses to represent rapacity and inhumanity, and the Sartorises * (or Sartoris equivalents, such as the Stevenses or the De Spains) to represent the old virtues of honor, courage, and tradition. In *The Town*, however, it is clear that the old aristocracy, as represented by Stevens and De Spain, scarcely offers a model of responsible conduct, being at best well-intentioned but morally ineffectual. The community itself, also heir to the standards of the old aristocracy, values the appearance of respectability but has little regard for genuine spiritual or human values, such as the love and fidelity between the "social sinners" Eula and De Spain during their eighteen-year-long affair. Thus, in spite of what everyone knows, or at least has strong reason to believe, everyone acts as if nothing had happened between De Spain and Eula after her death. With terrible and unconscious irony, Chick reports that De Spain's wearing a black armband to the funeral "was of course all right since the deceased was the wife of his vice president." (339) After this, the triumph of Flem Snopes seems a fitting comment on Jefferson's hollow morality.

The Mansion

The Mansion opens with Mink Snopes's sentence for the murder of Jack Houston in 1908, picking up the trial scenes from the final sections of *The Hamlet* and of the fourth chapter of *The Town*. It enlarges both on Mink's

---

* See "Faulkner's Mythology," by George Marion O'Donnell; reprinted in *Three Decades of Criticism*. According to Mr. O'Donnell, "the Sartorises act traditionally; that is to say, they act always with an ethically responsible will. They represent vital morality, humanism." Surely this is to oversimplify; to act traditionally, as is shown so clearly in *The Town*, is not necessarily to act responsibly.

conflict with his victim and on Flem's motives, fifteen years later, in having Montgomery Ward Snopes sent to Parchman for bootlegging, rather than to Atlanta for peddling pornography. Fearing that Mink, who in five years more will be eligible for parole, will come back to Jefferson and try to kill him, Flem persuades Montgomery Ward (by threatening him with false evidence of his having sent pornography through the mails) to contact Mink in prison and talk him into trying to escape. Montgomery Ward then tips off the guards, so that Mink's attempt at escape fails and he is sentenced to an additional twenty years. The first section of the novel covers the thirty-eight years of Mink's imprisonment, ending with his release and the beginning of his journey back to Jefferson to revenge himself on Flem.

Part II (LINDA) begins with Linda Snopes's return to Jefferson after an absence of nearly ten years, and recounts the history of her mother (a slightly different version from that given in The Hamlet) from her seduction by Hoake McCarron to her suicide in Jefferson in 1927, Linda's growing up and going away to New York, and her marriage to Barton Kohl, a Jewish sculptor. After Kohl's death in the Spanish Civil War and her own deafening by an exploding shell, Linda returns to Jefferson, where she continues her earlier platonic relationship with Gavin Stevens. The section ends in 1942, with Gavin's marriage to the widowed Melisandre Backus Harriss, to whom he had once been engaged as a young man.

Part III (FLEM) begins in 1946 with Mink's journey to Memphis to buy a pistol. It then continues the history of the Snopes clan in a manner reminiscent of the comic episodes of The Hamlet: Senator Clarence Snopes's elimination from politics, Flem's outwitting of Jason Compson in a deal over the Compson property, and Orestes Snopes's attempts to drive the crotchety Old Man Meadowfill out of his small corner of the former Compson property. As the novel draws to its conclusion, it is revealed that Linda is responsible for Mink's release two years before his sentence is due to expire. Mink finally reaches Jefferson, kills Flem, and is aided in his escape by Linda.

The difference in the accounts in The Hamlet and The Mansion of Eula's seduction by McCarron and of Mink's quarrel with Houston, and the additional information about Flem's actions in regard to Montgomery Ward are contributing factors in the growth of the legend, of the development of a Snopeslore. As the ancient legends of gods and heroes are variant and sometimes contradictory, so the Snopes saga becomes multifaceted. Filtered through the minds of a presumable variety of storytellers, modulated by the passage of time, it becomes perhaps less accurate in actual fact, more accurate in psychological reality, partaking both of the timeless validity of myth and the remembered, static reality of events in time. Similarly, there is a difference between the partial information given in *The Town*, in which Flem's planting bootleg whiskey in Montgomery Ward's studio is presumably an attempt to prevent the name of Snopes from being tarnished by an association with pornography, and the more complete account of his motives in *The Mansion*. In this instance, however, the additional information does not conflict, but is rather an example of a partial truth being made more complete by an additional perspective, that of Montgomery Ward himself. As in *Absalom, Absalom!*, no one person can be aware of, let alone fully grasp, the several motivations of any one action; only through the amalgamation of a number of different perspectives can a close approximation of truth be perceived.

The Mansion reflects, as, to a degree, does *The Town*, Faulkner's intellectual preoccupation in the last decade of his life with what he called in his Nobel Prize acceptance speech "the verities" of the human heart. It explains, too, his frequently stated belief, implicit in all of his major novels of the 1929–36 period, that life involves motion and change as the only alternative to stasis, nothingness, and death. However, in his late novels his concern with the verities and with the motion of life is expressed in an essentially undramatic form, in terms of explicit comments made by his characters rather than in action. There is a kind of dramatic tension in *The Mansion* created by the juxtaposition of the fast-moving, expertly balanced section on Mink and the slow, almost plodding section on Linda, and by the juxtaposition within the final section of the comedy of Clarence Snopes's elimination from the congressional race and the intense serenity of Mink's murder of Flem and his westward departure, both literally and metaphorically, in the final pages. Yet this dramatic tension is not quite enough to offset the results of Stevens' compassionate but antidramatic character, or his rational and almost sociological view of Flem, which reduces him from the status of an inhuman but marvelous villain to that of an impotent and friendless, aging man, from an "old fish-blooded son of a bitch who had a vocabulary of two words, one being No and the other Foreclose" (215–6) to one of "the poor sons of bitches that have to cause all the grief and anguish they have to cause." (430)

There are echoes in *The Mansion* of the dramatic themes of Faulkner's early writing, in particular of the major theme of *Absalom, Absalom!*: like Thomas Sutpen, the central figure of that novel, Flem Snopes rises from obscure origins to a position of social and economic importance. Both men hold to some nonhuman end above human obligations and responsibilities —in the one case, acceptance as a member of the ante-bellum aristocracy and a kind of immortality as the founder of a dynasty; in the other, the acquisition and control of money and the veneer of respectability. In doing so, both destroy the lives of others and are finally destroyed themselves. Unlike Sutpen, however, Flem is consistently a two-dimensional figure, totally lacking in any aura of tragedy, self-generated or otherwise. Also unlike Sutpen, he deliberately and calculatingly uses his family to engineer De Spain out of the bank and out of town, as he had used Linda as the means to ensure against Eula's leaving him and removing with herself any hope he might have of some day acquiring his father-in-law's money.

Though Flem is the nominal center of *The Mansion*, he remains almost entirely in the background, scarcely directly seen except for the remarks made upon his two new habits: his failure to spit, though he still goes through the motions of chewing, and his habitual placing of his feet on the specially attached wooden ledge on his Adam fireplace. Safely ensconced in wealth and respectability, he has lost his force as a shrewd and rapacious character that he had in *The Hamlet* and, to a lesser degree, in *The Town*. Having reached his small eminence as president of the bank and inhabitant of the town's most stately mansion, he has gone as far as he can go; there are no new worlds for him to conquer in Jefferson. Having achieved his ends, he seems to have outdistanced his motivations; his rapacity having devoured everything in sight, there is no longer much of anything for him to do, and he remains a rather small background figure, chewing—now that there is no longer anything left for him to gobble up— only empty air. Perhaps it is this dual sense of achievement and loss—the loss of further motivation once an end has been totally attained—that renders him so seemingly innocuous in *The Mansion*. He has become, if not quite pitiable, at least no longer an active threat to anyone. His core of active rapacity is gone, and only the Snopes shell remains.

It is Mink, a relatively minor character in *The Hamlet*, who moves to the fore as the major Snopes of the novel. Though called by Ratliff in *The Town* "the only out-and-out mean Snopes we ever experienced" (79), Mink becomes in *The Mansion* not only Flem's nemesis but a magnificently delineated character in his own right. His reputed meanness comes to be beside the point, and his plight as a man in irreconcilable conflict with his environment forms the center of his story. His sense of himself as a man and his need to be recognized as such drive him to see the killing of Houston (here retold) as the only possible way in which he can live with himself after Houston's arrogant treatment of him. Since in Mink's primitively simple moral code the injury to his manhood can only be effaced by the death of the man who insulted him, the conflict is not, essentially, an inner one; it is an external conflict between Mink's personal morality and the social morality that forbids murder. Mink is not unaware of the social code; he knows that he will be expected to pay for his murder of Houston. He also knows, however, that the social code has its loopholes, and he confidently expects that Flem, with his influence, not only can rescue him, but "would have to save him whether he wanted to or not because of the ancient immutable laws of simple blood kinship." (5) Flem, however, carefully avoids being available during the trial, and Mink feels that he has been deliberately betrayed by his kinsman. Thus, in wanting to kill Flem, he is not only seeking personal vengeance; he is also making himself an instrument of retribution for Flem's violation of the ancient laws of blood kinship—laws that are the basis of society, for they spring from the same need (the protection of the family) as that most fundamental of all laws, *Thou shalt not kill thy mother's child.**

Thus Mink is part Nemesis, harking back to the primitive roots of justice, part simple disaccommodated man, from whom all has been taken—freedom, wife, children, even citizenship. He is totally bereft of all but his condition as a human being. It is perhaps because of this that he becomes so sympathetic a character, so almost strangely moving. The level of basic humanity to which Mink has been reduced excludes both external judgment and accepted moral precept. One is no longer asked to view him or his actions in terms of right or wrong, but merely to see—to understand and accept—and in so doing to experience compassion and pity for one of the "poor sons of bitches" who are all mankind.

Mink as an isolated individual provides a part of one of the major themes of the novel. Physically isolated from the world for thirty-eight years, he returns to society to find himself an alien, the small world he had known gone and a new one in its place. Like him, Linda is isolated from the world by her deafness and from the Southern community by her marriage to a New York Jew, her Communist affiliations, and her attempts to improve the Negro schools. Flem, though accepted by the community, is isolated from humanity by his inhumanity, his placing of money above human values and relationships. However, the isolation of Linda and Mink is primarily external, something imposed upon them rather than something they have chosen, and is, to a degree, mutable and temporary. Though her deafness is permanent, Linda's isolation from the community need only last as long as she remains in Jefferson. Even Mink, still essentially isolated from society though free, is moving toward death and the anonymous brotherhood of "the beautiful, the splendid, the proud and the brave, right on up to the very top itself among the shining phantoms and dreams which are the milestones of the long human recording—Helen and the bishops, the kings and the unhomed angels, the scornful and graceless seraphim." (436) Only Flem, whose isolation is voluntary, even desired, is given no hope or expectation of its end.

In these three figures—who are, significantly, the title characters of the three sections of the novel—Faulkner has drawn a kind of parable of man's condition, both in broad outline and in detailed particular. Isolation is seen as a concomitant of man's existence, an adjunct of consciousness and of the

---

* Cf. Gavin Stevens' comments on murder in *Intruder in the Dust,* p. 129.

conscious striving to achieve selfhood. In order to realize oneself, one must of necessity recognize that one is separate, apart; in order to be whole, one must maintain one's integrity unbroken. Thus, one is isolated first of all by his very self-consciousness; if one's integrity conflicts with the accepted behavior of the community, he is doubly alone. Whether this conflict is dramatized in terms of murder or simple social disapproval, the result is the same: the individual is cut off from the community and, in its broadest extension, from humanity.

In comparison with his earlier treatment of individual isolation (see *As I Lay Dying*), Faulkner in *The Mansion* concentrates almost exclusively on man's sense of his anonymous membership in the brotherhood of humanity as a means of partially overcoming—or at least compensating for—the impossibility of establishing communion between individuals. Thus Mink and Linda both leave Jefferson for environments that will accept them, rather than in search of individuals with whom they can lose their sense of aloneness. Through the novel runs like a litany the phrase "poor sons of bitches"—poor men, poor mankind, all essentially alone, united only in their common need and striving to violate their aloneness, to somewhere, somehow, feel themselves at home. The contexts in which the phrase appears are particularly significant: Miss Reba, madam of a Memphis whorehouse, first invokes it: "All of us. Every one of us. The poor son of a bitches." (82) Goodyhay, the ex-marine turned preacher, repeats it: "Christ save us. Poor sons of bitches." Ratliff, speculating on Flem's passive acceptance of his death, echoes it: "The pore son of a bitch." (430) Each of the three contexts involves a situation offering some escape, partial or otherwise, from individual aloneness: sexual contact, religious experience, and death.

Playing on all possible meanings of his litany, Faulkner frequently places the phrase, in its derogatory sense, in the mouths of other characters. Indeed, the Snopeses themselves, as Montgomery Ward puts it, are "what you might call a family, a clan, a race, maybe even a species, of pure sons of bitches." (87) However, no Snopes is ever pure enough to make "the whole world recognize him as THE son of a bitch's son of a bitch"; the only true son of a bitch in the literal sense is Eck, who is "not a bitch at all but a saint and martyr." Ironically, because of the presumed "extracurricular night work" undertaken by Eck's mother nine months before he was born, the "one technically true pristine immaculate unchallengeable son of a bitch [the Snopes family] ever produced wasn't even a Snopes."

As "son of a bitch" is both an insulting epithet and a compassionate phrase encompassing and drawing together all men, it becomes a verbal equivalent of the complexity of human experience which, when seen in its totality, can never be reduced to simple and clear-cut moral distinctions. Thus, as there is no judgment passed on Mink's actions, there can be no moral judgment of Linda's complicity in Flem's death. This is not necessarily to say, as Stevens does, that there are no morals, but that accepted moral standards are inadequate to cover the infinite varieties of human needs and motivations. Traditional morality may provide a general guide for conduct, but it can never be regarded as an absolute without forcing human experience, with its necessary and constant motion and change, into a rigid and deadly pattern, robbing it of both vitality and meaning.

Stevens, despite his protestations to the contrary, is a moralist and a traditionalist; hence his difficulty in accepting the reality of the part Linda played in Flem's killing: " 'I wont believe it!' Stevens said. 'I wont! I cant believe it,' he said. 'Dont you see I cannot?' " (431) In refusing to admit her deed and the responsibility she has accepted for it, he denies her status as a mature and independent individual, hoping by thus reducing her to a projection of himself to make her "fixed, forever safe from change and alteration." (203)

Steven's unwillingness to accept Linda's moral responsibility for Flem's death is characteristic of his tendency to see life in terms of an established, unmoving pattern. In *The Town* and *The Mansion* he has represented the forces of tradition, as embodied in the law, which is by its nature in opposition to the constant growth and change of life. Significantly, his lifelong advocation has been to translate the Old Testament back into its original but dead and changeless language. Similarly, he is attracted to young girls just entering puberty, loving that moment of motion but unwilling to look beyond it to the next, toward the adulthood which the living girl must reach. As an idealist, Stevens seems to seek in life the kind of timeless and deathless beauty that can be found only in art; he would like to capture a moment of motion and enshrine it forever—immobilized in an ideal pattern that is, ultimately, irrelevant to life. In thus falsifying the nature of life itself, he limits his own apprehension of the reality of the lives of others and becomes merely a meddler in their affairs, never fully a participant. Though a compassionate man, capable of offering devotion with no expectation of reward, he remains incapable of deep involvement. He is caught between the traditionalism to which he is intellectually sympathetic and the dance of life to which he is emotionally drawn, unable to reconcile completely the emotional and intellectual aspects of his personality. He is a prototype of the intellectual and rationalist, which even as an ideal is a kind of failure, for in disregarding the emotions it crucially limits the possibilities of both perception and experience.

The Mansion explores the varieties of human attitudes from the primitive morality of Mink to the highly civilized and educated outlook of Stevens. Neither is set forth as preferable; both are presented simply as aspects of man's behavior. No major character is seen as either entirely good or entirely bad: even Montgomery Ward Snopes, who in *The Town* was only another example of Snopes industry making money out of the less desirable inclinations of members of the community, is seen in *The Mansion* as a man capable of pity and cognizant of his failings. Stevens, whose characterization in *The Town* was almost entirely uncritical, is put into better perspective through the comments of Ratliff and Charles Mallison; they speak of him, critically but fondly, as a "meal-mouthed sanctimonious Harvard- and Europe-educated lawyer that never even needed the excuse of his office and salaried job to meddle in anything providing it wasn't none of his business and wasn't doing him no harm" (55), and a "good man, wise too except for the occasions when he would abberate, go momentarily haywire and take a wrong turn that even I [Charles] could see was wrong, and then go hell-for-leather, with absolutely no deviation from logic and rationality from there on, until he wound us up in a mess of trouble or embarrassment that even I would have had sense enough to dodge. But he is a good man. Maybe I was wrong sometimes to trust and follow him but I never was wrong to love him." (230)

The conflict between man and society, between the motion of life and the staticity of institutions, is implicitly present but rarely emphasized, except in such vignettes as the story of Tug Nightingale, whose rigidity, inherited from his unreconstructed father, is expressed in his stubborn belief that the world is flat. As a member of society, Faulkner implies, the individual can and must find room for growth within its framework. As was shown in *The Town*, even so socially disruptive a force as Eula was able to exist in her "splendid unshame" with the complicity, if not always the approval, of the community, until Flem forced her to choose between death and open scandal. However, in *The Mansion*, institutions and traditions are not, as was frequently the case in the early novels, in direct opposition to individual growth. Even Gavin, the most tradition-oriented of the major characters, is capable of growth, acceptance, and understanding, as is made most evident in the two critical episodes involving Eula and Linda. Despairing over the loss of Eula but not understanding her choice of death, he comes to the realization, with tears, that "she loved, had the capacity to love, to give and to take it. Only she tried twice [with McCarron and De Spain] but failed twice not jest to find somebody strong enough to deserve it but even brave enough to accept it." (150) Similarly, Ratliff's explanation of Linda's motives in releasing Mink to kill Flem brings Gavin, again with tears, to an acceptance of her acts:

> She could a waited two more years and God His-self couldn't a kept Mink in Parchman without He killed him, and saved herself not jest the bother and worry but the moral responsibility too, even if you do say they aint no morals. Only she didn't. And so you wonder why. If maybe, if there wasn't no folks in heaven, it wouldn't be heaven, and if you couldn't recognize them as folks you knowed, wouldn't nobody want to go there. And that

someday her maw would be saying to her, "Why didn't you revenge me and my love that I finally found it, instead of jest standing back and blind hoping for happen-so? Didn't you never have no love of your own to learn you what it is?" (431)

If *The Mansion* is less powerful than the earlier major novels, it is also more optimistic, more explicitly confident that, in the conflict between the humanitarian values and the a-human drives toward power and possessions, the verities of human life will endure, that the Flem Snopeses of the world are, after all, poor sons of bitches too, equally deserving of pity in spite of the destruction they bring. Snopesism does not die with Flem— there are still Orestes and Watkins Products Snopes to cope with, not to mention Jason Compson, who is a Snopes in all but name—and the old order is not restored with the simple return of the De Spain relatives to an outsize and rather uselessly expensive mansion. Life goes on; there will always be a change and growth and adjustment, always the plight of man in conflict with himself and with others and with his world.

GO DOWN, MOSES [1942]

Characters

LUCIUS QUINTUS CAROTHERS MC CASLIN [1772–1837], *founder of the Mc-Caslin family in Yoknapatawpha County*

UNCLE BUCK [THEOPHILUS] MC CASLIN [1799–1879], *his son*

UNCLE BUDDY [AMODEUS] MC CASLIN [1799–1879], *Uncle Buck's twin*

ISAAC [IKE] MC CASLIN [1867–1947], *Uncle Buck's son*

HUBERT BEAUCHAMP, *Isaac's uncle*

SOPHONSIBA BEAUCHAMP, *Isaac's mother and Uncle Buck's wife*

MC CASLIN [CASS] EDMONDS [1850–   ], *grandson of L. Q. C. McCaslin's daughter*

ZACHARY [ZACK] EDMONDS [1873–   ], *Cass's son*

CAROTHERS [ROTH] EDMONDS [1898–   ], *Zack's son*

LUCAS BEAUCHAMP [1874–   ], *L. Q. C. McCaslin's part-Negro grandson*

MOLLY WORSHAM BEAUCHAMP [1874–1945?] *his wife*

HENRY BEAUCHAMP [1898–   ], *their son*

NAT [NATHALIE] BEAUCHAMP [1924–   ], *their daughter*

GEORGE WILKINS, *Nat's husband*

SAMUEL WORSHAM [BUTCH] BEAUCHAMP [1915–41], *Molly's grandson*

GAVIN STEVENS, *a lawyer*

SAM FATHERS [1808–83], *son of an Indian chief and a slave woman, the mentor of young Isaac McCaslin*

BOON HOGGANBECK, *a white man with some Indian blood*

RIDER, *a Negro*

In a strict sense, *Go Down, Moses* is not a novel at all, but a series of seven short stories, five of which were previously published in magazines. They are connected by certain dominant themes and all concerned with the descendants, white or black, of Lucius Quintus Carothers McCaslin. The history of this family, which is gradually revealed in the course of the stories, particularly in the often-confusing Section IV of "The Bear," is summarized below.

HISTORY

In the early nineteenth century, Lucius Quintus Carothers McCaslin migrated from the Carolinas to northern Mississippi, where he acquired a large grant of land from Ikkemotubbe, the Chickasaw chief of the area. Later, he bought from the Indian a quadroon slave woman and her young child, Sam Fathers, the chief's unacknowledged son. McCaslin was the father of three legitimate children—the twins Uncle Buck (Theophilus) and Uncle Buddy (Amodeus), and a daughter—and of two illegitimate children by his Negro slaves: Tomey (Tomasina), the daughter of Eunice, and Tomey's Turl (Terrel), his son by his own daughter Tomey. He provided a legacy of one thousand dollars to be given to his part-Negro son upon Turl's request as soon as he came of age. Turl never claimed the money, and McCaslin's legitimate sons increased the legacy to one thousand dollars each for Turl's three children—Tennie's Jim (James), Fonsiba, and Lucas Beauchamp. Tennie's Jim ran away to the North when he came of age, Fonsiba married at seventeen and went to live in Arkansas, and only Lucas remained on the plantation.

After McCaslin's death Uncle Buck and Uncle Buddy moved out of the half-completed plantation house and into a cabin they had built themselves. Not believing in slavery, they tried to let each slave work out his purchase price on the plantation and thereby earn his freedom; however, once freed, the Negroes refused to leave. Both the twins remained unmarried until their sixties, when Uncle Buck married Miss Sophonsiba Beauchamp, who bore him a son, Isaac, in 1867. Orphaned of his mother as a young child and of both his father and his uncle when he was twelve, Isaac was partly raised by his cousin McCaslin (Cass) Edmonds, sixteen years his senior and the grandson of old McCaslin's daughter. Under the tutelage of Sam Fathers, Ike learned as a boy to be a better hunter and woodsman than most grown men. At sixteen, he discovered, through his father's old ledgers, the miscegenation and incest his grandfather had committed, and came to believe both that the South was cursed with the guilt of slavery and that his family in particular was cursed by his grandfather's acts. When he was twenty-one he refused to inherit property that was rightfully his, believing that the land is the common property of all men and that his grandfather had had no more right to bequeath it than Ikkemotubbe to sell it. Because Ike renounced his patrimony, the property went to his cousin, Cass. Ike married, but his wife, thwarted in her attempts to make him accept the inheritance, denied him her bed and left him childless at her death. He spent the rest of his life in his wife's house in Jefferson, receiving a small monthly allowance from the Edmondses.

Cass Edmonds died and his son Zack inherited the McCaslin plantation. Both a friend and a rival of his Negro cousin Lucas Beauchamp, Zack kept Lucas' wife Molly at his house for six months to care for his infant son, his own wife having died in childbirth. Molly raised Zack's son Roth and Lucas' son Henry together, almost as brothers, but soon young Roth came to realize the external social distinctions between black and white. Each

generation of Edmonds men proved to be of less stature than the one preceding it: Cass was a better man than Zack, as Zack was a better man than
Roth. In the 1940s Roth had an affair with a light-colored Negro woman,
whom he refused to marry but by whom he had a son. The woman was
revealed to be the granddaughter of James Beauchamp, and the black
and white McCaslin lines were again joined.

PLOTS

"WAS"

The introduction is a brief summary of Isaac McCaslin's life up to the
present. The action of the following three sections, which take place in
1859, is seen through the eyes of young McCaslin (Cass) Edmonds, who
is referred to, for the most part, only as "he." A boy of nine, Cass is initiated into the comic complexities of the McCaslin family as he, with Sam
Fathers, will later guide Ike's initiation. The story opens with the discovery
that Tomey's Turl, old McCaslin's mulatto son, has again run away from
the plantation to court his sweetheart Tennie, a slave on the Beauchamp
plantation in the next county. The McCaslin brothers have refused to buy
Tennie because they already own more Negroes than they know what to do
with, and Hubert Beauchamp won't buy Tomey's Turl because he
"wouldn't have that damn white half-McCaslin on his place even as a free
gift." (11) Uncle Buck's and young Cass's pursuit of the runaway Negro is
conducted in terms of a mock fox hunt: "You stay back where he won't
see you and flush. I'll circle him through the woods and we will bay at him
at the creek ford." (13) There are references to hunting throughout the
story—and more than one kind of hunt, for Miss Sophonsiba, Hubert Beauchamp's spinster sister, is out to capture Uncle Buck just as surely as he is
out to get Turl. After spending the day in unsuccessful pursuit of Turl,
Uncle Buck and young Cass creep into the darkened Beauchamp house in
search of a bedroom. They enter Miss Sophonsiba's room, and Uncle Buck
gets into bed with her. To escape the calamitous result of this mishap—the
demand that he marry Miss Sophonsiba—Uncle Buck challenges Hubert
to a game of poker, with his own freedom as part of the stakes. Uncle
Buck loses, and Cass runs away to fetch Uncle Buddy to rescue his brother.
Uncle Buddy and Hubert play, and Hubert passes; by the terms of the
stake, Uncle Buck is free, but the McCaslins must buy Tennie.

"THE FIRE AND THE HEARTH"

Two sections of what was to become "The Fire and the Hearth" were
published as "A Point of Law" (Collier's, June 22, 1940) and "Gold Is Not
Always" (Atlantic Monthly, November, 1940). The former story deals
with the humorous clash of Lucas Beauchamp and George Wilkins, the

latter with Lucas' outsmarting of the mine-detector salesman in the search for buried gold. "The Fire and the Hearth," as it appears here, combines the humor of the magazine stories with the serious presentation of Negro-white relations, and sketches the growth of the black and white branches of the McCaslin family.

Lucas Beauchamp, the part-Negro grandson of old McCaslin, is sixty-seven at the time the present events of the story take place. He sets out to hide his still so that it will not be found when the sheriff comes looking for the still of young George Wilkins, Lucas' prospective son-in-law. While burying his equipment in an old Indian mound, Lucas finds a part of an old churn in which there is a single gold coin. Feeling that Wilkins has overstepped himself in setting up a still in what has been for years Lucas' territory and fearing, moreover, that Wilkins' amateurish operation will be discovered and lead to the discovery of his own, Lucas tries to have Wilkins put out of business, and goes to the plantation house to tell Carothers (Roth) Edmonds that Wilkins is making bootleg whiskey. The present action is interrupted by Lucas' memories of Roth's birth: Lucas had risked his life crossing the river during a storm to fetch a doctor for Roth's mother, but by the time he and the doctor arrived the woman was dead. Zack Edmonds, Roth's father, had kept Lucas' wife Molly at his house to care for the infant. After six months Lucas, not content to be a "nigger" first and a man second, demanded that Zack return her to him, and then realized that he would either have to kill Zack or go away. He had confronted Zack, but the tense scene had ended when the pistol Lucas held misfired.

Lucas' plan to get Wilkins arrested for bootlegging backfires when Wilkins and Nat, Lucas' daughter, carry his still to Lucas' backyard and it is found there by the sheriff sent by Edmonds. Wilkins and Nat reveal that they have been secretly married; thus Nat cannot testify against Wilkins, and both Wilkins and Lucas are dismissed by the judge and told to destroy their stills. Wilkins, however, buys a new still with the money Lucas had given him to fix up his house so that Nat would consent to live in it.

Obsessed with the idea of finding a treasure in the old Indian mound, Lucas sends for a salesman who has a contraption for locating buried metal, probably a mine detector. To avoid paying for it with his own money, he first tries vainly to borrow money from Roth Edmonds, then swaps a valuable mule belonging to Roth for the box. Caught by Roth with the missing mule and ordered to return it, Lucas tries a new trick: he sends Wilkins into town for fifty silver dollars, which he buries in the orchard. When he and the salesman "discover" the buried money, Lucas agrees to give the salesman half of it, as well as half of the money they still expect to find, if the salesman will give Lucas the box and return the bill of sale for the mule. For a few days the salesman continues to hunt for more buried money, renting the box from Lucas at $25 a night. When he leaves, Lucas and Wilkins go back to their nightly searches for the gold at the Indian mound. Molly goes to Roth Edmonds saying that she wants a divorce; she is afraid that Lucas will find buried gold and be punished by God for removing what He has rendered to His earth.

The progress of the action in the present is again held in abeyance while the McCaslin and Beauchamp history is recounted. Lucas had come to Ike McCaslin on his twenty-first birthday and demanded the legacy due to him. He had married and moved into a house Cass Edmonds had built for him on ten acres of McCaslin land that Lucas could farm as long as he remained on the plantation. Lucas' oldest son Henry and Zack Edmonds' motherless son Roth had been raised together almost as brothers, sharing the same table and the same bed until Roth, at seven, had come to realize the social gulf between black and white—"the old curse of his fathers, the old haughty ancestral pride based not on any value but on an accident of geography, stemmed not from courage and honour but from wrong and shame. . . ." (91) Growing into his white heritage, Roth had preempted the bed for himself, forcing Henry to sleep on a pallet on the floor.

Again in the present, Molly, despite her age and frailty, tries to discourage Lucas from searching for the buried money by going into the swamp with the mine detector herself. When she is found, nearly dead from exhaustion, Roth decides to get her the divorce she wants; but, at the last moment, Lucas appears in the courtroom saying he has changed his mind and doesn't want a divorce. That night he surrenders his machine to Roth, telling him to get rid of it.

"PANTALOON IN BLACK." First published in *Harper's Magazine*, October, 1940.

"Pantaloon" is a reference to a stock character (Pantalone) in an old Italian comedy, an emaciated old man who played the part of dotard and buffoon; in English pantomime this character was transformed into Pierrot, the tall, gangling clown who hides his real emotions behind a comic mask. In some versions he is in love with Columbine, a fairy immortal who lives with him for a time but finally leaves him to rejoin the invisible world of spirits.

Rider, the Pantaloon-Pierrot of the story, is grief-stricken at the death of Mannie, his young wife, but the acts of his anguish are misinterpreted by the white townsfolk as unseasonable haste to have his wife buried and a lack of respect for her memory. Drunk on bootleg whiskey and grief, he enters a crap game run by a crooked white man named Birdsong, and, catching Birdsong with a pair of loaded dice, slits his throat with his razor. Rider is summarily lynched by Birdsong's relatives.

"THE OLD PEOPLE." First published in *Harper's Magazine*, September, 1940.

The present action of the story takes place in 1879, when young Ike McCaslin, "the boy," is initiated by Sam Fathers into manhood through the ritual of the hunt. He kills his first buck, and is ceremonially marked by Sam with the blood of the animal. Sam Father's history is given: he is the unacknowledged son of Ikkemotubbe, or Doom (from *du homme*, meaning "the man"), the last Chickasaw chief on the area. Doom, whose right to the chieftainship came through his mother and was therefore not direct, returned from a seven-year visit to New Orleans with, among other things, a basket full of puppies and a box of white powder which, when administered to a puppy, would kill it instantly. The next day the young son of the present chief died suddenly and the chief himself hastily abdicated. Doom became chief, or The Man, as the Indians called him. He married to a black man the quadroon he had got pregnant and brought with him from New Orleans, and later sold the woman and her child to old McCaslin. The child, Sam, grew to manhood and worked in the plantation blacksmith shop, but he was primarily a hunter, going each November on the annual expedition to Major de Spain's hunting camp in the Tallahatchie River Bottom. In 1877, Sam left the plantation to live at the hunting camp, and that winter young Ike was allowed for the first time to be a member of the party.

Two years later, in the present, Ike kills his first buck, and shortly afterward the party breaks camp. As the wagon is leaving, Boon Hogganbeck spots an enormous buck and the party waits until sundown for it to return to its bedding place. Sam takes Ike into a little thicket, and—after Walter Ewell's horn has sounded, announcing that a deer has been killed—the great buck appears before them. Sam salutes it as "chief" and "grandfather." The other hunters, looking at the small buck killed by Walter, believe that Boon imagined the great buck he claimed to have seen. Later, Ike tells his cousin Cass that he and Sam had actually seen the animal. He thinks that Cass does not believe him until the latter reveals that Sam had shown it to him, too, when, as a boy, he had killed his first deer.

"THE BEAR." An abridged version of "The Bear," lacking the complex fourth section, was published in *The Saturday Evening Post*, May 9, 1942, two days before the publication of *Go Down, Moses*.

The present action takes place in 1883, when Ike is sixteen. Each year the hunting party unsuccessfully tracked Old Ben, an enormous bear. A few years previously Sam had taken Ike into the woods and shown him the bear's print. At twelve the boy began trying to track the animal, but never saw him. On Sam's advice, Ike went out unarmed, but had no luck until he abandoned the other marks of civilization he carried: his watch and compass. At last he came upon the bear's fresh footprints and then saw Old Ben himself. Later, Ike saved his small, foolhardy dog, snatching it from almost directly under the bear. Though both were armed, neither he nor Sam Fathers shot at the bear. During a later summer Sam trapped an enormous dog that had killed a colt, and starved it until the animal would let him approach. The dog, named Lion, was to be used to bring down Old Ben. Boon Hogganbeck took over the dog's care, and that November Lion led the hunt. The following year Lion bayed Old Ben, and General Compson drew blood; later that night Boon missed the bear five times.

Ike, sixteen now, waits in camp for the weather to break. He is sent to accompany Boon to Memphis to replenish the supply of whiskey. The next morning Old Ben is pursued across the river and bayed on the opposite bank. Lion rushes at the bear, which grabs him in both arms, and Boon leaps on the bear's back and searches with his knife for the animal's heart. The bear is killed, but Sam has collapsed, for no apparent physical reason and Lion is mortally wounded. Though camp is being broken up, Ike begs Cass to let him remain at the hunting lodge until Sunday, for he senses that Sam is dying. On Saturday, Cass and Major de Spain find Boon and Ike in the woods, sitting between Lion's grave and a raised platform on which is Sam's body.

The fourth section is a long mediation (almost half the length of the entire story) centered on Ike's consciousness and embracing the past history of the family and reaching some years into Ike's future. Biblical, sometimes almost incantatory in tone, the long conversations between Ike and Cass that frame the dramatic interludes of memory and future happening reveal that Ike, at twenty-one, is renouncing his inheritance because he believes that land is given by God to all men in common, and that ownership, rather than stewardship, goes against God's ordinance and brings a curse upon the land.

The history of the family is recounted with Ike's discovery, at sixteen, of the mysterious notations in his father's and uncle's ledgers referring to a Negro slave who drowned herself. He realizes that not only did his grandfather have a Negro son, but that that son was gotten on his own mulatto daughter. Two years later, at eighteen, Ike tries to locate the vanished Tennie's Jim (James Beauchamp), who had run away from the plantation on the night of his twenty-first birthday. As McCaslin's mulatto grandson, Jim is entitled to a share of the legacy left by old McCaslin to, but never claimed by, Jim's father, Tomey's Turl, which had been increased to one thousand dollars for each of Turl's descendants. Later the same year Ike travels to Arkansas in search of Turl's daughter Fonsiba, and leaves her share of the money with a bank, which is to send her three dollars a week as long as the thousand dollars lasts. Lucas, Turl's third and last living descendant, claims his money at twenty-one and remains on the plantation.

A legacy was left to Ike himself by his uncle, Hubert Beauchamp. Just after Ike's birth Hubert had taken a silver cup, filled it with gold pieces, wrapped it in burlap and sealed it with his ring. The cup was to come to Ike on his twenty-first birthday, but, as Hubert's money dwindled, he had "borrowed" from the cup, so that when Ike opened the gunny sack he found only a handful of pennies and a sheaf of IOU's. Though having, now, no money at all of his own, Ike only reluctantly accepts Cass's offer of the sum owed him by his uncle. Ike becomes a carpenter, using the money to pay his board and rent and buy tools, and takes on as a partner a dipsomaniac ship's carpenter. He marries a girl who hopes to become mistress of the McCaslin plantation, knowing that Ike is entitled to it. When he refuses all her appeals to claim his inheritance, she refuses him her bed and any hope of children.

Set earlier in time than the fourth section, the fifth tells how Ike, in about his eighteenth year, goes out to the Bottom to hunt with Boon. Major de Spain's annual hunting parties have stopped two years before with the deaths of Sam Fathers and Lion, and a new planing mill, now half-completed, is about to spoil the wilderness. Ike stops at the graves and places as an offering to his old mentor "the twist of tobacco, the new bandanna handkerchief, the small paper sack of the peppermint candy which Sam had used to love." (250) Just beyond the graves he is confronted by an enormous rattlesnake, which he salutes as it moves away from him as Sam had saluted the great buck six years before. He finds Boon sitting beneath the tree full of frantic squirrels, violently beating his dismembered gun in order to dislodge a jammed shell. His mental balance already destroyed by the "mine" and "thine" concepts of civilization, as the wilderness is about to be destroyed by progress, Boon screams at Ike: " 'Get out of here! Dont touch them! Dont touch a one of them! They're mine!' " (252)

"DELTA AUTUMN"

The story takes place in the early 1940s. Ike, now over seventy, goes with his young kinsman Roth Edmonds and several other men of Edmonds' age on their annual hunting trip—no longer to the Big Bottom, long since timbered or cultivated, but to the nearest wilderness two hundred miles away in the Delta region. Early in the morning Roth slips in to tell Ike that he expects a message and asks him to give the messenger an envelope with the answer "No." Later that morning a young woman with an infant child appears; Ike gives her the envelope, containing money, and Roth's answer. As she tells him about herself Ike realizes, with a sense of pity and outrage, that she is part Negro. His emotional reaction to this recognition, and to the thought that Roth might have married her, is intense and almost involuntary:

> Maybe in a thousand or two thousand years in America, he thought. But not now! Not now! (272)

She tells him what Roth does not know—that she is the granddaughter of Tennie's Jim, old McCaslin's Negro grandson who ran away to the North when he came of age. As she leaves, Ike gives her, to keep for her son, the hunting horn left to him in General Compson's will. Later Will Legate, one of the hunters, returns to fetch Roth's knife, saying that Roth has killed a deer. Ike, left alone in the tent, realizes that the deer was a doe.

"GO DOWN, MOSES." First published in *Collier's* January 25, 1941.

Molly Beauchamp, now an old woman, asks the lawyer Gavin Stevens to help her find her grandson, Samuel Worsham Beauchamp, locally known as Butch, a tough young Negro who, unknown to Molly, is about to be executed for murder in Chicago. Old Miss Worsham, a white spinster with whom Molly had been raised almost as a sister, tells Stevens that Molly would want Butch's body brought home. Miss Worsham pays him a small sum—more than twice what she can afford—to help cover the funeral expenses, and Stevens makes up the rest, with help from the editor of the newspaper and a few local merchants. Though Stevens persuades the editor not to print the story, so that Molly need not know how her grandson died, Molly—even if she had known the truth about his death—would not have cared; she only wanted his body brought home and interred with the proper rituals and accoutrements, a casket, flowers, and a hearse.

Though essentially a collection of short stories and not a novel, Go Down, Moses as a whole has a unity maintained by the theme, present in each of the stories, of the social relationship between whites and Negroes, and by the recurrent metaphor of the hunt, which is both an analogy to life—a pursuit, a condition that moves and changes—and a ritualistic act by which man defines his position between civilization and the wilderness. All the stories deal with the members, black and white, of the McCaslin family (a partial exception to this, "Pantaloon in Black," concerns a Negro who, though not a McCaslin by blood, is a sharecropper on the McCaslin plantation).

The book is given further unity by the theme of initiation, which appears in all the stories except "Pantaloon in Black" and "Go Down, Moses." In "Was," young Cass Edmonds is initiated into the rituals of plantation life—a preparation necessary for his regency during the years between the deaths of Uncle Buck and Uncle Buddy and Ike's coming of age, and for his own inheritance, by Ike's default, of the McCaslin property.

Ike, at twelve, is initiated into manhood in the wilderness under the guidance of Sam Fathers and through the ritual of the hunt. Young Roth Edmonds, guided by the attitude of the white world in general, undergoes initiation into his white heritage when he becomes aware of himself as a white boy and of his friend Henry as a Negro. Each of these characters is initiated into a specific aspect of life in accord with the role he is to play in adulthood: Cass, who becomes the head of the McCaslin family, grows into manhood as a rational, almost paternal individual, loyal to social values of plantation and town but not enslaved by them. Ike's initiation into the ways of the wilderness and his full acceptance of its values is completed when, at sixteen, he assists at the death and burial of Sam Fathers; it is as if Sam, by permitting him to be present, passes on to Ike the mantle of the Old People and the wilderness with which they are identified. Roth fulfills the heritage he had come into at seven when, as a man of forty, he abides by his white man's code and rejects his part-Negro mistress and son.

Taken in its totality, Go Down, Moses presents a microcosmic view of the entire South from the time of first settlers—who wrested the land away from the Indians, destroyed the wilderness, and thus established the pattern from which their descendants could not escape—to the early 1940s. The microcosm—the McCaslin-Edmonds plantation—reflects in miniature the growth of the South, the progress of civilization, and the Southern Negro-white relationship. As L. Q. C. McCaslin arrogated the right of ownership both of land and of other men, so did others of his kind throughout the South, thereby perpetuating the curse on the earth, which, according to Ike, was intended by God to be the common property of the brotherhood of men.

Each generation of McCaslin men must come to terms with old McCaslin's acts; each must, essentially, be faced with the situations he first created and either reenact them or repudiate the ancestral act. Thus, Uncle Buck and Uncle Buddy repudiate the fact of slavery by manumitting their slaves, but maintain the pattern of the master-slave relationship with the Negroes who remain on the plantation. Ike, in his turn, renounces his inheritance—the plantation, the land that Isaac believes was never his grandfather's to own or bequeath. On the other hand, Zack Edmonds takes Molly from Lucas Beauchamp, reenacting old McCaslin's taking of a Negro girl into his bed; Roth Edmonds, old McCaslin's last and weakest avatar, recommits his ancestor's act of incest and miscegenation in his affair with and his subsequent rejection of the light-colored Negro woman who, like Roth, is McCaslin's great-great-great-grandchild.

The Southern problem of the relationship of whites and Negroes is made more compelling by the fact that the Negroes in Go Down, Moses are not simply Negroes rejected because of their race from what should be the "communal anonymity of brotherhood," but literally brothers and uncles and cousins—blood relatives—of the whites. Tomey's Turl, the object of the foxhunt in "Was," is the half-brother of his hunters, but to them he is only a "nigger" with whom they are playing a game, a comic version—almost a parody—both of the actual hunt for an animal whose death will end the chase, and of the serious pursuit of a slave trying to escape to freedom. Zack Edmonds, in his relationship with his Negro cousin Lucas Beauchamp, regards him not as a man and a relative but as a "nigger"; the question of Lucas' rights as a man simply does not enter the white man's thinking. Thus, for Zack to take a white man's wife away from him would be a social and moral offense of great magnitude, but to take a black man's wife is no offense at all. Lucas, however, regards himself as an individual, a man, a paterfamilias whose rights are the same as Zack's, not because the latter is a white man and Lucas is aping white men's ways, but because both are men. Lucas demands his wife back, but her simple return is not enough to set right the wrong Zack has done him—in many senses the most heinous affront one man can give another—by failing to consider Lucas as a human being. Zack's son Roth, in his turn, grows into an awareness of the social distinctions between black and white, and allows—even arrogantly assumes—these to be of greater significance than the human claims of friendship and affection between him and the Beauchamp family.

Even Ike McCaslin is emotionally incapable, despite his intellectual convictions, of accepting the Negro as a human being. It is not merely for social reasons that he rejects the possibility of a marriage between Roth and his nearly white mistress, but because of his deeply ingrained Southerner's horror of miscegenation formalized by marriage, his inherited belief that a trace of Negro blood makes its owner a member of an inferior race. Even his feelings about the divinity of love are not strong enough to sanction a marriage between black and white; he tells the woman to go back to her home in the North, to her own people, to marry a man of her own race. Yet, who, if not the McCaslins and the Beauchamps, are her own people? And who, by consanguinity, is more of her own race than Roth?

Ike, in renouncing his patrimony, has escaped the guilt accruing to those who hold the land as private property, but, as his renunciation is negative, so is the freedom he believes he gains: he is not free, but merely unencumbered. Ike's freedom is as illusory as that of Fonsiba and her Northern husband, who exist in "baseless and imbecile delusion," believing that "we are seeing a new era, an era dedicated . . . to freedom, liberty, and equality for all." "Freedom from what?" Ike retorts. "From work?" Without work, without positive action, freedom is only escape from responsibility, a withdrawal from any kind of active commitment in the world of men.

The decline of the old Southern virtues of courage and love of the land is accompanied by the destruction of the wilderness, and this, in turn, is linked to the gradual moral decay of the white McCaslins. Ike, at the killing of his first buck, found in the death of the animal a kind of rededication of his life: "*I slew you: my bearing must not shame your quitting life. My conduct for ever onward must become your death.*" (265) Similarly, he found in the pursuit of Old Ben a pattern that became crystalized in his mind as a pure and timeless moment of truth. Roth, however, the last of the Edmonds line, has none of the hunter's regard either for the ritual aspects of the hunt or for the animals he kills. Ike has a passive faith that the Negro will endure, that the curse upon the land will be worked out by its very ravishers; but this faith is removed, like Ike, from the world of action. Feeling himself coeval with the wilderness, the spiritual inheritor of Old Ben and Sam Fathers, he is content to relegate the responsibility for the destruction of the wilderness to others, and to match his age and approaching death with the gradual disappearance of the forests.

INTRUDER IN THE DUST [1948]

Characters

LUCAS BEAUCHAMP, an elderly Negro
GAVIN STEVENS, a lawyer
CHARLES [CHICK] MALLISON, Steven's sixteen-year-old nephew
ALECK SANDER, Chick's Negro companion
MISS EUNICE HABERSHAM, a spinster of nearly eighty
VINSON GOWRIE, the murdered man
NUB GOWRIE, Vinson's father
CRAWFORD GOWRIE, Vinson's brother

PLOT

When he was twelve years old, Chick Mallison (the "he" with whom the story opens) had fallen into a partly frozen creek while hunting. Lucas Beauchamp, happening on the scene, had taken Chick home with him, dried his clothes, and given him dinner. When Chick tried to pay him for his hospitality, Lucas had refused to take his money. Chick had considered this an insult, since it put him, a white boy, under an obligation to a Negro. In the years that followed, Chick had repeatedly tried to repay Lucas—first with a Christmas present of cigars and snuff; later with a dress for Molly, his wife—but Lucas had replied by sending a gift to Chick. So the initial obligation still stood.

As the novel begins, Lucas, whom the townsfolk resent for his failure to "act like a nigger," has just been arrested for the murder of a white man, Vinson Gowrie. Lucas has been found near the scene, moments after Gowrie's shooting, carrying a pistol from which one bullet has been fired. Accused of the crime, Lucas neither protests nor explains. He is taken to a nearby house for safekeeping, for the townsfolk expect that the relatives of the murdered man may try to lynch him. Taken to jail the next day, Lucas sends for the lawyer Gavin Stevens, who brings Chick with him. Lucas says that he "wants to hire somebody," but does not say what for, and when Stevens and Chick leave he asks for some tobacco. On the excuse of getting him tobacco, Chick goes back to the jail and is told by Lucas that Vinson was not shot with Lucas' Colt 41. Chick tries to tell his uncle, who will not listen, that Lucas' pistol did not kill Gowrie; finally he and his friend Aleck Sander, together with the old spinster Miss Eunice Habersham, sneak out to the graveyard late at night, passing on their way a man on a mule carrying something in front of his saddle. At the graveyard they dig up Gowrie's coffin. The body it holds is not Vinson's but that of a lumber dealer named Jake Montgomery.

Told of Chick's discovery, Stevens tells Sheriff Hampton; they go back to the churchyard, where they are met by Vinson's father, Nub Gowrie, and his twin sons. When the grave is opened again, the coffin is found to be empty. They deduce that the mysterious man on the mule the night before was responsible both for Montgomery's body being in the grave and for its now being missing, and that he probably buried both bodies in the sand of a nearby creek. They find Montgomery's body hastily buried in a shallow grave and Vinson's sunk in four feet of quicksand. The bullet wound in Vinson's body was made by a Luger automatic, the type of gun owned by his brother Crawford.

Lucas reveals to the sheriff that, during his walks late at night, he had discovered that Crawford Gowrie was systematically stealing lumber from the mill which he operated in partnership with his brother. Crawford had tried to bribe Lucas, who refused, saying he would make up his mind whom he had seen stealing lumber when Crawford proved that he had paid his brother for the timber he had been removing. Crawford had sent for Lucas to meet him at Fraser's store, tricking him into shooting at a stump on his way there. Crawford had then told Vinson that Lucas knew the identity of the thief and he and Vinson had gone to meet Lucas at the store, Crawford walking behind. When they were in sight of Lucas, Crawford shot his brother and fled, expecting that Lucas would be accused of the murder. When Montgomery, the buyer of the stolen lumber, tried to blackmail him, Crawford killed him as well.

The mob in town have been waiting for the Gowrie kin and other inhabitants of Beat Four to come to avenge Gowrie's murder by burning Lucas, but they immediately disperse when word comes that Gowrie's brother, not Lucas, was the killer. Recoiling in horror from the violation of the most basic of all social codes—that a man must not kill his mother's child—the townsfolk effectively excommunicate Crawford Gowrie from the human race by refusing even to lynch him. Crawford recognizes this and, somehow coming into possession of his gun while in jail, commits suicide. Lucas, his innocence proven, continues in his habits as before, with the difference that the white people are finally forced to accept him as he is.

Intruder in the Dust immediately invites comparison with *Go Down, Moses* because of the presence of Lucas Beauchamp and the theme of Negro-white relations, which occurs in both books. Part detective story and part apologia for the South's resistance to any non-Southern intervention on behalf of Negro rights and equality, the novel suffers from a failure to fuse the dramatic reality of its material with Gavin Stevens' moralizing. The tone of the action is essentially comic, while the rhetoric of the ninth and tenth chapters is at best serious and at worst unnecessary. Though the loquacious Stevens is physically present at most of the scenes of the book, the silent, patient figure of Lucas Beauchamp looms out of the background of his jail cell to dominate the action. Lucas' lifelong attitude toward the white people gives the situation—his supposed murder of a white man—its dramatic intensity: not only has a "nigger" killed a white, but one who has for years infuriated the whites by his quiet refusal to act like a "nigger." Thus, the town shares Chick Mallison's belief that "they are going to make a nigger out of him once in his life anyway" (23) by lynching him. Even Aleck Sander, as spokesman for the feelings of his race, says that "it's the ones like Lucas makes trouble for everybody." (57) The old man's dignity and his impassivity, his total acceptance of both his black and his white blood (Lucius Quintus McCaslin was his grandfather) and of himself as an individual, make it impossible for the townsfolk to categorize him, and they resent their inability to do so. Because Lucas does not play according to the rules laid down by white society, his very existence is a threat to the ordered structure of Southern life. Thus, the townsfolk are only too willing to believe in Lucas' guilt, thinking he had finally acted like a nigger, "blew his top and murdered a white man . . . and now the white people will take him out and burn him, all regular and in order and themselves acting exactly as he [a white man] is convinced Lucas would wish them to act: like white folks; both of them observing implicitly the rules: the nigger acting like a nigger and the white folks acting like white folks and no real hard feelings on either side." (33–34) Because of this predisposition, no one doubts his guilt, which Lucas has not even bothered to deny. Even his lawyer assumes him to be the murderer and talks not of a defense but of a plea of manslaughter, a term in Parchman Penitentiary, and a possible parole if Lucas should live that long. The question of Lucas' guilt or innocence is left to Chick and Aleck Sander, boys on the verge of manhood and thus not fully a part of adult society and its accepted modes of self-deception, and to Miss Eunice Habersham, whose age has carried her beyond purely social responses and whose feminine mind is less subject to the domination of reason and apparent fact than are the minds of men. For Chick, the task of proving Lucas innocent is both expiation and initiation: expiation of Chick's childhood attempt to pay Lucas for a meal and thus to assert himself as a white boy and to place his would-be host in the position of a mere hired servant, a Negro and an inferior; initiation into an individual's role in an adult world in which unanimity of opinion does not always guarantee truth, nor tradtional reactions justice. Chick's first impulse, out of his child's need to feel safe and to see his world as a coherent whole, is to run, to put miles between himself and the question

Lucas' position poses, to return only when all is over and there is no need
for him to choose between two obligations—that of a white man to his
upbringing and his white blood, and that of any man to prevent the shedding of innocent blood, even that of an arrogant old nigger. Chick is at
first not consciously willing to permit the suspicion that Lucas might,
after all, not be guilty. When he tells Miss Habersham that Lucas said
that the murdered man was not killed by his pistol, she immediately replies: "So he didn't do it." Chick reserves his doubts: "I don't know . . .
I'm just going out there. . . ." (59) Chick leaves his sentence uncom-
pleted, but he is obviously hoping that he may prove Lucas guilty, or, at
least, if Gowrie was indeed shot with another gun, not find evidence that
Lucas was not the killer. In this way, he can both assuage his conscience
and hope that he will not be forced to renounce his loyalty to white society.

For better or worse, however, Chick is responsible for the discovery that
not only clears Lucas of suspicion but indicts a white man—and that man
the brother of his victim. Reacting from the realization of what he has
done, he thinks again that his first impulse to run was the right one, that
he is now "responsible for having brought into the light and glare of day
something shocking and shameful out of the whole white foundation of
the county which he himself must partake of too since he too was bred
of it, which otherwise might have flared and blazed merely out of Beat
Four and then vanished back into its darkness or at least invisibility with
the fading embers of Lucas' crucifixion." (90) Thus his act, his almost
accidental discovery of the truth, separates him from the oneness of his
people, which appears to him as a Face, "the composite Face of his native
kind his native land, his people his blood his own with whom it had been
his joy and pride and hope to be found worthy to present one united un-
breakable front to the dark abyss the night." (125) Significantly, however,
Chick's discovery of Lucas' innocence confronts the townspeople with a
dilemma similar to that which Chick had faced four years before in trying
to pay Lucas for his hospitality: the realization that the Negro was in
the right and they, the white people, in the wrong. And, as Chick had tried
to do, the white townsfolk, unable and unwilling to admit their fault, will
spend the rest of their lives trying to even up the obligation between themselves and Lucas by sending a can of tobacco to the Negro who has become
a "tyrant over the whole county's white conscience." (128)

As it was a meal that first threw Chick as a white boy in opposition
to Lucas, the Negro, so it is the act of eating dinner with his own family
that restores Chick to a sense of his identity and oneness with the white
world, feeling now that he has "expiated his aberration from it, become
once more worthy to be received into it since it was his own or rather he
was its." (134) By assuming a guilt that is no longer personally his, he is
accepting responsibility for his white world rather than rejecting it for its

failings. He realizes that it is his, that its shame and its need for expiation are his, and that he can demand perfection of it, but not passively, himself removed from its imperfection. In Go Down, Moses, Ike McCaslin had repudiated the failings of the white world and, by withdrawing from it, had refused to carry on the traditions of plantation society. Unlike Ike, Chick feels "a fierce desire that they should be perfect because they were his and he was theirs . . . [a] furious almost instinctive leap and spring to defend them from anyone anywhere so that he might excoriate them himself without mercy since they were his own and he wanted no more save to stand with them unalterable and impregnable." (135)

Chick's active sense of oneness with his people is the dramatic parallel to Stevens' lectures on the "homogeneity" of the white South and the necessity that the South alone free the Negro, without outside help and advice. Unfortunately, Stevens' words become an apologia for existing conditions in the South, whereas Chick actively assumes responsibility for those conditions in order that he may work toward their improvement. Thus Chick's actions are a dramatic indication that the white South can and possibly even will achieve a day when Lucas Beauchamp—"Sambo"— "can shoot a white man in the back with the same impunity to lynch-rope or gasoline as a white man," when "he can send his children to the same school anywhere the white man's children go and travel anywhere the white man travels as the white man does it." (100)

Meanwhile, Lucas, through the intervention of Chick, has "beaten" the white community (as he had "beaten" Zack Edmonds, another white man who had expected him to "act like a nigger" some forty years before in Go Down, Moses). Not only are the townsfolk no longer able even to try to force him to accept a "nigger's" place in Southern society, they are not able, because of their recognition of their guilt toward him, even to resent that fact. As Stevens at the end of the book is forced to accept payment for his services—and that in pennies which he himself must count—the townsfolk, too, must take Lucas at his own valuation: that of a man.

KNIGHT'S GAMBIT [1949]

In compiling *Knight's Gambit* Faulkner followed the pattern he had used in *The Unvanquished:* to a collection of previously published stories on the same general subject he added a longer, unpublished chapter. In *The Unvanquished* the addition of the final chapter, "An Odor of Verbena," succeeds in transforming a group of charming but slight stories into a book (one is almost tempted to call it a novel) of some significance. *Knight's Gambit*, however, despite the addition of the title story, remains simply a collection of independent detective stories strung together on the thin thread of Gavin Stevens as the sleuth, and Charles Mallison as his Dr. Watson.

"SMOKE." First published in *Harper's Magazine*, April, 1932; reprinted in *Doctor Martino* (1934) and in *Golden Book*, April, 1935.

Anse Holland, a cantankerous old man and the owner, through his dead wife, of a large portion of valuable farmland, is found dead, his foot caught in the stirrup and his body apparently having been dragged by his bolting horse. Stevens, having no actual proof with which to confront the killer, tricks him into revealing his guilt in the courtroom.

"MONK." First published in *Scribner's Magazine*, May, 1937.

Monk Odlethrop, a feeble-minded white man, is given life imprisonment in the penitentiary for murder; five years later another man confesses to the crime, and Gavin Stevens gets a pardon for Monk, who is happy in the penitentiary and begs to be allowed to stay. Shortly after this, Monk inexplicably kills the warden who has befriended him, and Stevens discovers the circumstances that led up to this act.

"HAND UPON THE WATERS." First published in *The Saturday Evening Post*, November 4, 1939.

Lonnie Grinnup, the feeble-minded last descendant of Louis Grenier, one of the original settlers of the County, is found dead, caught on his own trotline. Stevens, suspecting foul play, lays a trap for the possible killer. He also goes out to Lonnie's cabin, where he finds two men ransacking it, and comes near to being killed himself.

"TOMORROW." First published in *The Saturday Evening Post*, November 23, 1940.

Homer Bookwright, a farmer from Frenchman's Bend, kills a man named Buck Thorpe to prevent his seventeen-year-old daughter from running away with him. Because of Thorpe's reputation, the fact that he had a gun in his hand when he was killed, and the discovery that he already had a wife, the town expects Bookwright to be acquitted. One man on the jury, however, refuses to vote for acquittal; a mistrial is called, and Bookwright is acquitted when the case is retried. Stevens tries to find out something about the juror, Jackson Fentry, who voted against Bookwright's acquittal, and by talking to various country people discovers why Fentry acted as he did.

"AN ERROR IN CHEMISTRY." First published in *Ellery Queen's Mystery Magazine*, June, 1946. "An Error in Chemistry" was one of 838 manuscripts submitted for the First Annual Detective Short-Story Contest; it was awarded the second prize of $500, and missed first prize by one vote.

Joel Flint, an ex-carnival man, marries the daughter of Wesley Pritchel and settles in the county. Two years later, Flint calls the sheriff and announces that he has killed his wife; he is taken to jail, from which he escapes and disappears without a trace, and the country folk try to look after his sour and cantankerous father-in-law. Old man Pritchel sends for Stevens and the sheriff, telling them he is going to sell his farm for a high price to a Northern company that wants it for its clay deposits. Though not at first suspecting anything, Stevens discovers the truth about the murder and the disappearance of the murderer.

"KNIGHT'S GAMBIT"

The title refers to a move in chess in which the knight checks the opponent's queen and castle simultaneously; the proper reply to the knight's gambit is to save the queen and let the castle go.

While Chick Mallison and Gavin Stevens are playing a chess game, they are rudely interrupted by young Max Harriss and his sister; Harriss demands that Stevens do something about getting Captain Gualdres, Mrs. Harriss' house guest, out of Jefferson, telling him that Gualdres has jilted his sister and that he doesn't want him to marry his mother for her money. They leave, and a half-hour later the girl returns alone, telling Stevens that Captain Gualdres is in danger from her brother, who hates the older man because he had beaten him at both riding and fencing, in which the young man considered himself to be expert.

The next day, Chick learns that Max has bought a mad stallion from Rafe McCallum, the only man who can handle the animal. Stevens, anticipating the obvious denouement, races out to the Harriss place with Chick and Rafe and prevents the unsuspecting Gualdres from being killed by the horse, which had been placed in the stable normally occupied by Gauldres' own gentle and half-blind mare.

The following day, Saturday, Stevens strongly suggests to Max Harriss that he enlist in the army; he then receives a visit from the just-married Gauldres and the Harriss girl. Later that day Stevens and Chick go to pay a visit to Mrs. Harriss. On the way, Stevens tells his nephew how he had once courted Mrs. Harriss, then Melisandre Backus, when she was sixteen and he was thirty. The next day is Sunday, and Pearl Harbor Day; soon after, Chick leaves for the service. When he returns the following spring, Stevens and Melisandre Harriss are married.

REQUIEM FOR A NUN [1951]

Each of the three acts of this stylized drama is preceded by a long narrative section that is parallel in physical context; thus "The Courthouse" and Act I take place in Jefferson, "The Golden Dome" and Act II at the Governor's Mansion in Jackson, and "The Jail" and Act III at the Jefferson jail. However, the narrative and dramatic sections are contrasting in tone and style, the rich, occasionally humorous or grandiloquent prose of the narrative balancing the hard, spare dialogue of the play. The play has been performed in several European countries, notably France, where it was adapted by Albert Camus in 1956. The American production, largely based on Camus' adaptation, opened in New York City in January, 1959.

THE PLAY

Characters

TEMPLE DRAKE STEVENS
GOWAN STEVENS, *her husband*
GAVIN STEVENS, *a defense attorney, Gowan's uncle*
NANCY MANNINGOE, *the Negro nursemaid of Temple's children*

The story takes place eight years after the events of *Sanctuary*, in which Temple Drake, a seventeen-year-old college girl, was taken to a bootlegger's hideout at the Old Frenchman Place by her drunken escort, Gowan Stevens. After witnessing a murder, Temple was kidnapped by the murderer, a gangster named Popeye, and taken to a Memphis brothel for six weeks. Upon her release, she was taken by Popeye's lawyer to testify against the bootlegger, wrongfully accused of having killed Popeye's victim, and immediately thereafter went to Europe with her father. In order to make up for his drunken conduct and his partial responsibility for Temple's kidnapping, Gowan has married her and they have returned to live in Jefferson.

As the play opens, Nancy Manningoe is sentenced to hang for the murder of Temple's infant daughter. Almost immediately afterward, Temple herself leaves for California. A week before Nancy's execution, she is summoned back by Gavin Stevens and by her own uneasy conscience. She attempts to persuade Gavin to save Nancy from death by offering to swear that Nancy is crazy, but Gavin relentlessly forces her to admit her own responsibility for Nancy's act. In hopes of obtaining a pardon for Nancy from the Governor, Temple drives with Gavin to Jackson, the capital, and there relates events she had previously kept secret to the Governor, to Gavin, and, unwittingly, to her husband, who is present by secret arrangement with Gavin. Whereas she had previously maintained that the Temple Drake who had spent six weeks in a whorehouse and loved it was dead and that Mrs. Gowan Stevens had taken her place, she now confesses that she took Nancy, a "nigger dopefiend whore," out of the gutter to be nursemaid to her children not as an act of charity but because she needed someone to talk to and Nancy was "the only animal in Jefferson that spoke Temple Drake's language." (266) She confesses that she had been blackmailed by the brother of the lover she had had in the Memphis brothel and, though given the chance to pay him off and get rid of him, had chosen instead to run away with him, planning to take her infant daughter with them and leave her four-year-old son with Gowan. Nancy, when she found that Temple was determined to leave in spite of everything, had smothered the baby in order to prevent Temple from ruining her home and the lives of both her children.

The Governor refuses—has refused, even before Temple came to plead with him—to pardon Nancy and thus annul the meaning of her act, and Temple realizes that Nancy is giving her life "To save my soul—if I have a soul. If there is a God to save it—a God who wants it—." (295)

THE NARRATIVES

"The Courthouse (A Name for the City)" deals with the early days of Jefferson, emphasizing its transition from a nameless settlement, a Chickasaw agency trading post, to a town whose newborn sense of community is symbolized by the building of the courthouse, to which all contribute their labor. However, the events leading up to the establishment of the town are largely fortuitous, less the result of deliberate intent to introduce a sense of community into the wilds than an attempt to get around the difficulties raised by the theft of Alec Holston's fifteen-pound lock which, having been attached to Pettigrew's mail sack, presumably belongs to the United States government—and, as Pettigrew blandly and imperturbably reminds Compson, Peabody, and Ratcliffe, there is a stiff penalty attached to defacement or felonious use of government property. Faced with the strict and unbribable morality of Pettigrew, Peabody attempts to conciliate him by covering the cost of the lock, by building a courthouse adjacent to the jail, and, as a final stroke, by naming the new town after the childless and kinless Thomas Jefferson Pettigrew: in effect, bribing him with a kind of immortality that his name would never otherwise achieve.

As "The Courthouse" centered on the local history of Jefferson and its inception as a town, "The Golden Dome (Beginning Was the Word)" reaches back into the beginnings of geologic time and encompasses an area out of which was made twenty states. Moving forward through the time of the Indians and the first wilderness frontiersmen, the section focuses on the conflux of events that led to the building of the statehouse in Jackson in 1821, passes on through the burning of the city during the Civil War, and continues up to its present state in 1950. Though serious and almost ponderous compared to the roistering folk humor of some of the events in "The Courthouse," "The Golden Dome" also reduces to a concern with the establishment of government and law, the transition of the area from wilderness to ordered and civilized communities. "The Jail (Nor Even Yet Quite Relinquish—)" encapsulates Jefferson from its settlement days of the old lean-to jail up to the present, recounting the dispossession of the Indians, the partial history of some of the town's famous families, the outbreak and end of the Civil War, Reconstruction (and the unreconstructed and irreconcilable women still capable, seventy years later, of walking out in the middle of *Gone with the Wind*), the new century, and the new war and the war after that. All of these are summed up in the jail that witnessed the progression of time, and in a girl's name scratched on a windowpane in 1861, the windowpane still intact and speaking to the present out of long ago.

Thematically, the emphasis in the narrative sections on the establishment of the courthouse and the capitol—the symbols of law and legal justice—is paralleled in the play in Temple's conviction that she is legally innocent of any responsibility for Nancy's crime, and in her later attempts to countermand Nancy's death sentence by legal means—a plea of clemency from the bereaved mother, an affidavit certifying that Nancy is crazy. Similarly, the sense in the narrative of the immanence of the past in the present is echoed in Stevens' comments that there is no such thing as past —that the past is always present, and cannot be separated or compartmentalized—in the face of Gowan's attempt to live down his past drunken irresponsibility by marrying Temple and giving up liquor, and Temple's insistence that the provocative and foolish Temple Drake of eight years ago has given place entirely to the respectable and socially prominent young wife and mother, Mrs. Gowan Stevens. Essentially, the play deals with the refutation of legal justice as the sole standard of morality and with the inseparability of past and present, the existential necessity of recognizing the reality of one's own actions and living with their consequences.

The play suffers from excessive, undramatic talk and a general failure to express its themes in significant action. However, its skeletal structure is well conceived and the interaction of its characters, though primarily verbal, points out with nearly allegorical simplicity the extremes of responsible and irresponsible action. Both accepted social morality and legal justice permit—and in some cases encourage—irresponsible action. Gowan does "right" by his standards as a Virginia gentleman in marrying Temple, for whose abduction by Popeye eight years previously he was at least partially responsible. Yet this conventional sacrifice of his bachelor freedom as partial reparation for his behavior—even his giving up of alcohol as a means of buying immunity from his past and ensuring his future—is only a selfish action by means of which he can live with himself according to his social standards. As purely social action it is perhaps commendable; as evidence of his awareness of his responsibility it fails completely, for Gowan still demands that Temple consider his marrying her a sacrifice for which she should be grateful and his forgiveness of her an act of generosity. Unsatisfied with her gratitude, he reveals his feeling of moral superiority by doubting the paternity of their child. In believing that he has done "right," that his past actions have been paid for in full, he contributes nearly as much as Temple to the tragedy that finally befalls them, just as he had contributed, eight years earlier, to the tragedy at the Old Frenchman Place.

Temple, who desires social approval as much as the irresponsible freedom to flirt wth evil, played the role (at the trial in *Sanctuary*), of Southern Womanhood forcibly defiled and constrained, even though her false testimony sent an innocent man to his death. In marrying Gowan she further demonstrated her yearning for respectability. In *Requiem*, the bereaved mother, her child murdered by a "nigger dopefiend whore" can seem as much the innocent victim as she did in the hands of the pervert and gangster Popeye; she is still free of legal or social guilt.

But Temple's "innocence" has more than merely social implications. Through her inability or unwillingness to accept responsibility for her actions, or to face her own emotional participation in the events they provoked, she was able to spend six weeks in a brothel, "hanging bone dry and safe in the middle of sin and pleasure like being suspended twenty fathoms deep in an ocean diving bell." (258) Now, isolating herself from life in the unhallowed, if inviolate, sanctuary of her self, she continues to hang bone dry and safe in the middle of life, denying not only the significance but the very reality of her past. When Red, her Memphis lover, dies, she finds that her relationship with him was "as though it had never been, [never] happened." (263) She is like "the woman in Hemingway's story" who destroyed the reality of her experience, and no matter who remembered or bragged of it, it remained effectively erased, as if it had never happened. In Temple's case, those who could remember, Popeye and Red, are both dead, and her experience does not even have a twilight existence in the memory of others. Yet, Temple Drake's existence, however inviolate, respectable, and even normal, is totally without meaning. In one sense, when she insists that the Temple Drake of eight years ago is dead, she is speaking the truth—not that she has changed, or that Mrs. Gowan Stevens has reformed, but that her refusal to accept and assimilate her own experience is tantamount to a rejection of her reality as an individual.

The difference between the external responsibility demanded of an adult by society and the more profound existential responsibility is exemplified in the two types of sacrifice in the story: Gowan's sacrifice of his bachelorhood, and Nancy's sacrifice of her own life and that of Temple's baby. Gowan responds to purely social and external standards—a gentleman who allows a young woman to find herself in a compromising situation should offer to marry her—and his assumption of responsibility for his acts goes no further than the social context. Whereas Gowan tries to protect Temple's reputation, Nancy, on the other hand, tries to save her soul. She tries to force Temple to think of the life of the remaining child whom Temple was ready to abandon to a man who might at any time tell the boy that he had no father, as well as to make her recognize herself as she is rather than simply as she chooses to appear to be. Nancy's act, though socially and legally reprehensible, can yet be interpreted as having the greatest possible moral validity: having chosen to save Temple and her four-year-old son, rather than herself and an infant, Nancy acts on her decision and accepts the moral guilt and legal punishment that must follow it. She stands before the Judge as before the Judgment, upsetting "the whole edifice of corpus juris and rules of evidence we have been working to make stand up by itself ever since Caesar" (289) by replying "Guilty, Lord" when asked how she pleads, and "Yes, Lord," when her sentence is passed.

The primitive, intuitive Nancy, the "Nun" of the title, is able to see through to the heart of the situation, to transcend the mere legal apparatus of justice. With her inarticulate faith, her urgent but unspecific injunctions to "suffer" and "believe," she transcends narrow doctrinal limits and witnesses to the fundamental striving of the human spirit toward meaning--whether this be expressed in traditional religious belief or in simple affirmation. Faulkner, in the explicitly affirmative pose he adopted more and more in his later work, uses Nancy's primitive faith to show that human life can be endowed with meaning, without risking, as he would with a more sophisticated protagonist, comments on the nature of that meaning. "The salvation of the world is in man's suffering. Is that it?" asks Stevens, putting into words what Nancy can only hint at. It is left to the reader, however, to attach a more precise interpretation to this somewhat ambiguous statement, reading it as traditionally but vaguely religious or as a Camus-like affirmation of man's ability to infuse meaning into life in the face of an indifferent universe. The suffering of which Nancy speaks can easily be seen as the existential anguish of living responsibly—suffering that is not repentance or contrition but a full realization of one's own guilt and an acceptance of responsibility for one's acts. Only through this suffering can one's past be redeemed from insignificance, one's present from meaninglessness. "Hope" is opposed to "salvation," for to hope that someone (Temple's father, the Governor, God, all of whom are to some degree invested with the protective power of a father-deity) will relieve the individual of the necessity of accepting responsibility for himself is essentially to reject the salvation—the possibility of living meaningfully—that is within man's grasp.

THE REIVERS [1962]

Characters

LUCIUS PRIEST, the narrator, who tells the story as it happened to him when
he was an eleven-year-old boy in 1905
LUCIUS [BOSS] PRIEST, the narrator's grandfather
BOON HOGGANBECK, a part-Chickasaw employee of the Priest family
NED MC CASLIN, a Negro, Boss Priest's coachman
MISS REBA, the madam of a Memphis brothel
MR. BINFORD, her husband
EVERBE CORINTHIA [CORRIE], a girl in Miss Reba's house
OTIS, her fifteen-year-old relative

PLOT

As a result of a city ordinance forbidding automobiles passed by
Colonel Sartoris, the president of the second oldest bank in Jefferson, Boss
Priest feels it incumbent upon himself, as president of the oldest bank, to
put Colonel Sartoris in his place by buying an automobile—in spite of the
fact that he disapproves of the new-fangled machines as wholeheartedly as
Sartoris. Boon Hogganbeck, who works in the Priest livery stable, becomes
immediately enamored of the automobile and manages to persuade Boss
Priest, who intends to keep it idle in the carriage house, that the car must
be driven for the health of its engine and that he, Boon, is the man to
drive it.

Not long after this, young Lucius' maternal grandfather dies in Bay
Saint Louis, Louisiana, some three hundred miles away. Lucius' parents
and paternal grandparents leave for the funeral, planning to be gone at
least four and possibly up to ten days, and the children are sent off with
their nurse to their cousin Zack Edmonds' place, some miles out of town.
Boon, who wants to drive the automobile to Memphis, seduces young
Lucius into going with him. Letting the Edmondses believe that Lucius is
to stay in town with old Ike McCaslin, they leave the rest of the children
at the Edmonds' place and take off for Memphis. Before they have gone
far they discover that Ned McCaslin, the Negro coachman, has stowed
away in the back seat.

After an adventure with the operator of a car-trapping mudhole, they
arrive in Memphis, where Boon takes them to Miss Reba's brothel. The

place—and particularly Mr. Binford, the landlord—is upset due to the presence of Otis, the strange young relative of Miss Corrie, one of the residents of the house and Boon's girlfriend. Before the evening is over Ned has swapped the automobile for a horse named Lightning, which he plans to race in the town of Parsham against a horse that has already beaten it twice. Ned is convinced that he can make the horse run, and thereby win back the automobile, but the immediate problem is to get the horse, which obviously did not belong to the man who swapped it for the automobile, out of town before someone recognizes it as stolen. With the help of a railroad flagman Corrie knows, they get the horse onto a train leaving for Parsham in the morning, and go back to the house for a few hours of sleep. Otis and Lucius share the attic, where Otis tells Lucius that he is blackmailing Corrie a nickel a day by threatening to tell that her real name is Everbe Corinthia. He then goes on to elaborate on less innocent ways in which he has made money out of Corrie back home in Arkansas. Lucius, enraged at Otis' lewd invasion of Corrie's privacy, begins hitting him; Otis pulls a knife, and Lucius cuts his own hand in getting it away from him. Boon and Corrie stop the fight, and Corrie is so touched by Lucius' fighting for her that she promises him to give up her profession.

In Parsham, Lucius, his damaged hand wrapped in a sock, rides the horse, which shows a remarkable indifference to racing and merely gallops obediently around the track and back to Ned. A predatory deputy sheriff named Butch arrives on the scene, trying to make trouble for Boon and Ned and ogling Corrie. Miss Reba takes care of him temporarily, but there is more trouble—Otis has fled, absconding with a gold tooth belonging to Minnie, Miss Reba's servant.

The first race of the three-heat contest is run, and Lucius, under instructions from Ned, makes no attempt to make Lightning get in front of Acheron, the competing animal. At the end of the race, however, Butch makes trouble about the ownership of Lightning, gets into a fight with Boon, and has Boon and Ned arrested. Ned is released early the next morning and told to get the horse out of town. It turns out that Butch, unable to get at Corrie any other way, has bribed her into giving herself to him in order to get Boon, Ned, and Lightning out of jail so that Lightning can run in the race and win back Boss Priest's automobile, without which none of them would dare to go home. As soon as Boon is released, he beats up both Corrie and Butch. Mr. Poleymus, the constable, takes all the participants, including the women, into nearby Hardwick to be jailed. Lucius is distraught and incredulous that Corrie would have broken her promise and taken up prostitution again.

Despite all their other problems, Ned and Lucius manage to race Lightning in the second heat, but the results are suspended because Acheron breaks out of the track and completes the race on the wrong side of the rail. It is decided that the winner of the third heat will be considered the winner of the second, and therefore of the entire race. Ned, seemingly miraculously, makes Lightning run at breakneck speed to get back to where Ned is waiting behind the finish line, and the race is his. They then discover that Boss Priest has arrived, and soon all the confusion about the ownership of the horse and the automobile is straightened out. Otis is caught and persuaded to part with Minnie's gold tooth by an ingenious means of torture. A final race is run, with Lightning's real owner, Mr. van Tosch, setting the stakes: if Lightning wins, Boss Priest is to get the horse and Mr. van Tosch is to get Ned's secret of making it run; if Lightning loses, Boss Priest will give Mr. van Tosch five hundred dollars, either taking or leaving the horse, as he chooses. Lightning loses, and the *status quo ante*—except that Boss Priest has paid five hundred dollars for not taking Lightning—is resumed. Boon marries Corrie, who takes back the name Everbe and, in due time, produces a son named Lucius Priest Hogganbeck.

Faulkner's last novel, *The Reivers* is aptly subtitled "A Reminiscence." Beginning with the words "Grandfather said," the story is presented as an old man's recollections of his childhood. In it, Faulkner recalls many familiar inhabitants of Yoknapatawpha country—the Sartorises, the Sutpens, the McCaslins—with fragments of their histories. The novel is Lucius Priest's reminiscence of a highly comic and moving adventure—and of childhood's innocence, no sooner discovered than lost, of the child's growing awareness of the irretrievability of one's actions. As Boss Priest tells the boy Lucius at the conclusion of the book, "A gentleman accepts the responsibility of his actions and bears the burden of their consequences, even when he did not himself instigate them but only acquiesced to them, didn't say No though he knew he should." (302) This, in a nutshell, summarizes the burden of much of Faulkner's total work, whether told in terms of the suffering and finally enlightened Hightower of *Light in August*, of the failure of responsibility of Temple Drake in *Sanctuary*, or of the quasi-withdrawal from responsibility for the guilt of others by Isaac McCaslin in *Go Down, Moses*.

The book is a comic novel in much the same sense as *Huckleberry Finn* is a comic novel: uproarious, sometimes ludicrous adventure and excitement mixed with the very serious business of a boy's initiation into moral adulthood, of his realization of evil and injustice; it is all viewed with the freshness of a child's eye that, still undistorted by shortsighted moralism, sees good in a prostitute and wholeheartedly takes her side. As Huck Finn accepts the solemn consequences of loyalty to his Negro friend Jim above his loyalty to white society, so Lucius learns to accept and live with the consequences of deceiving his family, knowing that no whipping can ever undo the wrong or make him forget it. Both Lucius and Huck effectively leave childhood behind them, emerging from the cocoon of innocence and unawareness—perhaps more accidentally than deliberately—into a realization that, though there are things which they do not yet understand, they must act; they must learn to choose for themselves, and stand by their decisions.

There are several elements in the novel connecting it with the earlier Yoknapatawpha County books, notably the scenes at Miss Reba's brothel (cf. *Sanctuary* and *The Mansion*), the connection of the Priest family with the McCaslin family of *Go Down, Moses*, and the episode of the horse that will run only for one man, which is reminiscent of the horse stolen by the Cockney groom in *A Fable*.

SOLDIER'S PAY [1926]

Characters

DONALD MAHON, *a lieutenant in the R.A.F.*
MRS. MARGARET POWERS, *a 24-year-old war widow*
JOE GILLIGAN, *a private in the Army*
JULIAN LOWE, *a young air cadet*
CECILY SAUNDERS, *Donald's fiancée*
RECTOR MAHON, *Donald's father*
JANUARIUS JONES

Donald Mahon, returning home to Georgia after the First World War, sick and with a terrible facial scar, comes into contact with Private Joe Gilligan and Cadet Julian Lowe. Though these two have been previously drinking and making nuisances of themselves on the train, they begin to develop a sense of responsibility for the badly ill Mahon, and, with Mrs. Margaret Powers, a young war widow also traveling on the train, adopt Mahon as their charge. Lowe, an adolescent enamored of death and glory, imagines that he is in love with Mrs. Powers, but soon leaves the party to go on to his mother in San Francisco, while Gilligan and Mrs. Powers take Mahon home to Georgia.

Mahon's arrival at home, where he had been presumed dead, provides the central focus of the story. His fiancée, Cecily Saunders, faints at the sight of his badly scarred face. His father, an Episcopal rector, accepts the situation with stoic dignity, though he tends to be overoptimistic about Mahon's chances of recovery. Emmy, the serving girl who had had a brief and romantic affair with Mahon before he left for the war, is heartbroken over his failure to recognize her. Neighbors flit through to see the War Hero, indifferent or curious and wrapped up in their own concerns. Januarius Jones, a coarse satyrlike figure, nimbly pursues every available young female.

Only Mrs. Powers and the no-nonsense, somewhat hard-bitten Gilligan recognize that Mahon is dying; only they, the Rector, and Emmy are genuinely concerned for his welfare. Mahon lives in a semicomatose state, almost unaware of or completely unconcerned with his surroundings, unable to remember how he was wounded, and slowly going blind. The response of the other characters to him reveals their isolation from him, as well as from one another, and the gap between the illusory civilian idolization of the War Hero and the embittering reality of war. Thus young Cadet Lowe (who never appears on the Mahon home scene but whose presence intrudes from time to time in the form of adolescent love letters to Mrs. Powers) subscribes to the civilian death-and-glory complex, for the war had ended before he could see action. Mrs. Burney, whose son Dewey is dead, comforts herself effusively with thoughts of his bravery and scorns those whose loved ones were cowardly enough not to get themselves killed. The irony of this situation is heavily underscored by the repeated musings of Sergeant Madden, who saw Dewey, crazed with fear that the morning mist on the battle front was poison gas, leap onto the fire-step and shoot Lieutenant Powers—Margaret Powers' husband—for leading them into what Dewey believed was certain death. Cecily Saunders, who had become engaged to Mahon when he was going away to become a War Hero, feels nothing but revulsion for the Mahon who has returned from the war. Finally, Januarius Jones acts as the epitome of civilian indifference to the reality of war, so much so that, though constantly in and out of the rectory, he rarely even lays eyes on Mahon.

Mahon's isolation becomes alienation both from himself and from the world. He is unable to connect his present, dying existence with his living— and now effectively dead—past. Several characters think of the old Donald, who is dead, as one individual and the invalided, dying Donald as another. Indeed, this separation between the Donald they remember and the man who has come home to die becomes so sharp that on one occasion the Rector speaks in Donald's presence of the objections of Cecily's parents to her marrying him; he, too, has come to think of the invalid as an insentient, almost nonexistent thing.

As Donald's isolation is emphasized by the physical and mental condition that has effectively removed him from the world, the isolation of the civilians is made ironically sharper by their going through the motions of love without experiencing the sense of communication that real love brings. Thus Cecily, engaged to Donald and occasionally protesting her love for him, is completely without feeling for him, save a sense of revulsion. Provocative but sexless, vain, epicene, she first leads on and then repulses the lecherous Januarius Jones. Though she surrenders once to the sophomoric George Farr, she runs weeping from the scene and tortures him thereafter with her flirtatious behavior with other men. The goatlike Jones pursues first Cecily, then Mrs. Powers, and finally the distraught Emmy, who, though she surrenders to the person of Jones on the night of Donald's death, is actually reliving her experience with the "old" Donald. Mrs. Powers and Gilligan, more perceptive and with more human potential than the rest of the characters, seem to be fighting their way out of the no man's land of aloneness. Mrs. Powers' concern for Donald, and, ultimately, her marriage to him when Cecily runs away to marry George Farr, is best seen as an act of expiation for her first marriage, into which she entered in much the same way as Cecily entered her engagement to Mahon—a meaningless, impersonal relationship springing out of the cult of the War Hero.

Only Emmy and the Rector, of all the characters who had known the "old" Donald, have an inner dignity and strength that enables them to adjust to the change and endure the situation that Donald's return creates. They can accept what they cannot change. Mrs. Powers thinks of Emmy: "The Donald she had known was dead; this one was but a sorry substitute, but Emmy was going to make the best of it, as women will." (187) The Rector, speaking to Gilligan after Donald's death can say, "Well, Joe, things are back to normal again. People come and go, but Emmy and I seem to be like the biblical rocks." (219) Which, indeed, they are. Some of their characteristics foreshadow those of Dilsey in *The Sound and the Fury*, who can bear suffering with fortitude, and the many other characters in Faulkner's later work who embody the virtues of the human heart—compassion, sacrifice, and endurance.

Faulkner's first novel, *Soldier's Pay* was written in New Orleans in 1925. According to legend, Faulkner admired the life led by his friend Sherwood Anderson, who wrote in the forenoon, strolled about the city in the afternoon, and drank in the evenings. Faulkner, deciding that this was the life for him, tried his hand at it, discovered that writing was fun and six weeks later finished *Soldier's Pay*. Meeting Faulkner on the street, Mrs. Anderson asked how the book was doing, and said, "Sherwood says that he will make a trade with you. If he doesn't have to read your manuscript he will tell his publisher to accept it." (ID, 77) Faulkner agreed, and the manuscript was taken by Horace Liveright of Boni and Liveright, which also published his second novel, *Mosquitoes*. (1927)

Soldier's Pay was not an especially auspicious beginning for Faulkner's career as a novelist; the book was favorably reviewed, but it did not sell well. Though the writing is competent—occasionally quite good, frequently overromantic—the characterization is sometimes stereotyped and two-dimensional, particularly that of Cecily, the apotheosis of the flapper. The major charge that can be brought against the book, however, is that it is not Faulkner writing from the heart, but diligently imitating other successful novelists of the time. There are echoes of F. Scott Fitzgerald in the "jazz age" scene at the dance, and of Aldous Huxley in the flippant, satiric conversations of Cecily and Jones. Drawing-room witticisms are simply not Faulkner's métier, and there is sometimes a tone of coy artificiality which, however deliberate, does not suit the over-all tone of the book. There is, to be sure, a good deal of satiric humor in the caricature of Jones, and there are positive steps in the direction of Faulkner's later work, notably the closing, melancholic, and peaceful description of the singing coming from the Negro church, which anticipates the Negro Easter service in the fourth section of *The Sound and the Fury*. All in all, *Soldier's Pay* is the work of a promising young novelist, but one would scarcely expect such a major work as *The Sound and the Fury* to follow it in only three years.

MOSQUITOES [1927]

Characters

GORDON, a *sculptor*
MRS. PATRICIA MAURIER, *a wealthy widow who cultivates artists*
PAT ROBYN, *her niece*
THEODORE [JOSH OR GUS] ROBYN, *Pat's twin brother*
ERNEST TALLIAFERRO, *a widower employed in the women's clothing business*
DAWSON FAIRCHILD, a *novelist*
MARK FROST, a *poet*
MAJOR AYERS, *an Englishman*
JENNY STEINBAUER, *a last-minute guest invited by Pat*
PETE GINOTTA, *Jenny's boyfriend*
MRS. EVA WISEMAN, *a divorcée*
JULIUS KAUFFMAN, *her brother*
MISS DOROTHY JAMESON, *a spinster*
DAVID WEST, *a steward on Mrs. Maurier's yacht*

PLOT

Mrs. Maurier invites a party for an excursion on Lake Ponchartrain in her yacht. To the invited guests are added, at the last moment, Jenny—a soft, placidly voluptuous and utterly mindless girl whom Pat, Mrs. Maurier's niece, has met only that morning—and her boyfriend Pete, who refuses to let her go without him. Despite Mrs. Maurier's attempts to make the voyage gay and busy, most of the male guests, led by Dawson Fairchild, abandon the women to drink in Fairchild's cabin. The nephew, carving a pipe, finds that he needs a piece of metal and removes one from the engine room. In the morning the ship's steering gear is found to be inoperative, and the yacht drifts toward land and runs aground. Pat, having made a conquest of the young steward, goes ashore with him early the following morning, planning to go to Mandeville, which they believe to be nearby. They spend the day first lost in the swamp and then trekking in the wrong direction on a scarcely used road, suffering from mosquitoes, the blazing heat, and lack of water. On board, meanwhile, Mr. Talliaferro makes tentative passes at Jenny, while she makes up to the taciturn but somewhat responsive nephew, as does Miss Jameson, whose obvious advances he evades coldly. Intermixed with the conversations that take up the better part of the book are a few other incidents, an attempt to pull the yacht off its sand bar, and the disappearance of Gordon and the search for him. On their return to New Orleans, the members of the party continue, more or less separately, to pursue the futilities they had followed on board. Mr. Talliaferro, believing he has found the secret of success with women, tries to practice it on Jenny; he fails miserably but resumes his endless speculation on the subject. Miss Jameson makes an abortive attempt to get herself seduced by Mark Frost. Gordon, Fairchild, and Julius wander the streets of New Orleans in an alcoholic haze.

A satire on the artists and literary lion hunters in New Orleans of the twenties, *Mosquitoes* is more important as a document of Faulkner's literary apprenticeship in New Orleans than as a novel in its own right. The idea of setting the major part of the story aboard a pleasure yacht probably came as a result of Faulkner's trips with Sherwood Anderson (the model for Dawson Fairchild in the novel) on Lake Ponchartrain. The tall tales told by Fairchild were cooked up by Faulkner and Anderson for their own amusement during their leisure hours.

Mosquitoes is marred by faults that were apparent, but milder, in *Soldier's Pay*, published the year before: imitativeness in style and content, particularly of the satiric "twenties" novels of Aldous Huxley, and an attempt at sophisticated satire, at which Faulkner is, at best, only competent. Smacking occasionally of Eliot ["Spring and the cruelest months were gone, the cruel months, the wantons that break the fat hybernatant dullness and comfort of Time" (10)] and of a rather outdated *fin de siècle* world-weariness, the novel is certainly a failure by Faulkner's later standards. Its only redeeming feature is the author's obvious ability to handle words.

Words form the main theme: specifically, that moral and emotional paralysis (Eliot again) result when words are substituted for deeds, when men are able to talk but not to act—when, indeed, action is refined out of existence by drawing-room conversation. Accordingly, Talliaferro, the most absurd of the major characters, is the one most concerned with the efficacy of words. He feels (apropos of advice to be silently bold with women) that "to try to do anything without words . . . was like trying to grow grain without seed." (104) So convinced is he of the power of the word to change the dimensions of reality that he has changed the spelling of his name from Tarver to its more precious form. The majority of the characters are word-oriented rather than action-oriented to various degrees. Most of the voyagers on the yacht are artists, dabblers, or aesthetes of one stripe or another, but Gordon, the sculptor, and Dawson Fairchild, the novelist, are the only two who are genuinely creative. Though Fairchild contributes a good deal to the weary conversation, his superiority to the rest of the

characters is evidenced partially in his awareness of the emptiness of talk
and of the paradoxical nature of words.

> Well, it is a kind of sterility—Words. . . . You begin to substitute words
> for things and deeds, like the withered cuckold husband that took the
> Decameron to bed with him every night, and pretty soon the thing or the
> deed becomes just a kind of shadow of a certain sound you make by shaping
> your mouth a certain way. But you have a confusion, too. I don't claim
> that words have like in themselves. But words brought into a happy con-
> junction produce something that lives, just as soil and climate and an acorn
> in proper conjunction will produce a tree. (173)

Bearing out this theory of the "happy conjunction of words," Fairchild's
tall tales of the Jacksons and the swamp-sheep are among the best sections
in the book.

Fairchild's tales serve as examples of Faulkner's ability as a humorist,
later to flower in *The Hamlet*. The satire of the rest of the book, however,
becomes as tedious as the conversations that make it up, and as effete as the
hollow characters that posture and prattle through its pages. With a few
exceptions the characters are stereotypes, two-dimensional figures such as
the rich and rattlebrained Mrs. Maurier, patroness of the arts; the pompous,
vain, and ineffectual Mr. Talliaferro; the frustrated spinster Miss Jameson;
and so on. Perhaps in an attempt to create a satiric distance between himself and his characters, Faulkner robs many of them of what little individuality they have by referring to them not by name but as "the Semitic
man" (Julius Kauffman) or "the niece" and "the nephew" (Pat and Theodore Robyn). The conversations are largely on sex and art, the two topics
in which the characters seem to be most interested, but the several weak
attempts at actual sexual encounters come to nothing except mild frustra-
tion, and art remains uncreated in the void of talk. The center of much of
the sexual interest is Jenny, who becomes "like a heavy flower, pervading
and rife like an odor lazier, heavier than that of lilies." (69) Though a relatively minor character in *Mosquitoes*, Jenny is interesting as the forerunner
of Lena Grove in *Light in August* and Eula Varner in *The Hamlet*, both
of whom are fertility symbols and placid, voluptuous earth-mother figures.
The major example of initiative and action in the book—the niece Pat's
elopment with the steward—serves to emphasize the ineffectuality of all the
members of the group. Confronted with the uncompromising reality of
nature—the mosquitoes, the heat, the uninhabited and unmarked land, and
the lack of water—Pat and David find their thoughtless pleasure jaunt
turned into a nightmare of discomfort with which Pat is particularly unable to cope. The conclusion seems to be that even the young and relatively uninitiated niece is unable to exist outside of the artificial world of the
yacht.

PYLON [1935]

Characters

A REPORTER
ROGER SHUMANN, *a racing pilot*
LAVERNE SHUMANN, *his wife*
JACKIE SHUMANN, *his six-year-old son*
JACK HOLMES, *a parachutist*
JIGGS, *an airplane mechanic*

PLOT

Set in New Valois (obviously New Orleans) during Mardi Gras, the novel deals with a "family" of air circus people—Roger, Jack, Laverne, their mutual "wife" (though legally married to Roger), and little Jackie, her son by one of the men, though no one knows for sure which. Jiggs, Shumann's mechanic, is a more or less tangential member of the group. A nameless reporter, tall and cadaverous in appearance, is sent to cover the stunt show held at the new Feinman Airport. He develops an infatuation for Laverne and a fascination for what he at first considers to be the inhuman bloodlessness of people connected with flying.

Roger, by turning dangerously close to the pylons that mark the race course, manages to come in second in a race even though his plane does not have the speed of his competitor's crafts; however, he cannot pick up his prize money until Saturday, two days later. Jack, counting on the money won by Roger, lets Jiggs take twenty dollars the group owes him out of the twenty-five he earns for the day's parachute jump. After Jiggs buys a pair of fancy riding boots, the group, including Jiggs, finds itself with no money and no place to spend the night. The Reporter takes them home with them, first buying a gallon of New Valois absinthe on which he and Jiggs get thoroughly drunk.

The following day Jiggs, considerably the worse for the night before, continues drinking; largely because of his failure to finish the job assigned him on the plane, Roger and Jack do not have time to check the engine completely before the afternoon race. The engine fails during the race and Roger crash-lands the plane, damaging parts of the body. There is no chance of repairing the plane to fly in the following day's race, so the Reporter helps Roger, through various mildly illegal means, to get a plane belonging to Matt Ord, a champion pilot and part owner of an aviation company. Ord had refused to let them buy the plane on the grounds that it was dangerous, having too powerful an engine for the strength of its body, as well as a tendency to go out of control during landings. Despite Ord's attempts to stop them they buy the plane from his associate and succeed, again over Ord's protests, in getting it qualified for the race.

With the larger plane Roger is qualified for the Trophy Race, with a first prize of two thousand dollars. He is just catching up with Ord's own record-setting plane when the fuselage of his craft collapses under the strain. Roger uses what little control of the plane he has left to get out of the way of the other racers and head the plane out into the lake, away from the grandstand full of spectators. After an extensive search, his body is resigned to the lake and a wreath dropped over the spot at which he crashed. Laverne, Jack, and little Jackie leave for Ohio, the home of Roger's parents, and Jiggs teams up with another pilot to become a parachutist himself. Before they leave, however, he sells his precious boots and buys toys for Jackie with the money. The Reporter, knowing that Laverne will not accept money from him, hides one-hundred and seventy-five dollars in a toy plane for Jackie to tide the group over until some dim time when he can join them. When he discovers that Laverne is going to leave the boy with Roger's parents and go off with Jack, he is disillusioned with the group's solidarity. Actually, the "family" had been held together only by Roger, who accepted the responsibility for them to such a degree that he made the flight that ended in his death in order to have the money to pay for the child that Laverne now carries—even though that child is Jack's, not Roger's.

Though written while Faulkner was at work on *Absalom, Absalom!*, one of his finest novels, *Pylon* is one of his least successful works. Where *Absalom* is verbally rich, sometimes almost a jungle of hallucinatory prose, *Pylon* is simply overwritten and turgid. Where *Absalom* is a haunting, mythopoeic evocation of the South, *Pylon* attempts, but largely fails in its attempt, to create a "folklore of speed" and of the modern mechanized wasteland of cities. Part of Faulkner's difficulty with *Pylon* might be explained as a result of his leaving the world of Yoknapatawpha for an urban setting; Faulkner is not a novelist of cities. An even more important source of the book's failure, however, is its heavy load of symbolism—largely derived from T. S. Eliot—which generally seems pasted on, rather than a dynamic and integral element in the novel's structure.

"Created out of the Waste Land" reads the sign on the new Feinman Airport. The action alternates between the airfield and city, between the world of fliers—rootless, pastless, seemingly inhuman, who yet have a kind of commitment to their work and to one another—and the world of New

Valois peopled by mindless, joyless Mardi Gras merrymakers. The Reporter, as a representative of the city, is repeatedly described as corpselike, cadaverous, skeletal—one of the spiritually dead who populate the "Unreal City" of Eliot's Waste Land.

The fliers, to whom the Reporter is drawn, have in a sense escaped the dehumanization and death of the city by repudiating the way of life of modern society. They are, as Faulkner later put it, "ephemera on the face of the contemporary scene," (36, F IN U) pastless, existing of and for the moment, living briefly and intensely in flying. They recognize no ties of geography or kin, and the center of their family unit is not the child but the airplane, the acknowledged leader of their group the man who flies it. Within this anomalous structure they have a kind of integrity, and show themselves, particularly Roger, capable of a degree of responsibility for the preservation of the group. They have, on the whole, a discipline and vitality—even a strange but coherent morality—that the Waste Land, the dead city of New Valois, lacks.

Faulkner repeatedly describes the litter from the Mardi Gras festivities as "spent tinseldung of Momus' Nilebarge clatterfalque." This, aside from being a bad example of his use of Joycean compound and portmanteau words, comprises images of glitter, excrement, ridicule, voluptuous sex, noise, and death. Two sacrifices that are offered up to the Mardi Gras revelers—Lieutenant Burnham's death by fire and Shumann's death by water—are powerless to touch them. The first is shouted by newsboys "as oblivious to the moment's significance as birds are aware yet oblivious to the human doings which their wings brush and their droppings fall upon." (35) The second draws only a crowd of curiosity seekers who, with the impersonal lust of spectators for bloody diversion, pay a quarter to be ferried out to the spot where the dredgers are hunting for Shumann's body.

Several elements in the novel are suggestive of other pieces of Faulkner's work, particularly Light in August. Laverne, like Lena Grove, is a kind of earth-goddess, a personification of fertility in a sterile and death-imbued world. The young lust-maddened deputy trying to get at Laverne suggests the mad avenging angel, Percy Grimm, who pursues and kills Joe Christmas in Light in August, and also the young men who were irresistibly attracted to Eula Varner in The Hamlet.

References to time and clocks recur frequently, usually in conjunction with newspapers, which are described as a "cryptic staccato crossection of an instant crystallized and now dead." (53) Like the dead instant trapped in the newspaper, time has about it a quality of death, of sterility, in which the characters are bound. Time and newspapers—the one, which directs the activities of men, the other, which tersely record the facts of those activities —become ever-present reminders of the reduction of human experience to trivia. Related to clock time is the idea of the past, which in most of Faulkner's writing is of extreme importance as the shaper of the present—in a sense, there is no such thing as *was*, since the past is immanent in the present; all time exists in a condition of *is*. In *Pylon*, the characters have disavowed their pasts, and exist in a kind of unanchored present, much, as Faulkner later described them, as does "the butterfly that's born this morning with no stomach and will be gone tomorrow." (36, F IN U)

There is thus both a sense of futility and a feeling of slightness or ephemerality to the lives of the fliers which undercuts the Waste Land symbolism of the city; the protagonists become merely May flies flitting over the corpse of a dead world, powerless to save even themselves. The Reporter, attracted by their momentary life, at least achieves a sense of his own spiritual barrenness, which is perhaps a beginning. After he learns that Laverne is going to leave the child Jackie with Roger's parents, and thus destroy the group, he drives out to the airfield, apparently hoping to find in the simple physical existence of the field some escape from the sterility of his ghostly life. Yet he realizes that "if he were moving, regardless at what terrific speed and in what loneliness, so was it [the city], it outlay all gasolinespanned distances and all clock- or sunstipulated destinations." (170)

THE WILD PALMS AND OLD MAN [1939]

In the original edition of the novel *The Wild Palms*, the two stories of the doomed lovers and the convict were arranged in alternating chapters. Editions currently in print present the stories as separate units, the convict's story called *Old Man*. In the plot summaries, therefore, each will be treated as an independent whole, and the relationship between them discussed afterwards.

The Wild Palms

Characters

HARRY WILBOURNE, a 27-year-old *interne*
CHARLOTTE RITTENMEYER, *a young married woman*
FRANCIS [RAT] RITTENMEYER, *her husband*
MC CORD, *a Chicago newspaperman*
A DOCTOR AND HIS WIFE, *owners of the beach cottage that Harry and Charlotte rent in Mississippi*

Having lived an ascetic, almost monastic life in order to get through medical school, Harry Wilbourne is ill-prepared to cope with the world of love and rebellion from conventional society offered him by Charlotte Rittenmeyer. Because Charlotte cannot bear the necessity of sneaking out to cheap hotels in New Orleans to be with Harry, and they have no money with which to run away, they come to the verge of never seeing each other again. However, Harry finds a wallet containing nearly thirteen hundred dollars, and he and Charlotte—with her husband's knowledge and even a kind of consent—run away together to Chicago, where they work intermittently and live as long as their money lasts. In September, having nearly run out of money, they go north to live in a Wisconsin lakeside cabin loaned to them by McCord, a newspaperman and friend of Charlotte's. In December, having run out of food, they return to Chicago, where Charlotte works as a window designer in a department store and Harry writes stories for the confession magazines. Soon, however, Harry realizes that they are heading toward a kind of "normal" life of respectability, relative security from want, and relatively little time, because of their jobs, to be together. In order to preserve their love, or to keep love from leaving them for being unworthy of it, Harry takes a rather questionable job as a doctor in a remote Utah mining camp. However, the corruption of the cities has penetrated even to the wilds of Utah. Harry and Charlotte learn that the owner has not met his payroll in five months and in all likelihood never will again, and that all of the miners except the Poles, who do not understand their predicament, have left. Harry and Charlotte live in a one-room cabin with the manager and his wife, and Harry is finally persuaded to perform an abortion on the woman, since the couple cannot afford to have a child. The manager and his wife leave, but soon Charlotte accidentally becomes pregnant, and asks Harry to perform an abortion on her as well. He refuses, and after opening the commissary to the Polish miners and sending them away, he and Charlotte go to the Gulf Coast of Mississippi, where they can live cheaply. Harry finally agrees to give her an abortion, but complications follow and Charlotte dies of toxemia. Harry is turned over to the police by their doctor-landlord, and though Charlotte's husband urges him to jump his bail and flee the country, Harry refuses. After his trial—at which Rittenmeyer, having promised Charlotte, tries to speak in his behalf—Rittenmeyer offers him a cyanide tablet, but Harry destroys it, preferring to live in prison and keep the memory of his love alive than to die and have it die with him.

Old Man

A tall young convict, in Parchman Penitentiary for attempted train robbery, is sent with a group of other prisoners to aid rescue parties during the great Mississippi flood of 1927. He is sent out in a skiff with a plump convict with instructions to pick up a woman stranded in a tree and a man on a cotton-house, but the skiff is caught in a current and overturned. The plump convict climbs to safety. Picked up along with the man on the cottonhouse, he reports that the tall convict has been drowned.

Actually, the tall convict manages to recover the boat, though it smashes into his nose, and he tries to go back for his partner and the man and woman he was told to rescue. Helping the woman from a cypress clump, he realizes that she is far gone in pregnancy. He follows the current, believing he is going downstream and expecting to pass a town, but in reality the floodwaters are carrying him up the Yazoo toward the terrific crest formed by the force of the backed-up river water. Somehow the boat survives the impact of being caught by the crest, and the Yazoo, heading downstream again, carries it past Vicksburg and out into the Mississippi. Later the convict finds himself in a second tributary which, like the Yazoo, is flowing backwards. He meets a shantyboat and is given some canned food and bread, and, sensing that another massive wave is building up ahead of him, flees before it into the Atchafalaya River basin. Making his way into Baton Rouge, he tries to surrender, but is shot at and flees. Again hit by a wave, he finally finds a snake-infested Indian mound above the water. Almost as soon as the boat is beached the woman gives birth, the convict assisting with the sharp edge of a tin can to cut the umbilical cord and a piece of shoelace to tie it. Having lost his paddle, the convict spends six days burning a sapling into a rough paddle shape before he and the woman and child can set off again. With no idea where he is, he hears again the sound of "deliberate and irresistible and monstrously-disturbed water" (200) and thinks it is a third wave. Fortunately, it is a steamboat on its way to New Orleans with a boatload of Cajuns. The convict also asks to be taken to Parchman, but is misunderstood and taken to Carnarvon.

Somehow he manages to drag his boat down the sixty-foot levee into a bayou, in which he comes upon the stilt-supported shack of a Cajun alligator hunter. The Cajun takes in the convict and his passengers, though the two men cannot speak each other's language. The Cajun teaches the convict to hunt alligators, with the unspoken understanding that they will divide the money they make equally. After ten days the Cajun leaves precipitously, trying to explain his sudden departure and encouraging the convict and the woman to come with him, but they remain behind. The following morning a motor launch appears at the shanty to take them away, since the levee is to be dynamited to prevent Baton Rouge from being flooded. The convict, still refusing to leave his skiff behind, is taken with the woman and child to New Orleans, from whence they slowly make their way back up the Mississippi, still flood-swollen but no longer dangerous, to Parchman. The convict completes his seven-week journey by meeting the deputy with the words, "Yonder's your boat, and here's the woman. But I never did find that bastard on the cottonhouse." (228) Though he had been officially discharged from the penitentiary as drowned, he is given an additional ten-year sentence for attempted escape—which the tall convict accepts philosophically: "All right. . . . If that's the rule." (233)

Faulkner claimed that he had alternated chapters of the two short novels in order to emphasize the story of the doomed lovers through contrast with the story of the convict: "I would write the chapter of one and then I would write the chapter of the other just as the musician . . . puts counterpoint behind the theme that he is working with." (171, F IN U) However, he said elsewhere that the two stories had both been rejected by a publisher as too short, and he had struck on the idea of alternating the chapters to make one book of the requisite length. This format was not retained after the original hardcover edition; perhaps following the lead of Malcolm Cowley, who published "Old Man" as a separate piece in *The Portable Faulkner* in 1946, recent reprintings have appeared in which the stories are presented as two separate novels under one cover. There have also been separate paperback publications of each.

For whatever reason the two stories were joined, there is little question that they operate as a study of thematic contrast. In the alternating chapter form, the stoic endurance of the convict and the frequently dead-pan comic tone of his story offer a welcome relief from the depressing and painful adventures of Charlotte and Harry. However, the combined effect of the two stories is not lost by reading them consecutively. Strangely enough, although the majority of critics agree that "Old Man" is the better work and quite able to stand alone, critical opinion on the two stories as a unit is mixed. A few critics consider it one of Faulkner's best novels, but most view it as one of his more minor works.

In the double novel the story of Harry and Charlotte is of greater importance, although, of course, each story is modified and intensified by its relation to the other. Read singly, the story of the lovers seems to be only an example of the destructiveness of romanticism carried to an extreme degree. Similarly, the story of the convict, by itself, seems an over-simplification and near-glorification of primitive mentality and unimaginative endurance pitted against the unleashed forces of nature. When seen as a complementary part of a whole, however, each story is an extreme example of man's attempt to live in a hostile environment. Ironically—and it is from this irony that the book derives much of its power—each set of protagonists is striving toward a condition that the other strives to avoid: the lovers seek to escape from a loveless and empty world of security and respectability, and search for solitude and a free, natural environment in which love—and they—can survive; the convict, thrust out into the flood, wants nothing more than to get away from unharnessed nature and back to the secure and ordered world of the prison. Charlotte and Harry repudiate the claims of social duty, she by leaving her husband and children, he by abandoning his internship and career, for the sake of their love; the convict is faithful to his duty to an extreme degree, caring for the woman and the skiff in his charge with the same impersonal concern—a concern less for their safety per se than for carrying out the orders given him. Harry avoids working as much as possible, and quits a job he has come to enjoy (writing for the confession magazines) because it is threatening to make him a respectable member of society; the convict finds, during his stay with the Cajun, the joy of working, and realizes that during his seven years in prison he has "been permitted to toil but not to work." (218) Harry eventually is sentenced to fifty years in prison as a result of his love for a woman; the

convict's story ends with his contemptuous comment, "Women—!" (239)
These parallels and contrasts, only roughly sketched here, form the back-
bone of the novel, giving it a structure and depth that each story, taken
individually, lacks.

The middle-aged moralistic doctor with whom "The Wild Palms"
opens provides a partial key to the characters of both Harry and the convict. Living inside a rigid, puritan world order, the doctor has, in a negative
sense, retained a kind of innocence, the result of a refusal to see evil and
suffering. Neither he nor his wife speak the fact that they both sense—that
Harry and Charlotte are not married—for to do so would be to give the fact
a reality that they could not ignore, and they would be forced to throw the
couple out. Similarly, the doctor resists his dawning realization of the
cause of Charlotte's illness: "the veil was going now, dissolving now, it was
about to part now and now he did not want to see what was behind it; he
knew that for the sake of his peace of mind forever afterward he did not
dare and he knew that it was too late now and that he could not help himself." (16) It is this type of puritanistic eclipse of reality, the negative
innocence of the penny-pinching, ascetic life he has led up to the time he
met Charlotte, that Harry seeks to escape through love. He thus deifies love
and the sexual experience (both he and Charlotte regard love as a gift that
will not remain with those who are unworthy of it, a visitation of divine
grace, as it were) as the means of achieving a timeless state of prelapsarian
innocence, a condition that antedates guilt rather than atones for it. Unfortunately, though Harry can escape to a certain degree the respectable
life that he believes will kill love, he cannot escape from the puritan within
himself, the guilt-ridden fallen Adam whose conscience demands confession, sacrifice, and punishment for his rebellion against the mores of his
world. Thus Harry is literally pitted against himself; he is his own destroyer.
During his sojourn by the Wisconsin lake, he tries to escape from time by
slipping into a passive, foetuslike condition—yet he occupies himself by
constructing a calendar based on Charlotte's menstrual periods. Thus he
himself brings time into his Eden, cunningly using the very nature which
has lulled him through the timeless and imperceptibly merging days. During
his second stay in Chicago he partially exorcises his guilt by writing for the
confession magazines but, finding that he enjoys his work and relative security, panics at the thought of being caught up in respectability and packs
himself and Charlotte off to the mining camp in Utah. When he finally—
and almost inevitably—bungles Charlotte's abortion, he explains that it is
because he loves her, because "a miser would probably bungle the blowing
of his own safe too. Should have called in a professional, a cracksman who
didn't care, didn't love the very iron flanks that held the money." (129)
But it is also that, as both the partner in his guilt and his most precious
possession, Charlotte must be sacrificed. In his search for the punish-

ment his conscience demands, he evades Charlotte's pleas for him to leave, readily admits having performed the fatal abortion, and accepts his sentence. He refuses a chance at suicide, not only to keep alive the memory of their love but to endure the punishment his sense of guilt thirsts for.

If the story of Charlotte and Harry is an allegory of the crippling effects of guilt and the inability of the modern puritan to escape his conscience, the story of the convict in 'Old Man" is an allegory of innocence, of "natural," almost unconscious man whose social responses are little beyond those of an automaton, and whose reactions to the dangers of the chaotic river are—aside from a fervent desire to get back to the security of prison— the instinctive processes of an animal. Significantly, he is bothered by no guilt over his attempted robbery; he merely feels that he had been betrayed by the western dime novelists, on whose fictitious robberies he had based his own poor crime—no crime to him, but "a chosen gambit in the living and fluid world of his time." (152) Having proved to his own satisfaction that he had failed to be the best in his chosen career in that fluid world, he accepts the security and order of prison life happily, and has no particular desire to leave his comfortable niche for the chaos of the outside world. Turned out of his snug heaven to help with flood relief, his one concern is to fulfill his obligation and return.

Harry's need to escape from the world, spurred by an internal conflict that he can neither reconcile nor evade, creates a frantic tension, a sense of despairing urgency, in both his flight and his relationship with Charlotte. Balancing this is the convict's unresisting acceptance of his situation—an acceptance so unimaginative that even fear is lacking—and the comic tone that results from his absurd imperturbability in the face of an unknown and dangerous world.

As an innocent, the convict passes unscathed and almost unconcerned through the chaos of the flood, except for the absurd comedy of his persistent nosebleeds. The water moccasins of the snake-infested garden-mound ignore him, and even the surly shantyboat people give him and the woman food. His sojourn with the Cajun provides another example of men in a state of primitive innocence. Having no language in common, they nevertheless manage to understand each other and, without even a spoken compact, let alone a written agreement, each trusts the other in the matter of the dividing of the skins. In this pre-Edenic world none of the commercial appurtenances and guarantees of civilization are necessary; man is able to meet man on a mutual basis of understanding and trust.

The cyclicity of the stories—each opens at the same location in space (though not, in "Old Man," in time) that it ends—suggests a parallel to the cyclicity of life. In "The Wild Palms" the protagonists resist, in the name of love and freedom, the rigidity of their society that forces its members "to conform, or die." (81) The convict, at the opposite pole of experience, finds even the preprison world "fluid"; cast out on the flood—symbolically and almost literally the dark, faceless sea of the Creation myths—he yearns for the order and regimentation of the prison. It is not simply ironic that the protagonists in each of the stories long for a condition that their environment does not provide; more important, they embody the constant striving of life from stasis to fluidity and on again.

A FABLE [1954]

Characters

THE MARSHAL, also called The Old General, commander-in-chief of the
   Allied Forces
THE CORPORAL, his illegitimate son
MARTHE, the Corporal's half-sister
MARYA, Marthe's feeble-minded older sister
A YOUNG WOMAN, formerly a Marseilles prostitute, affianced to the Corporal
THE QUARTERMASTER GENERAL
A BRITISH RUNNER, formerly an officer
A BRITISH SENTRY, formerly a horse groom
THE REVEREND TOBE SUTTERFIELD, also known as "Monsieur Tooleymon," a
   Negro, formerly a lay preacher and stablehand
DAVID LEVINE, a young British Airman
GENERAL GRAGNON, commander of the division which includes the Cor-
   poral's regiment
GENERAL LALLEMONT, the corps commander over Gragnon, and his only
   friend

A Fable opens in medias res—on Wednesday, the middle of the week, as
well as the midpoint of the chronological action in the present. At first, action is recounted with no explanation: the townsfolk converge on the Place
de Ville in Chaulnesmont (the seat of the Allied headquarters), moving
in an almost hypnotic rhythm in response to an unspoken but deeply felt
sense of urgency that is transmitted but not yet made clear. Gradually, the
events leading up to the situation on this Wednesday morning are revealed: on Monday morning a French regiment refused to carry out an attack; their refusal was taken up by other regiments, and by Tuesday evening
all gunfire in France—on both the German and Allied sides—had stopped.
General Gragnon, the commander of the division to which the initial
mutinous regiment belonged, is bringing the regiment into town to be
imprisoned and executed.
   The mutiny that has touched off a three-day recess in the war and the
execution of the leader of the group of thirteen men who first refused to
attack form the central concern of the story. Surrounding it are several

subplots which, though occasionally apparently unrelated to the dominant action except perhaps by propinquity, explore different aspects of the philosophical problem implicitly raised by the mutiny and its resultant temporary truce. Like the primary situation, the tangential action is also often introduced in the middle or even at the end, gradually working back to its beginnings from which the meaning of the action can be inferred. Ultimate meaning is also withheld by the technique of nonjudgmental presentation of the main characters of the subplots; not until parallel or at least complementary patterns of behavior or attitudes of thought emerge from the action of the subplots do their relatedness and their significance become clear.

A *Fable* is less a novel, in the traditional sense, than a group of set pieces collected around a modern allegory of Passion Week and intended to intensify its meaning. As such, it draws heavily on a number of more or less obvious parallels to Christ's mission and death: the Corporal, like Christ, is born in a stable in winter; he comes into the fullness of his mission when he is approximately thirty-three, has a group of twelve close followers, of whom one, Polchek, betrays him, and another, Pierre Bouc,* denies him. As Christ was tempted by the devil in the wilderness with the offer of power over the cities of the world, the Corporal is tempted with secular power by the Marshal. Christ was crucified between two thieves for sedition against the Jewish state; the Corporal is executed between two thieves for what amounts to traitorous action against the ruling military power. Christ's crown of thorns becomes a circlet of barbed wire accidentally entangled around the head of the dead Corporal, and the former's resurrection and disappearance from his tomb is paralleled by the disappearance of the Corporal's body from his grave after it has been struck by mortar fire. Christ's Magdalene was a former prostitute who become one of his devoted followers; the Corporal's fiancée was formerly a Marseilles whore. Mary and Martha, the sisters of Lazarus in the New Testament, become Marya and Marthe, the Corporal's half-sisters. The Runner, who tries to carry on the Corporal's attempt to end the war, plays Paul to the Corporal's Christ.

The character groups and the situations through which this allegory is presented will be treated separately as set pieces in the plot analysis.

1. General Gragnon, having ordered an attack that he knew was intended by his superiors to fail, considers the mutiny of one of his regiments to be a personal failure of himself as a general, and a dishonor to his reputation and his division's record. He asks to have the entire regiment—and therefore himself—placed under arrest and executed. Wishing to minimize the

* There is some apparent confusion over the name of this character. The Corporal urges him to "be a Zsettlani," which is often taken to be his real name. It is possible, however, that "Zsettlani" refers to the man's nationality. Cf. Marthe's question to the Corporal's betrayer (Polchek): "You are Zsettlani?"

importance of the mutiny in the official records, his superiors order his executioners to shoot him from in front with a German pistol so that he will appear to have been killed by the enemy while leading the attack that had never materialized. Gragnon, however, insists that he be shot as a traitor, and, with an almost superhuman effort, succeeds in twisting around in time to take the bullet in the back of his head. The American soldiers delegated to kill him are forced to disguise the original wound with wax and shoot his dead body in the proper place.

2. Two British privates—a Sentry and a Runner—are introduced. The events leading up to the Sentry's violent attack on the Runner at the end of this section go back to 1912. The Sentry, then a horse groom, was purchased as the handler of a race horse and taken first to Argentina, then to the United States. En route from New Orleans to Kentucky, the train carrying the horse crashed through a flood-weakened trestle. The groom, together with a Negro lay minister and stablehand and the latter's young grandson, rescued the injured horse and hid it in a bayou, where they set its broken hip. When it was well, they entered the horse in races repeatedly over a period of fifteen months; even crippled it easily outran every sound animal in the country. During this period, they were pursued by five separate groups of police or other officials all over the Mississippi watershed. When the pursuers finally caught up with them, the groom killed the horse in order to prevent an animal that had known and loved only running from being incarcerated in a stud farm for the rest of its life. The groom was taken to jail, but the two Negroes mysteriously disappeared.

After eight months of pursuing the thieves, an ex-Federal Deputy from New Orleans resigned his position and began following the three men no longer in order to capture them but to aid them. He visited the groom in jail and hired a lawyer to defend him. However, when the lawyer appeared, the prisoner and the body of the horse had vanished so that there was neither a felon nor evidence of any crime. Both had apparently been spirited away by local Masons, into whose mystic brotherhood the groom had recently been accepted. A week later the Negro appeared at the jail's kitchen door, having come back to tell the groom good-by. The Negro was taken away from the turnkey by a mob that freed him and put him on a train out of town.

After the outbreak of the war in August, 1914, the groom returned to Europe. The Negro and his grandson followed him later (under the auspices of a philanthropic group established by a wealthy American matron), but were unable to find him until 1916, and then the Sentry, embittered by his experiences, refused to see them. It was at this point that the Runner first crossed the Sentry's path. He learned that the Sentry was conducting a kind of gambling-and-loan association in which a man could borrow ten shillings and gradually repay fifteen—providing he was not killed first. The

Sentry was also the beneficiary of a number of soldiers' life-insurance policies—a situation that one officer felt could be explained only by the word "love." The Runner, curious to know the connection between the foulmouthed, sour Sentry and the obviously important Negro who arrived in great state to see him, joined the loan association, borrowed ten pounds, and went to Paris, where he came across the society with which the Negro is associated—Les Amis Myriades et Anonymes a la France de Tout le Monde—and learned from the Negro the story of the crippled race horse. The Runner, like the ex-Federal Deputy four years before, recognized the Sentry as a man who, in spite of his grimy and bowed exterior and his morose and sullen taciturnity, has an amazing capacity for love and an ability to command the love and complete loyalty of others.

In the present action, when the Runner has heard of the mutiny, he dares to hope that he, with the aid of the Sentry and his loyal friends, can carry on the mission begun by the Corporal. He tries to persuade the Sentry to lead the whole battalion unarmed out into the no man's land between the now-silent lines to meet the Germans. The Sentry, fiercely unwilling, attacks him, kicking him in the face and beating him with his rifle butt. The Runner, however, refuses to give up, and on Thursday meets with the old Negro and the boy to tell them of his plan to meet the Germans unarmed, to climb "through the wire and then just walk on barehanded, not with our hands up for surrender but just open to show that we had nothing to hurt, harm anyone; not running, stumbling: just walking forward like free men . . . and maybe, just maybe that many Germans . . . or maybe just one German who doesn't want more than that, to put his or their rifles and grenades down and climb out too with their hands empty. . . ." (312–13) They free the Sentry, who is under arrest for beating the Runner and attacking a sergeant who tried to interfere. Still resisting, the Sentry is bodily hauled over the parapet and through the wire by his companions. As they go through the passageway out into the strip between the lines, they are joined by the others in the battalion; the Germans, also empty-handed, advance from their lines to meet them. This attempt to create a permanent peace fails, however, for the unarmed men of both armies are fired upon by barrages from both sides—"no barrage by us [the French] or vice versa to prevent an enemy running over us with bayonets and hand grenades or vice versa, but a barrage by both of We to prevent naked and weaponless hand touching opposite and weaponless hand." (327) The Sentry is killed and the Runner badly burned and maimed.

3. A young British airman, David Levine, is called in from a flight on Monday morning as a result of the temporary cease-fire on the French front. Obsessed with the idea of heroics and valor, he feels that he has been deprived of his first—and, if the war should really end, his last—chance at joining the ranks of the illustrious and glorious heroes of the air. On Wednes-

day, however, he is sent out on a patrol over the lines, shot at with blank German artillery, and himself shoots—though he does not know his tracer is also blank—at a German plane carrying a general to the French lines for a conference among the leaders of both sides. After his return to the airfield he has the tracer fired at himself to find out what is wrong with it; though the pellets bounce off him, their phosphorous coating burns his flying overall, which he takes off and carries about, still quietly smoldering, with him. Unable to bear the situation created by the truce, disillusioned in his dream of the glory of war and his faith in discipline and regulations, he commits suicide on Thursday night.

4. Picking up the scene in the Place de Ville with which the book opened, Faulkner returns to the figure of the young woman as a means of introducing the relationship between the Corporal who led the mutiny of Monday morning and the Marshal, the commander-in-chief of the Allied Forces, who is to hear and decide on General Gragnon's request that the regiment be executed. The young woman is the Corporal's fiancée, who has traveled with his sisters from their distant village to the city where, somehow, the populace of the countryside knew that the mutinying regiment would be taken and sentenced. The various strands of the story begin to be drawn together as the division commander, General Gragnon, is brought under arrest to the Marshal's headquarters in the city. In the following subsection the Marshal's history is recounted—his hereditary right, temporarily held in abeyance by him, to secular power and glory; his friendship with the Norman who was the first to recognize the other's future greatness and later received the quartermaster generalship as a gift of the Marshal; his career in North Africa; his disappearance, for many years, into a Tibetan lamasery. The next subsection brings the Marshal and the Corporal together for the first time, as three officers—an American, a Briton, and a Frenchman—are brought in to identify the Corporal. The Briton, Colonel Beale, recognizes him as a man whom he himself saw killed in 1914; the American, Captain Middleton, identifies him as a man who had died at sea of influenza and whom he himself had buried in 1917; and the Frenchman, Major Blum, tells how the Corporal raised enough money from the soldiers to pay for an operation to save the eyesight of a little girl going blind, and how he collected money for the wedding of a young American soldier and a French orphan girl. The Marshal then meets with the three women—the two elders sisters of the Corporal and his young fiancée—and the relationship of the two men is revealed: some thirty-three years before, the man who was to become the Marshal had appeared in a remote village of middle Europe, where he met and seduced a married woman who died in giving birth to his son. Nine-year-old Marthe and the eleven-year-old idiot Marya, the woman's daughters, had raised the child. When she was nineteen, Marthe had taken her charges with her to Beirut, where she married

a Frenchman, making it possible for them to get to France, where she sensed in some obscure way her half-brother's destiny was to be found.

The following night, Thursday, the Quartermaster General, horrified at the realization that he has tacitly agreed to—by not preventing—the murder of both the Germans and the Allies who met unarmed in no man's land, attempts to hand his resignation to the Marshal, but the Marshal refuses to accept it. Then the Marshall tempts the Corporal to repudiate his acts and those who followed him by foregoing his martyrdom and thus negating the effect of the mutiny. The Marshall offers him first liberty, then temporal power as the Marshal's heir; finally he appeals to his love of life itself. The Corporal refuses. Back in his cell, he is visited by a priest who tries to persuade him to renounce his martyrdom in order to save the life of General Gragnon. After talking with the Corporal, the priest realizes that he himself has been serving the world—Caesarism—while seeming to serve God; in despair he commits suicide. On Friday morning the Corporal is executed between two thieves; his body is taken by his sisters back to their farm near St. Mihiel, and he is buried on Saturday beneath an enormous beech tree. Early Sunday morning fighting breaks out nearby, and in the course of the barrage the tree and the Corporal's grave are struck by a shell. Though the sisters find some fragments of the coffin, the body itself has disappeared.

5. The concluding section picks up, at different points in time, the final threads in the careers of the Corporal, the Marshal, the Runner, and the former Quartermaster General. After the armistice, a group of twelve soldiers, with a sergeant in charge, is delegated to go to Verdun and bring back an intact but unidentifiable body to be entombed as France's Unknown Soldier. As a result of a series of coincidences, they obtain a body that is almost certainly the Corporal's. Some four years later the Runner, badly burned and crippled, arrives with a companion * at the Corporal's sisters' farm, and is given his Médaille Militaire. Some time after this the Marshal dies and is buried in state. His funeral cortege is interrupted by the crippled Runner, who flings the medal at the Marshal's coffin, and bitterly denounces him until he is attacked and nearly killed by the crowd.

Faulkner's only major novel set outside of Yoknapatawpha County, A Fable deals with the themes implicit in the novels of the 1929–36 period, but in a theoretically universal rather than a local framework. Like the early major novels, A Fable is experimental in form; however, it seems to

* This character is ambiguous. He is clearly a Judas-figure, for he attempts to pay for his soup with thirty pieces of silver, and the feeble-minded but strangely perceptive Marya knows he is "looking for a tree" from which to hang himself. Though logically he should be Polchek, the Corporal's betrayer, his mannerisms do not seem to match those of Polchek that were revealed in the symbolic "last supper" scene.

reflect a conscious and deliberate attempt at both novelty and universality in which the creation of individual characters and the revelation of meaning through their interaction is largely sacrificed to philosophical abstraction and to a kind of vagueness that is probably intended to emphasize the universal by avoiding the particular. It is unfortunate that Faulkner, certainly a master of characterization through relevant and revealing dialogue, has chosen to depersonalize the characters of A Fable, to give them speeches that, instead of helping to delineate distinct personalities, sound like lines in the mouths of allegorical figures. A certain amount of confusion, both of motivation and of fact, results from this blurring of characterization. The reader is frequently puzzled, particularly in the first half of the book, by the introduction of amorphous characters whose place in the development of the action is revealed extremely slowly. There is, moreover, a tentativeness in the action itself, which, though essentially simple, is presented fragmentarily and sometimes hazily. Faulkner has used this technique—the withholding of meaning—far more successfully in Absalom, Absalom! and As I Lay Dying, forcing the reader to participate in the development of the action, to discover for himself the manifold nature of human reality, and finally to achieve, at a higher level than would otherwise be possible, an approximation of a multidimensional, perhaps inexhaustible truth. In A Fable, however, this obfuscation of fact seems to serve very little purpose, since the final process of clarification makes the reader aware not so much of the bias and lack of perspective of the characters as of their allegorical and representative functions.

It is always extremely difficult to write a philosophical novel in which the development of a complex, abstract idea, rather than the development of character, dominates and determines the action. Except in the "Notes on a Horsethief" * section, Faulkner has stylized the action to such a degree that the book is imbued with a quality of the dance, formal and patterned. All the characters and subplots, however seemingly removed from the central conflict (the Greek word agon expresses the idea of stylized confrontation or contest better than the English "conflict"), move toward the center in different yet complementary attitudes, expressing the multitudinous ramifications implicit in the critical point of the action—the meeting of the Corporal and the Marshal.

The setting of A Fable is the First World War—an event in history that marked the turning point at which man's material progress and his control over the forces of nature became no longer an index of his strength but an indication of his failure to achieve an equivalent spiritual growth. This dilemma, though never directly emphasized in the book, is implicit

---

* The long section dealing with the groom and the stolen race horse was previously published under this title in 1950.

in the subtly underlined sense of deracination of those characters—particularly young David Levine—whose lives are bound up with machines rather than with the land, whose roots in both the earth and in humanity have been chopped off, leaving them isolated and essentially inhuman puppets for whom war is the only justification for existence. The state of war becomes an artificially created means both of positing man's sense of identity as a member of a group (we against them) and of shielding him from the realization that he is no longer—if he ever was—the master of himself and his environment, but a puny and defenseless thing at the mercy of the weapons he himself has invented, a frightened soul unable to face his self-created alienation from nature, from God, and from humanity.

War, in A Fable, is also an analogy for the condition of the modern world as Faulkner sees it. If we lack an elaborate military hierarchy and idealistic pretensions to glory and patriotism, we have their peacetime equivalents in the law, traditionalism, and codes of social morality—ideals which, being abstract, all too often run counter to individual human obligations and needs. The secularization of A Fable, in which the Marshal assumes the power and position of an earthly deity, is paralleled in the modern world in which the secular ends of power, wealth, and prestige have come to overshadow ethical and humanitarian goals. The Marshal's power and society's secular emphasis are not necessarily wrong in themselves, but they become evils when man allows himself to be totally possessed by them. The war is purposeless in so far as it exists of and for itself, not as a means of establishing a more permanent peace, or even simply of conquering the enemy. It is a state of equilibrium in which the respective countries, and their individual members, are able to define themselves. "Can't you understand?" Lallemont asks Gragnon. "The boche doesn't want to destroy us, any more than we would want, could afford, to destroy him. Can't you understand: either of us, without the other, couldn't exist?" (28)

This condition of war as an end in itself is an expression of one of man's most innermost needs: a structure in the hierarchy of which he can believe and feel at home. In this sense it is a modern substitute for the office once performed by the Church and by the concept of the world that placed man and the earth at the center of the universe, protecting him from his folly by placing him in a well-defined niche, higher than some but lower than others, and giving him his appointed tasks and obligations. The war is an expression of a kind of Nietzschean Will to Power, a last-ditch effort to create a dynamic and self-perpetuating system of values to replace those earlier systems which, in the modern scientific age, are no longer tenable. As Nietzsche's Will to Power sprang from his belief that God was dead and, with Him, the entire religio-ethical system of moral imperatives and proscribed acts, so the secular consciousness and will to power of the military leaders in A Fable springs from the failure of moribund world views, no longer tenable in a scientific age, to give man a sense of importance in his universe. But the result is the spiritual death of humanity—as must occur in any system whose rigidity denies human freedom. Thus the enlisted men are spoken of as being dead since the war began, and the military leaders, like General Gragnon, have had to "Abdicate [their] right in the estate of man," in order to "gain the high privilege of being a brave and faithful Frenchman and soldier." (135–36)

The complex philosophical structure of A Fable is perhaps best seen in terms of the dialectic of paired opposites in the persons of the Marshal and the Corporal. As characters, both are larger than life—as if they wear the Greek tragedian's cothurni (elevated boots) and oversized mask. In a sense, they are also simpler than life, refined, purified, in order that no human indecision or weakness detract from their roles as both quintessentially human and superhuman figures. There is some justification for viewing the mountaintop meeting of the Marshal and the Corporal as paralleling, on one level, Christ's temptation by Satan. As in the prototypical scene two thousands years before, the Marshal tempts the Corporal to forego his martyrdom, thereby betraying those who believe in him, and offers him secular power over the earth—for the Marshal is, metaphorically if not literally, the Caesar and supreme commander of the modern world. He also offers liberty and, most precious of all, life itself. However, the Marshal is not only the tempter; he is also the physical father of the Corporal, as well as a kind of secular Father-God to the children of the Western world. Thus the conflict is not between Good and Evil, Christ and Satan, but between father and son, and all that the conditions of fatherness and sonship imply. On the simplest level, the Corporal refuses to accept his father's way of life and renounce his own rebellion; similarly, the child, in developing his own identity, must transcend the limits imposed by the father's authority. The transition from childhood dependence upon the father to full adulthood and independence becomes on the anagogical level equivalent of the individual's emergence from dependence upon external authority for a system of values to a state of moral freedom and true selfhood in which the individual himself assumes responsibility for his acts. Thus the Marshal comes to represent Authority—the authority of the father over the dependent child, of the leader of the state over the citizens, of the Old Testament Father-God over his children. He is strongly reminiscent of the Grand Inquisitor in Dostoevski's The Brothers Karamazov, who, as leader of the Church, has corrupted—or corrected—Christ's attempts to give men the terrible burden of freedom, and given them, in Christ's name, what their weak hearts really crave—"a mystery which they must follow blindly, even against their conscience . . . [for] man prefers peace, and even death, to freedom of choice in the knowledge of good and evil." (305, 302, BK) The Grand Inquisitor confesses that he, and the Church as a whole, has been working "with *him*" (the devil) and not with Christ. To that end he has used the mysteries vested in the Church in order to relieve man of his responsibility for his own actions and his own life. He has used even the very things which Christ rejected when tempted by Satan: the miracle of changing stones into bread, in order to hold man both by the illusion of the miracle and the reality of the bread, which feeds the body but not the spirit; and the offer of secular power, with which he is able to satisfy mankind's need for a feeling of unity. Significantly, both the Grand Inquisitor and the Marshal act less out of a desire for power than from love of humanity, knowing its weaknesses, its fear of freedom, and its "deathless passion for being led, mystified, and deceived." (349)

The confrontation between the Marshal and the Corporal reduces, from all its multiple levels of meaning, to a presentation of two different but not necessarily mutually exclusive attitudes toward life: on the one hand, the fear of freedom and responsibility; on the other, the acceptance of the right of choice and of its consequences in one's own life and in the lives of others. Thus the Corporal must choose death for General Gragnon and for the entire regiment, as he must choose his own death. To do otherwise would be to annihilate the validity of his attempt to halt the war and his dedication to his entire mission for humanity. One's acts necessarily involve choosing for others as well as oneself; to remain in good faith and give his choice meaning, the Corporal cannot repudiate it for the sake of others.

Faulkner has remarked that to him the Marshal "was the dark, splendid, fallen angel. . . . Satan, who had been cast out of heaven . . . because God Himself feared him." (62, F IN U) However, this is to oversimplify—and, indeed, to distort—the significance of the Marshal's function in the book, for there is nothing essentially evil about him; he is rather a modern—and human—version of the Old Testament Jehovah, powerful and jealous of his power, paternalistic, aware of man's "ineradicable folly, his deathless passion for being led, mystified, and deceived." (349) As such, he is an ambivalent figure in which are mixed both positive and negative qualities. This ambivalence serves to underline one of the major themes of the novel, the philosophical dualism that sees both good and evil as inextricably part of the nature and experience of man.

The concept of dualism is reflected in many other aspects of *A Fable*. For instance, in the lives of most of the major characters, there is a significant absence of family ties—the most basic human relationship, out of which may grow the sense of responsibility to others outside the immediate family group, expanding, ultimately, to include the whole family of man. For the characters dedicated to the military hierarchy, the lack of family emphasizes their spiritual dehumanization, their tendency to place the

abstract claims of honor and obedience of military authority above purely
human considerations. Gragnon, an orphan, seems to "have been intended
by fate itself to be the perfect soldier: pastless, unhampered, and complete"
(21); he is mercilessly faithful to his concept of military honor, which
demands that not only his own life but the lives of three thousand men
be sacrificed to erase the blot on his record and his rank caused by the
Monday morning mutiny. The Marshal, also an orphan, refuses to exploit
—and thus, in a sense, to recognize—his relationship to his uncle and
guardian, a Cabinet Minister, and to his godfather, the chairman of the
Comité de Ferrovie (Ministry of Transportation). Both (along with the
future Quartermaster General) spend a part of their military careers in
remote outposts in the deserts of North Africa—an additional symbolic
sundering of their ties with humanity undertaken not (like Saint Anthony's retreat, which suggests an ironic parallel to theirs) for the futher-
ance of their spiritual growth, but as a necessary preparation for their
future roles as secular leaders. Even young David Levine is a half-orphan;
it is certainly significant that his attachment to his mother is less a personal
feeling than an extension of the idealism that is expressed in his longing
to be a member of the brotherhood of heroic flyers. Thus for a year he
acquiesced to his mother's pleas to remain with her, and he considers the
work of his first year in training a compensation "for his own inability to
say no to a woman's tears" (88). Thus, also, he prepares a letter for her
before his first mission, a "succinct and restrained and modestly heroic one
to be found among his gear afterward . . . [and] be sent back to his mother"
(91), thinking far less of her grief at losing her only son than of his own
proper entrance into the immortal halls of glory.

It must not be overlooked, however, that the characters who represent
the antithesis of the regimented world—the Corporal and the Sentry—are
also orphans. The Corporal was orphaned of his mother at birth and of
his father—for all he knows of him—until just before his death; he is, in
addition, only an adopted son of France, being a naturalized citizen. The
Sentry, an Englishman by birth, is both kinless and childless, utterly alone.
Yet the lack of family ties in the Corporal's case serves to emphasize his
love and compassion for all of mankind—he gives no more indication of
attachment to his half-sisters than to his twelve followers or, one is led to
infer, to any of the men in the trenches; his feeling for all men is equally
deep, without regard for extraneous considerations of kinship or the lack
of it to weigh the balance. Similarly, although the Sentry is totally without
kin, and presents to other men a singularly unappealing, almost misan-
thropic, exterior, he is able to command the loyalty of the men in his
battalion, as, in America, he had enlisted the sympathy of taciturn and ordinarily suspicious mountain men.

Despite the apparently considerable differences between the personalities of the Corporal and the Sentry, they actually represent two halves of the same coin. Though sullen, dirty, and inarticulate, the Sentry is, like the Corporal, capable of dedication and commitment and, most important, love. The contrast between the two characters is intensified by the treatment their stories are given: the Corporal's mission is presented seriously, infused with grandiose rhetoric, heightened by stylization and made more dramatic, paradoxically, by the almost antidramatic revelation of the Corporal's relationship with the Marshal and their subsequent meeting. The Sentry's story, on the other hand, is basically humorous, reminiscent of the tall tales of nineteenth-century American frontier writing, and tempered by irony and a degree of pathos. While the Corporal is profoundly spiritual, the Sentry embodies the very antithesis of the common conception of spirituality; he is sullen and profane, a gambler and a thief. Yet, when reduced to their basic elements, both their stories involve the same conflict between authority and freedom, law and love.

If the Corporal's mission is sacred, the absurd flight of the Sentry with the race horse is its profane equivalent. The Sentry's story is a love story, one made ironic yet strangely more moving by the fact that it concerns not the doomed love of a man and woman, but the mysterious and magical affinity between a bowed and crusty groom and a crippled horse. Thus the Sentry's flight with the horse is "not a theft, but a passion, an immolation, an apotheosis . . . the immortal pageant-piece of the tender legend which was the crowning glory of man's own legend . . . the world's oldest and most shining tale limning in his brief turn the warp-legged foul-mouthed English horse-groom as ever Paris or Lochinvar or any else of earth's splendid rapers." (153–54) Passion and dedication and love are superior to external moral and legal imperatives, as is recognized by the Negro minister who, though a servant of God and therefore a "sworn and dedicated enemy of man's lusts and follies . . . not only abetted theft and gambling, but [gave] to the same cause the tender virgin years of his own child as ever of old had Samuel's father or Abraham his Isaac." (159)

The Sentry is the dark complement of the Corporal's shining spirituality. Associated with the horse—traditionally a symbol of sexuality, of masculine freedom and animal strength—he is thereby associated with the earth, with physicality, and with a primitive, essentially presocial morality that sees life in its simplest terms. Thus, to him, the horse is an animal to which life means running; it may be valuable to its owners as a stud animal and nothing else, but such an existence is, to the groom who loves and understands the animal, a living death, a violation of the horse's nature. While the Sentry is concerned only with the horse and its need to run, the various groups in pursuit of the stolen animal are motivated partially by a desire for money, but primarily by strictly legal considerations: the horse belongs to its owner, and must therefore be returned to him. Only the ex-Federal

Deputy, of all the pursuers, recognizes the supremely moral validity of the Sentry's flight with the horse. Like the Runner, he is a former representative of Authority; both, like their prototypical Saint Paul, are converted from the dominant world view of their times to become quasi-evangelists of a way of life that is above and beyond the Law, that looks to the sanctity of individual life rather than to the inviolability of a legal structure. Thus the ex-Deputy comments on the escape of the Sentry and the disappearance of the body of the slain horse: "right perhaps, justice certainly, might not have prevailed, but something more important had—truth, love, sacrifice, and something else even more important than they: some bond between or from man to his brother man stronger than even the golden shackles which coopered precariously his ramshackle earth." (164-65)

Whereas the Corporal is aware of his mission and of the necessity of his death so that the meaning of his acts should not be abrogated, the Sentry acts instinctively, almost unconsciously, exercising his natural talents in much the same way as the race horse exercises its ability to run. The Negro, the ex-Deputy, and the Runner recognize the Sentry's mysterious ability to command the love and loyalty of men, as when he unites men in the trenches in the mystic brotherhood of Masons—a symbol, essentially, of brotherhood in its most basic sense, an appeal to the primitive and inarticulate foundations of common humanity—the Sentry himself balks fiercely at the idea of becoming personally involved in any of the larger, conscious issues of man's fate. He is an unwilling savior and an unconsenting sacrifice, yet he becomes the means by which the Runner is able to lead the battalion unarmed out into no man's land to meet the unarmed enemy. Significantly, however, the Sentry's forced leadership is not without consequences in the brief remainder of his own life, for, as the barrage strikes the battalion, he cries "No! Not to us"—saying " 'we' and not 'I' for the first time in his life probably, certainly for the first time in four years [since the death of the horse]." (321) Even though one of its agents has acted unwillingly, the mission begun by the Corporal is picked up and carried on, and this time it is not by means of a simple act of omission— the refusal to attack—but a positive act of commission, a massive and active going-forth that is miraculously met by a similar act on the part of the former enemy.

Although this second attempt of the enlisted men to stop the war ultimately fails, as did the first, the spirit of it does not die, nor is the attempt itself without consequences in the lives of others. Because of it the Quartermaster General is shocked into a realization of his responsibility—and that of the other military leaders—for a "barrage by both of We [Allied and Germans] to prevent naked and weaponless hand touching opposite naked and weaponless hand" (327) and, horrified at the way in which the military hierarchy has dehumanized itself, attempts to resign his generalship. His conversion to the Corporal's mission is far more dramatic than the Runner's, inasmuch as he loves the Marshal and has believed in him as the savior of man with an almost religious faith. Thus there is a note of real anguish in his realization of what he and the Marshal and "our whole unregenerate and unregenerable kind" have done to man, as well as to their own humanity, becoming a "small repudiated and homeless species about the earth who not only no longer belong to man, but even to earth itself, since we have had to make this last base desperate cast in order to hold our last desperate and precarious place on it." (327)

The Corporal is executed, the war plays itself out according to the rules, and the three-day truce in May is passed over almost as if it had never happened; the world has not changed, nor has Authority bowed before the simple free spirit of man. The situation poses a hypothetical question: if the Messiah were to come now, offering peace and brotherhood and freedom to a world literally or figuratively at war with itself, would He again be crucified? For a second time it is answered in the affirmative. Yet the pessimism of this answer is considerably modulated in the final scenes of the book: in the Corporal's ironic but strangely fitting entombment as France's Unknown Soldier—ironic in that the Unknown Soldier supposedly represents all those nameless Frenchmen who died for their fatherland; fitting in that the Corporal, in the anonymity of death, has become a symbol of the brotherhood of all the nameless dead, as in life he strove toward the brotherhood of the living. Nor has the Corporal's mission been forgotten; the Runner, badly burned and crippled, has found through his suffering the complete and intuitive understanding that makes it possible for him not only to endure but to laugh, to triumph. Confronting the coffin of the Marshal, he in one sense has the last word: "You too helped to carry the torch of man into that twilight where it shall be no more: these are his epitaphs: They shall not pass. My country right or wrong. Here is a spot which is forever England." (436) And, though nearly killed by the mob, he is still able to laugh, and to say to the crowd with full knowledge, "Tremble. I'm not going to die. Never." (437) The spirit of freedom, the deathless protest against those that would set man against brother and man against himself, the boundless hopes and aspirations of man's soul will not die. Man will endure—prevail—not only, as the Marshal said, because of his deathless folly, but because of his deathless spirit, "a spirit capable of compassion and sacrifice and endurance."

The Short Stories

THE SHORT STORY is generally considered to be a more demanding form than the novel, primarily because the limitations of its length require greater tightness and control. Though Faulkner began writing short stories (his first published story "Landing in Luck," appeared in *The Mississippian*, the University of Mississippi's student newspaper in 1919) long before he turned to the novel, and though the total number of his published stories is over seventy,* his contribution to the art of the short story as a genre is relatively slight. This is not to say that his stories are without great literary value, but simply that they have added little to the development of the genre, in contrast to the immense importance of his novels to the growth of American literature.

"A Rose for Emily," which appeared in *The Forum* for April, 1930, was the first of Faulkner's stories to be published in a national magazine. The following year he published his first collection of short stories, *These Thirteen* (1931); a second collection, *Doctor Martino and Other Stories* (1934), appeared three years later. Almost all of these and many of the stories that originally appeared in magazines have been reprinted in the thick volume of Faulkner's *Collected Stories* (1950). Others, such as the Gavin Stevens detective stories or the stories of the Sartoris family during the Civil War, have been published in book form as *Knight's Gambit* (1949) and *The Unvanquished* (1938), respectively, and are discussed under those titles.

The publishing history of the stories is interesting, inasmuch as it illuminates a facet of Faulkner's work as a novelist: his tendency to brood over his material, to approach a subject repeatedly from different points of view, to enlarge and develop a situation until its complexities, both stylistic and contextual, approximate the shifting colors and patterns of life itself. Faulkner is, in a sense, always rewriting, always returning to a vision not quite perfectly apprehended and adding another perspective. This can be seen even in the usually slight revision of the original stories as they are reprinted in the *Collected Stories*. It is particularly clear in the major overhauling of five uncollected stories—"Spotted Horses" (*Scribner's Magazine*, June, 1931), "Lizards in Jamshyd's Courtyard" (*The Saturday Evening*

---

* This figure includes all stories published separately in national magazines. Only forty-two appear in the *Collected Stories*. Not discussed in this work are the privately printed stories "Idyll in the Desert" (1931) and "Miss Zilphia Gant" (1932), or the early stories reprinted in *New Orleans Sketches* (1958).

Post, February 27, 1932), "Fool About a Horse" (*Scribner's Magazine*, August, 1936), and "Afternoon of a Cow" (written sometime during the thirties, published in *Furioso* in 1947)—that formed the genesis of the episodes in *The Hamlet* (1940). Similarly, the incidents related in "Wash" (*Harper's Magazine*, February, 1934), one of Faulkner's best stories, bloomed into the massive *Absalom, Absalom!* (1936). The two collected stories about the Snopeses, "Centaur in Brass" (*American Mercury*, February, 1932) and "Mule in the Yard" (*Scribner's Magazine*, August, 1934) were slightly revised as parts of the second volume of the Snopes saga, *The Town* (1957).

Still exploring the Sartoris legend after the publication of *Sartoris* (1929), Faulkner looked both forward and backward in time, writing of the situation of the family ten years after the conclusion of *Sartoris* in "There Was a Queen" (*Scribner's Magazine*, January, 1933), and recounting the Civil War boyhood of old Colonel Bayard Sartoris. The Bayard Sartoris stories were published in book form, with the additional chapter, "An Odor of Verbena," as the unifying piece, as *The Unvanquished* (1938). Five years later Faulkner added another incident to the Civil War Sartoris history with the story "My Grandmother Millard and the Battle of Harrykin Creek" (*Story*, March-April, 1943).

The rest of the Yoknapatawpha County tales (which account for about two-thirds of Faulkner's stories) add to the emerging picture of the county and its people. The stories of the Indians—some of them among Faulkner's best tales—show us the county before its settlement by the white man, and provide the first element of a major theme in the novels: the gradual alienation of man from nature through the progress of civilization. The majority of the contemporary county stories deal either with minor characters that appear in the novels or other small, nonaristocratic folk who, not mentioned in the novels, make up the population of Jefferson and the countryside. Most of these stories are less important as independent tales than as pieces of a large pattern, the Yoknapatawpha County saga as a whole.

Like the novels, the stories set outside of Yoknapatawpha County are generally of lesser interest and importance. Perhaps the major exception to this is "Mountain Victory," which is indirectly related to the county stories, though it takes place in Tennessee. Most of the noncounty stories fall into two general groups: those dealing with the war, and those with a supernatural tinge. The war stories run from the wry humor and excitement of "Turnabout" to the slight, almost plotless sketches on the theme of the figurative, if not literal, death suffered by fliers in "Ad Astra" and "All the Dead Pilots." The tales of the supernatural vary from the whimsicality of "Black Music" to the strange postmortal prose poem of "Carcassonne"; as a group, they are among Faulkner's least successful pieces. The dozen or so stories that fit into no particular category are primarily ironic and subtle sketches of various types of failures.

Faulkner's most frequently anthologized stories are "A Rose for Emily," "That Evening Sun," and "Barn Burning," roughly in that order. Although "That Evening Sun" is perhaps the best, it is the least easily accessible outside of the Yoknapatawpha County context, depending as it does on the subtle characterizations and tensions of the Compson family of *The Sound and the Fury*. "Wash," "Red Leaves," and "Mountain Victory" are also among Faulkner's best achievements in the field of the short story.

AD ASTRA. First published in *American Caravan*, Volume 4 [1931]; reprinted in *These Thirteen* [1931] and *Collected Stories* [1950].

"Ad Astra," like many of Faulkner's stories dealing with the First World War, is less a story in the accepted sense of the word than an evocation of a mood, an indirect suggestion of the futility and waste of war sketched in a glimpse of a group of soldiers on a drunk in France shortly after the armistice. The group is made up of an American of Irish extraction, an Englishman, two Americans from the South (the one named Bland is probably the Gerald Bland who appears briefly in the second section of *The Sound and the Fury*; the other, Bayard Sartoris, is a major character in *Sartoris*), an Indian officer or Subadar, and a German. The Subadar and the German are the major spokesmen of the themes (suggestive of Faulkner's later work in *A Fable*) that the concept of Fatherland is a "symbol of that hierarchy which [has] stained the history of man with injustice of arbitrary instead of moral; force instead of love" (417), and that those who have been in the war have come out of it morally and spiritually dead.

AFTERNOON OF A COW. Written during the thirties, published in *Furioso* in 1947; it contains the germ of what was to become the Ike Snopes episode in *The Hamlet*.

ALL THE DEAD PILOTS. First published in *These Thirteen* [1931]; reprinted in *Collected Stories* [1950].

Reiterating the theme frequently found in Faulkner's war stories, the title "All the Dead Pilots" refers to those who had "exhausted themselves psychically" (23, F IN U) in the war and were unable to cope with the postwar world. Thus, in a manner of speaking, they had ceased to be vitally alive after the armistice. The story deals with John Sartoris a few months before his death in July of 1918; slight, almost anecdotal, it concerns his conflict with Captain Spoomer over a French girl. Sartoris manages to get back at Spoomer when he catches him, quite literally, with his pants down during an enemy shelling of the cafe in which the girl lives and works. Sartoris takes Spoomer's clothes and dresses a drunken ambulance driver in them, leaving Spoomer to get back to the base as best he can. Transferred to another squadron for punishment, Sartoris is killed in action soon afterwards.

AMBUSCADE. Published in *The Saturday Evening Post*, September 29, 1934; see *The Unvanquished*.

ARTIST AT HOME. First published in *Collected Stories* [1950].

A quasi-humorous, subtle story, "Artist at Home" deals with a somewhat successful writer, Roger Howes, whose farm has become the refuge of occasional poverty-stricken artists whom Roger takes in and feeds—much to the despair of his wife, Anne. With the visit of John Blair, a Shelley-like poet, the situation becomes both ludicrous and critical. Blair, wanting to make love to Howe's wife, is too honorable to remain under his host's roof, and goes to stay in the nearby town. Howes puts this difficult situation to good advantage, however, by writing a story about it as it develops. Blair finally departs completely, sending Anne a poem scrawled on the back of a menu. Howes recognizes the poem as Blair's greatest achievement and sends it to the magazines, in which it enjoys a tremendous success. Blair, however, dies soon after, presumably of pneumonia contracted when he refused to come in out of the rain.

BARN BURNING. First published in *Harper's Magazine*, June, 1939; reprinted in *Collected Stories* [1950].

Ab Snopes, just evicted from another county for barn burning, arrives with his family in Yoknapatawpha County, where he goes to work as a sharecropper on Major de Spain's place. On the day of his arrival he deliberately tracks horse manure on the De Spain's valuable white rug and is ordered to repair the damage. He cleans the rug with harsh lye, ruining it, and Major de Spain charges him twenty bushels of corn to be taken from his crop. Young Sarty (Colonel Sartoris Snopes), Ab's son, is torn between his need to love his father and his innate honesty and regard for justice. When Snopes plans to burn Major de Spain's barn in revenge for his treatment of him over the rug, Sarty runs to the De Spain house to give warning. Having by this act betrayed his father, he runs away. However, he still grieves for the loss of his father, and makes a final attempt to see him as a brave man who fought in the Civil War—not knowing that Snopes was in the war only for booty, and did not even care from which side he was able to get it.

The events in "Barn Burning" are related at the beginning of *The Hamlet,* just after Ab Snopes has moved into Frenchman's Bend.

THE BEAR. Published in *The Saturday Evening Post*, May 9, 1942; reprinted in *Big Woods* [1955]; see *Go Down, Moses*.

A BEAR HUNT. First published in *The Saturday Evening Post*, February 10, 1934; reprinted in *Collected Stories* [1950]; a revised version reprinted in *Big Woods* [1955].

Ratliff, the sewing-machine salesman, tells how he was beaten up by Luke Provine, a local tough, and how he cured Provine's hiccups. Provine, having had hiccups for twenty-four hours, accepts Ratliff's joking suggestion that he go up to the old Indian mound, where the Indian John Basket may be able to cure him. But old man Ash, Major de Spain's Negro servant, learns where Provine is going, and sneaks out to the Indian mound before him, telling the Indians that Provine is a new revenue agent and that if they were to give him a good scare he would probably go away. The Indians pretend that they are going to burn Provine at the stake; he escapes, thoroughly frightened and cured of his hiccups, and rushes back to Major de Spain's hunting camp, where he attacks Ratliff for having set the Indians on him. The next day Ratliff forces Ash to tell him of his part in the business, and Ash reveals that he was one of the Negroes who had had his celluloid collar burned off his neck by Provine some twenty years before. It wasn't, says Ash, that he minded the white man's prank; he simply loved the collar, and had never been able to get another one like it.

In the version of the story that appears in *Big Woods*, Luke Provine becomes Lucius Hogganbeck, a former member of the Provine gang. Otherwise, the stories are essentially the same.

BEYOND. First published in *Harper's Magazine*, September, 1933; reprinted in *Doctor Martino* [1934] and *Collected Stories* [1950].

One of Faulkner's stories of the supernatural, "Beyond" deals with a Judge who dies and passes to a "beyond" region in which he meets various people—a young man killed on the morning of his wedding, the village agnostic, and others—while searching for his only son, who was killed when he was ten years old. He returns to the scene of his death and his funeral, and passes as if in sleep into a different state, apparently waiting for the Judgment, as in life he had waited for juries to pass judgment on the accused.

BLACK MUSIC. First published in *Doctor Martino* [1934]; reprinted *Collected Stories* [1950].

"Black Music" is a whimsical, quasi-supernatural story of a quaint little man who believes that for one day in his life he was transformed into a faun. On that occasion, twenty-five years ago, he had been an architect's draftsman sent to the wealthy Mrs. Van Dyming's newly built estate in Virginia to deliver a set of plans for an outdoor theater. The theater was to be built on a hillside covered with old grapevines—an area with a bad reputation among the local folk since two ventures to cultivate it had ended in disaster.

While on the train to the estate, the draftsman had experienced a kind of hallucination, believing that his reflection in the train window was a goatlike, horned face. He had fainted and been revived with whiskey, to which he was completely unaccustomed. Either drunk or possessed— "chosen," as he put it—he had got off the train, bought a flutelike tin whistle and, on the way to the estate, begun to take off his clothes.

Mrs. Van Dyming, finding him on the theater site, had mistaken him for a maniac and his whistle for a knife. She had fainted and the "madman" had vanished. However, the draftsman's portfolio was found near the scene, and it was assumed that he had been murdered by the maniac, since no trace of him could be found. When the "madman" woke up in the woods the following morning, he realized that he could not go back after what he had done, tried to make sure that his wife would get his life insurance, and then went away to spend the rest of his life in the little Caribbean town where, twenty-five years later, the narrator finds him.

THE BROOCH. First published in *Scribner's Magazine*, January, 1936; reprinted in *Collected Stories* [1950]; television adaptation presented on Lux Video Theater, April 2, 1953.

Howard Boyd is a man completely, and it seems willingly, under the thumb of his domineering mother. He marries, but his somewhat flighty wife Amy does not come up to his mother's exacting standards. Howard refuses to leave the old woman, who is bedridden as the result of a stroke, and takes Amy to live in his mother's house. Old Mrs. Boyd gives her a brooch, a family heirloom, which Amy always wears—but, as it were, sarcastically, pinning it even to her aprons. After her child dies in infancy and Howard still refuses to move into a house of their own, she begins to go out alone every Saturday night. Howard tries to deceive his mother into thinking that he accompanies Amy to her Saturday night dances, but the old woman soon realizes what Amy is doing, and has her suspicions confirmed when a phone call comes for Amy late one night and the girl is not yet home. The call is from Amy's companions, who leave a message that the brooch, which she had lost, has been found. When Amy finally arrives home, her mother-in-law orders her summarily out of the house. Amy goes and Howard refuses to move out with her. He calls a cab to take her to a hotel, and, after making sure that his mother will not hear the gunshot, kills himself.

BY THE PEOPLE. Published in *Mademoiselle*, October, 1955; slightly revised in *The Mansion* as Clarence Snopes's elimination from politics.

CARCASSONNE. First published in *These Thirteen* [1931]; reprinted in *Collected Stories* [1950].

"Carcassonne" is less a story than a prose poem of a postmortal flight of consciousness apparently undertaken by the same old man who was the central character in "Black Music." Haunting and poetic, it has little substance but some memorable lines.

CENTAUR IN BRASS. First published in *American Mercury*, February, 1932; reprinted in *Collected Stories* [1950].

Flem Snopes, having recently arrived in Jefferson with his wife, is made superintendent of the town power plant—an appointment the town believes is a result of his wife's adultery with the mayor. Snopes soon begins collecting odd bits of brass and tries to play the two Negro firemen of the plant against one another in order to make one of them, Tom Tom Bird, hide the brass for him, and the other, Turl Beauchamp, steal the hidden brass from Tom Tom's house for him. Turl, however, gets sidetracked from his mission by Tom Tom's young wife. Taken suddenly sick, she confesses to her husband, who waits in her bed for Turl. After a frantic run through the woods with the pursuer mounted piggy-back on the pursued, the two Negroes talk over their dispute and decide that Snopes is the cause of it all. Together they dump the brass into the water tank where, when challenged by Snopes, they claim that they had thought he wanted it. Thus Snopes, though he has already paid for the missing brass out of his own pocket, is unable to get at it, even after the tank is condemned because the brass has tainted the water. This story appears, relatively unchanged, in *The Town* (1957).

A COURTSHIP. First published in *Sewanee Review*, autumn, 1948; reprinted in *Collected Stories* [1950].

One of the stories of the Old Days when the Chickasaws still lived in the land that was to become Yoknapatawpha County, "A Courtship" has the cadenced style and fresh imagery typical of Faulkner's tales of the Old People. The story deals with the rivalry between Ikkemotubbe, later to become the Man, or chief, of his People, and David Hogganbeck, the helmsman on a steamboat that makes an annual voyage into the Indian land. Both Ikkemotubbe and Hogganbeck are in love with Herman Basket's sister, a lovely, indolent Indian girl whose placidity and beauty resemble that of Eula Varner in *The Hamlet*. The two young men compete in various contests for the right to the girl; Hogganbeck, an enormous man, outeats the Indian, but Ikkemotubbe cannot reconcile himself to his loss, so they plan another contest—a race to a cave a hundred and thirty miles away. The first man to reach the cave is to fire a pistol shot inside; if the roof does not collapse, that man is the winner. Ikkemotubbe reaches the cave first, but Hogganbeck rushes in after him as he fires the shot and supports the collapsing roof on his back. The Indian gets a pole with which to hold up the roof, and manages to pull Hogganbeck to safety before the pole breaks under the strain.

When they return to the village they find that Herman Basket's sister has married Log-in-the-Creek, a worthless Indian who could not race or dance or drink, and who sat all day long on her porch playing his harmonica. The two disappointed suitors have the Indians fire up the steamboat and depart. The embittered Ikkemotubbe is at the beginning of his change from the young Indian loved by all to the usurper of the title of the Man, from an honorable, proud boy to a man who would let nothing stand between him and the achievement of his desires.

CREVASSE.   First published in *These Thirteen* [1931]; reprinted in *Collected Stories* [1950].

A group of soldiers, one of them wounded, are skirting the edge of a barrage; they come to a ridge on which there are overlapping shallow depressions, like shellholes. Following a ravine in the ridge, they find on its floor skulls of men apparently buried in sitting positions. As the result of an earthquake or avalanche, the men are pitched into a cavern in which are the skeletons of troops trapped there and probably gassed. The soldiers manage to dig their way out, half-hysterical, into light and air and life.

The story evokes the desolation of war through the sterility of the landscape and the seemingly benumbed condition of the characters. There is an undertone of quiet horror throughout, particularly in the desperation with which the living fight their way out of the cavern of death.

DEATH DRAG.   First published in *Scribner's Magazine*, January, 1932; reprinted in *Doctor Martino* [1934] and *Collected Stories* [1950].

Narrated by an unidentified member of the community, "Death Drag" deals with the brief sojourn of three members of an aerial stunt show in Jefferson. Spiritually dead, embittered, and operating with little money and barely adequate equipment, they become the objects of both pathos and humor in their attempts to get a sponsor to pay them for risking their lives for the amusement of the townsfolk. Ginsfarb, the member of the team who performs the "death drag," is ludicrously and pathetically concerned with their fee, and demands that they be paid a hundred dollars; when, already in the air, he learns that the pilot has accepted less, he refuses to complete the "death drag." In his rage at not being paid and his hurry to get back to the ground to do something about it, he jumps from the death-drag ladder as the plane is going over a barn. He is almost miraculously uninjured. On the ground, he continues his tirade against the townsfolk who have "taken advantage of him" by making him risk his life for only sixty dollars. Finally, one of the townsfolk, with a mixture of pity and disgust for his plight, gives him the extra money, and the fliers leave town.

DIVORCE IN NAPLES. First published in *These Thirteen* [1931]; reprinted in *Collected Stories* [1950].

The title is an ironic reference to the temporary "divorce" between George, a burly and half-inarticulate Greek deck hand, and Carl, his young Scandinavian companion. Though Carl, who has a face like an angel, has been to sea for three years, he is still innocent—until one night in Naples, when George takes him and a woman to a cafe. George gets thoroughly drunk, Carl and the woman disappear, and in his haste to pursue them George neglects the check and winds up in jail. Carl does not return to the ship until the day after George is released from jail, and the two avoid each other like an estranged and angry husband and wife until the ship puts out to sea again, when their former relationship is resumed.

DOCTOR MARTINO. First published in *Harper's Magazine*, November, 1931; reprinted in *Doctor Martino* [1934] and *Collected Stories* [1950].

The narrator, Hubert Jarrod, a rather pompous young man from Yale, meets and decides to marry Louise King, who has been since childhood under the mysterious influence of the elderly and dying Dr. Martino. Dr. Martino has taught Louise that doing something of which one is afraid gives one a sense of being alive, and has given her a small metal rabbit "in the shape of being afraid" that she has promised to keep as long as she has the courage to challenge her fears. Her mother, resenting Dr. Martino's influence over Louise and fearing that he will make her ride a dangerous horse, is determined to get Louise away from him and married to Jarrod immediately. To get the old man to release his hold on Louise, Mrs. King sends him the metal rabbit, which he believes Louise has voluntarily relinquished. When, on the way to be married, Louise discovers that her token is missing and realizes what her mother has done, she is almost hysterical, but urges Jarrod not to turn back. That afternoon Dr. Martino dies.

DRY SEPTEMBER. First published in *Scribner's Magazine*, January, 1931; reprinted in *Collected Stories* [1950].

A Negro, Will Mayes, is accused of attacking a white woman, the forty-year-old spinster and former belle, Minnie Cooper. Though there is more than a hint that the attack existed only in Miss Cooper's slightly warped and hysterical imagination, and though the sensible and sympathetic barber, Hawkhurst, tries to speak in favor of the Negro, a small group of men take Mayes out and kill him. The character of McLendon, who had commanded troops in France and who leads the lynching party, is somewhat similar to that of Percy Grimm, the fanatic patriot and leader of the mob in *Light in August*.

ELLY. First published in *Story*, February, 1934; reprinted in *Doctor Martino* [1934] and *Collected Stories* [1950].

Elly, an eighteen-year-old girl who lives in Jefferson, is a unique female character in Faulkner's fiction; self-pitying, selfish, and hateful, a sexual tease, utterly cold and amoral, her main motive for her actions seems to be her hatred of her grandmother. She forms a relationship with Paul de Montigny, who supposedly has Negro blood. Her grandmother catches her in a clump of shrubbery with Paul, and Elly fears that the old woman will tell her father. She tries to persuade Paul to marry her, but he refuses, and within a week Elly becomes engaged to a childhood friend. Soon afterward, her grandmother leaves for a visit to Mills City, two hundred miles away. Elly and her fiancé are supposed to drive to Mills City to bring her home, but Elly arranges to go with Paul instead. On the way she tries to trap him into agreeing to marry her by having sexual relations with him. In Mills City, her grandmother, outraged that Elly has brought Paul into the house and has made her "sit down to table with a negro man," threatens to tell the girl's father. On the journey home Elly again asks Paul to marry her. When he refuses she attempts to kill her grandmother by jerking the steering wheel and sending the car off the road.

AN ERROR IN CHEMISTRY. Published in *Ellery Queen's Mystery Magazine*, June, 1946; see *Knight's Gambit*.

FOOL ABOUT A HORSE. Published in *Scribner's Magazine*, August, 1936; revised to become the Ab Snopes-Pat Stamper episode in *The Hamlet*.

FOX HUNT. First published in *Harper's Magazine*, September, 1931; reprinted in *Doctor Martino* [1934] and *Collected Stories* [1950].

The present action of the story deals with the wealthy Harrison Blair's almost monomaniacal pursuit of a fox, and the strangely parallel pursuit of Blair's wife by Steve Gawtry. The presentation of the action is oblique, the central figures being seen only through the consciousness of peripheral characters—two of the local poor whites and Blair's valet and chauffeur. Highly subtle and suggestive, the story comes into sharp focus only at the very end, when the poor-white youth accidentally confronts Blair's wife after she—and the fox—have been overtaken by their respective pursuers.

GO DOWN, MOSES. Published in *Collier's*, January 25, 1941; see *Go Down, Moses*.

GOLDEN LAND. First published in *American Mercury*, May, 1935; reprinted in *Collected Stories* [1950].

A subtle story of success and disillusionment, "Golden Land" deals with a middle-aged real-estate man who, having escaped from the primitive Nebraska town of his youth and built himself a prosperous business in Los Angeles, has arrived at an empty and materialistic existence, the futility of which he himself does not fully realize. His marriage is completely hollow, his son is hostile and effeminate, and his daughter is the center of a sex scandal which he allows her to exploit—and himself exploits—by accepting a thirty per cent cut of the front-page scoop. His only close tie is with his mother, whom he has brought to California from Nebraska, and whom he visits faithfully every morning. Though he is very generous to her in every other way, he will not give her money to return to Nebraska, and cannot understand why she should want to go. She, however, realizes how easy life and easy money in the "golden land" have ruined both her son and her grandchildren, giving them a life barren of the values she and her husband had learned during their hard existence on the Nebraska frontier.

GOLD IS NOT ALWAYS. Published in *Atlantic Monthly*, November, 1940; see "The Fire and the Hearth" in *Go Down, Moses*.

HAIR. First published in *American Mercury*, May, 1931; reprinted in *These Thirteen* [1931] and *Collected Stories* [1950].

Hawkshaw (alias Henry Stribling), a barber, comes to Jefferson, where he discovers a little orphan girl with "straight, soft hair not blonde and not brunette" whose hair he cuts and to whom he gives a small present each Christmas. One of the barbers discovers that each April Hawkshaw spends his vacation in a small town in Alabama, where he works on the house formerly belonging to the Starnes family, and pays off the yearly installments on the mortgage. The barber finds out that Hawkshaw had been engaged to the Starnes girl, whose hair was like that of the orphan girl in Jefferson, and who died just after their marriage. Hawkshaw, with dogged faithfulness, returned every year until the girl's mother died, and then continued to repair and pay the mortgage on the empty house. His orphan girl, meanwhile, grows up wild, but as soon as Hawkshaw has the mortgage paid off he takes her away with him and marries her.

HAND UPON THE WATERS. Published in *The Saturday Evening Post*, November 4, 1939; see *Knight's Gambit*.

HONOR. First published in *American Mercury*, July, 1930; reprinted in *Doctor Martino* [1934] and *Collected Stories* [1950].

Monaghan (a minor character in "Ad Astra"), a pilot during the war, becomes a wing-walker in civilian life, and falls in love with the wife of his pilot, Howard Rogers. Rogers and his wife talk the situation over and agree that the only thing for her to do is leave him and go with Monaghan, although Monaghan himself is not enthusiastic about this aspect of the affair. The following day Monaghan somewhat unwillingly performs his wing-walking stunts with Rogers as his pilot, taking fantastic chances and thinking how easy it would be for Rogers to let him fall; but when Monaghan, through his own fault, is about to fall off the wing, Rogers creeps out onto the wing and rescues him. Monaghan withdraws from the triangle he has created, and Rogers and his wife go back together, later naming him the godfather of their first child.

The story has some similarities to *Pylon* (1935), in which a pilot and a parachute jumper share the pilot's wife, by whom one of them (they do not know which) has a child.

THE HOUND. Published in *Harper's Magazine*, August, 1931; reprinted in *Doctor Martino*; revised to become the Mink Snopes-Jack Houston episode in *The Hamlet*.

A JUSTICE. First published in *These Thirteen* [1931]; reprinted in *Collected Stories* [1950].

The first and final sections are narrated by Quentin Compson, who, as a child, visits his grandfather's farm and listens to tales from Sam Fathers, the elderly part-Indian carpenter. The second, third, and fourth sections are told to Quentin by Sam Fathers, as he himself heard the story of his own birth and naming from Herman Basket, one of the Indians. In the old days, when Ikkemotubbe—or Doom, as he came to be called—had just returned to the Indians' Plantation from New Orleans and become chief, an Indian named Craw-ford desired one of the black women whom Doom had brought with him. This woman had a black husband, who complained to Doom of Craw-ford's attentions to his wife, but nothing constructive was done and soon the black woman gave birth to a copper-colored son. The black man went to Doom and demanded justice. Doom first gave the child a name—"Had-Two-Fathers"—and then gave the black man a justice: he ascertained the height of a fence that Craw-ford could not leap, and then set the Indian to build a palisade fence of that height around the black man's cabin; and by the time the fence was finished, the black man had a new son, this time as black as could be wished.

THE LEG. First published in *Doctor Martino* [1934]; reprinted in *Collected Stories* [1950].

Much of the effect of this story is gained from the straightforward narration of the mysterious, apparently supernatural events that take place. The story opens with Davy, the narrator, and his friend George, passing through a lock on the Thames; George falls overboard and is fished out by Simon, the operator of the lock. All during this episode George continues to apostrophize Everbe Corinthia, Simon's daughter, with quotations from Milton. The next year (1915) England is in the war and George is dead. Some time after this, Davy loses a leg, and while in the hospital is visited by George, whom he repeatedly asks to look for his leg and make sure that it is properly dead. Davy's dreams become frightening, but soon afterward the visitations from George cease.

Some time later Davy, now equipped with a wooden leg and working as an Observer, is attacked by Jotham Rust, Everbe Corinthia's brother. Davy is completely mystified by this attempt on his life by a man he does not know and has scarcely seen before. Rust is court-martialed and sentenced to death, and a padre tells Davy Rust's story. Some months before, Corinthia had begun to behave peculiarly, and Rust discovered she was slipping out of the house at night; following her one night, he heard a man's jeering laugh, but saw no one. He took her back to the house and locked her in her room, but the next morning she had disappeared; she was found unconscious on the doorstep at dawn the next day. She was revived, only to scream all that day and die at sunset. Her father, old Simon, died shortly afterward. Rust, seeking vengeance, left his battalion to find the man whom he had heard laughing, and kill him.

On the morning of Rust's execution, the padre brings Davy a photograph that was among Rust's effects, addressed to Corinthia and followed by an unprintable word. The photograph, dated from a time when Davy was still in the hospital, is a vicious parody of Davy's own face.

LION. Published in *Harper's Magazine*, December, 1935; incorporated in "The Bear"; see *Go Down, Moses*.

LIZARDS IN JAMSHYD'S COURTYARD. Published in *The Saturday Evening Post*, February 27, 1932; revised to become the final episode in *The Hamlet*.

LO! First published in *Collected Stories* [1950].

The President is discommoded by the arrival in Washington of Francis Weddel (or Vidal), the half-French half-Chickasaw chief who has brought his People from Mississippi to have the President judge whether Weddel's young nephew is guilty of the murder of a white man. The dead man, having discovered that a section of the Indians' land included the only ford of the river in three hundred miles, brought a small section of land that included the ford and set up a toll gate on it. Weddel's nephew challenged the white man to a horse race, in which the stakes were several hundred acres of land against the ford. The nephew's horse lost, but the white man died of a split skull.

The Indians in Washington are puzzled by the white men's ways, but being polite try to behave as "these people believe that Indians ought to act." The President, desperate for a way to get rid of them, finally delivers an impressive speech in Latin (most of which is made up of a reading of Petrarch's sonnets), at the end of which he pronounces Weddel's nephew innocent. The Indians are satisfied with the impressiveness of the ceremony, and depart. Soon, however, another white man "became obsessed with the idea of owning this ford, having heard tales of his own kind who, after the curious and restless fashion of white men, find one side of a stream of water superior enough to the other to pay coins of money for the privilege of reaching it." This white man is challenged to a swimming contest by Weddel's nephew in which the stakes are again the ford against a large parcel of land; the white man fails to come out of the river until after he is dead, and Weddell again plans to come with his People to Washington to have the President pronounce judgment in the case. The President replies with a document to the effect that no white man shall ever own the ford, and that the Indians shall never cross the eastern side of their river.

MISTRAL. First published in *These Thirteen* [1931]; reprinted in *Collected Stories* [1950].

Two Americans, a man named Don and the narrator, are on a walking tour through the mountains of northern Italy in October, the season of the Mistral, a cold northerly wind. While looking for a place to spend the night they talk to an Italian woman, who tells them to go to the priest's house, and mentions that there is a funeral that day. The dead man, she tells them, was engaged to marry the priest's ward, a young girl of dubious antecedents; the marriage had been put off for three successive harvest seasons because of the girl's unwillingness and her flirtations with a young man named Giulio—the soldier who had passed the two Americans on a bicycle at the opening of the story.

The Americans go on to the village and ask Giulio's aunt for lodging, but she says she has none. They watch the funeral, then go to the priest's house to see about a bed for the night. They are fed and go on to the cafe, where they see the girl, the priest's ward, with Giulio. Returning from the cafe they come upon the priest stretched out on the ground beside a wall making soft whimpering noises; nearby, they see the bicycle belonging to Giulio.

MONK. Published in *Scribner's Magazine*, May, 1937; see *Knight's Gambit*.

MOUNTAIN VICTORY. First published in *The Saturday Evening Post*, December 3, 1932; reprinted in *Doctor Martino* [1934] and *Collected Stories* [1950].

Saucier Weddel, a Confederate major of Choctaw Indian and French descent, and his Negro servant are on their way home to Mississippi after the end of the war. They ask lodging for the night of a family of Union-sympathizing Tennessee mountaineers. The daughter of the family is shyly struck with Weddel's gracious manners and his obvious nobility, but the elder son is fanatical in his hatred of Confederates. The father urges Weddel to leave, but his Negro servant has gotten drunk on corn whiskey and cannot ride, and Weddel refuses to abandon him. The younger son tries to help Weddel, and asks the major to take him and his sister home to Mississippi with him. Weddel refuses, but the following morning the boy, knowing that his brother and father are waiting in ambush, joins Weddel and the Negro and asks to go part of the way with him, taking them along a little-used path. When he realizes that his brother has covered the path as well as the road, he knocks the Negro off his horse, leaps on the animal, and forces it ahead of Weddel, telling him to get back off the path. Both are shot off their horses and killed by the boy's father and brother, who kill the defenseless Negro as well.

The boy's conflict between his loyalty to his father and brother and his admiration for Weddel, and his final choice to betray his family and try to save Weddel, even at the risk of his own life, is suggestive of the conflict of young Sarty Snopes in "Barn Burning." Like the young boy in "Mountain Victory," Sarty is caught between loyalty to his father and a recognition that his father's actions are wrong, and finally betrays him by warning the owner of a barn that the elder Snopes has set on fire.

MULE IN THE YARD. First published in *Scribner's Magazine*, August, 1934; reprinted in *Collected Stories* [1950].

The story opens with the apparitionlike appearance of a mule in the yard of Mrs. Hait, whose connection with the mule business is then recounted. Some ten years before, her husband had been employed by a man named Snopes to place a string of mules on a blind railroad curve at night so that Snopes could collect damages from the railroad company for their destruction. One dark night, however, Hait met the same fate as the mules, and Mrs. Hait collected over eight thousand dollars in damages. Now, with the mule running wild in the yard, Snopes appears on the scene. The mule evades their combined attempts to capture it, and in the process of its mad galloping kicks a scuttle of live coals from the cellar steps into the cellar. The house catches fire and burns to the ground.

Mrs. Hait offers to buy the mule, which has now fled, and Snopes asks a hundred and fifty dollars for it. Later in the afternoon Old Het, an elderly colored woman and friend of Mrs. Hait, delivers ten dollars to Snopes as payment for the mule; Snopes takes the money, and returns in the evening to claim the rest of the price of his mule. Mrs. Hait reminds him that he never paid her husband his fifty dollar fee for leading the mules onto the railroad track the night he was killed, and that the ten dollars Snopes accepted was the difference between the fifty he owed her and the sixty the railroad paid him per mule killed. Complaining that he has done all the work of defrauding the railroad company while she was the one to benefit financially from the death of her husband, Snopes finally returns her ten dollars and agrees to take back his mule—not knowing, when he leaves to get it, that Mrs. Hait has shot it.

This story, slightly revised, appears in *The Town* (1957).

MY GRANDMOTHER MILLARD AND THE BATTLE OF HARRYKIN CREEK. First published in *Story*, March-April, 1943; reprinted in *Collected Stories* [1950].

Narrated by young Bayard Sartoris and dealing with the same characters and setting as the stories of *The Unvanquished* (1938), "My Grandmother Millard" is a humorous account of Sartoris adventures in Civil War days. Granny (Mrs. Rosa Millard) drills the other members of the household in getting the silver into a trunk and buried in the orchard as quickly as possible. However, when a small group of Yankees arrives at Sartoris, Granny tries a ruse already successfully employed by Mrs. Compson, and puts Cousin Melisandre and the trunk in the outhouse. The Yankees, wise to this gambit, knock down the outhouse and send Cousin Melisandre into hysterics, but are soon routed by a Confederate officer named, unfortunately, Philip St.-Just Backhouse. Philip falls promptly in love with the beautiful Melisandre; the very mention of his name, unfortunately, sends Melisandre into screaming fits. He returns to his battalion and annoys his commander, General Forrest, by leading private charges and licking four times his weight in Yankees; to put an end to this—and to get rid of Philip's objectionable name—General Forrest and Granny conspire to have him killed at the mythical battle of Harrykin Creek in the Sartoris pasture, and commission a new officer named Lieutenant Philip St.-Just Backus. Colonel John Sartoris returns in time for Cousin Melisandre's wedding to Philip Backus, and things return to normal—including the nightly drill of burying the trunk.

A NAME FOR THE CITY. Published in *Harper's Magazine*, October, 1950; incorporated in "The Courthouse (A Name for the City)" in *Requiem for a Nun*.

THE OLD PEOPLE. Published in *Harper's Magazine*, September, 1940; reprinted in *Big Woods* [1955]; see *Go Down, Moses*.

PANTALOON IN BLACK. Published in *Harper's Magazine*, October, 1940; see *Go Down, Moses*.

PENNSYLVANIA STATION. First published in *American Mercury*, February, 1934; reprinted in *Collected Stories* [1950].

An elderly man who has fallen from mere poverty to the status of a bum sits in Pennsylvania Station to rest and escape from the winter cold. He tells a younger bum the story of his sister and Danny, her no-good son. With the idle loquaciousness of the old, he hovers over the story of Danny and the death of his sister, insisting that Danny's scrapes were never Danny's fault; he wasn't bad, just wild. The bum finally tells how Danny gypped his mother out of the money she was setting aside with the undertaker for her coffin. He, the narrator, had sent word to his sister in New York that he needed money to help Danny out of some trouble, and when his sister went to the undertaker to borrow money on her investment in her coffin she found that Danny had been there a year before with a forged note from her requesting the money. This incident brought on her final illness and death. Danny, having gotten a "good job" in Chicago, was unable to attend the funeral, but sent a wreath that the credulous narrator thinks must have cost two hundred dollars.

A POINT OF LAW. Published in *Collier's*, June 22, 1940; see "The Fire and the Hearth" in *Go Down, Moses*.

RACE AT MORNING. First published in *The Saturday Evening Post*, March 5, 1955; reprinted in *Big Woods* [1955].

Faulkner's only post-1950 story not to be incorporated in a novel, "Race at Morning" is strongly reminiscent of the stories dealing with young Ike McCaslin's coming of age in the wilderness. Essentially a story of initiation, "Race at Morning" is humorous in style, dealing with the annual pursuit by the boy narrator and his guardian Mr. Ernest of a great buck that has eluded them for years. When after a day-long hectic chase they come upon the buck, Mr. Ernest shoots at the animal with a rifle he has previously emptied. "All right," he asks the boy later, "which would you rather have? His bloody head and hide on the kitchen floor yonder . . .

or him with his head and hide and meat still together over yonder in that brake, waiting for next November for us to run him again?" (197, BW)

RAID. Published in *The Saturday Evening Post*, November 3, 1934; see *The Unvanquished*.

RED LEAVES. First published in *The Saturday Evening Post*, October 25, 1930; reprinted in *These Thirteen* [1931] and *Collected Stories* [1950].

One of Faulkner's finest stories, "Red Leaves" deals with the autumn of the Old Days, the time of the Indians in Yoknapatawpha County. Issetibbeha, the Man, has just died, and his Negro body servant, to escape the traditional burial of the slave with the dead chief, has fled. The second section recounts the history of Issetibbeha's father, called Doom,* who, though descended on the distaff side of a family whose rulers came from the male line, succeeded to the chieftainship when his uncle and cousin died suddenly and mysteriously. Doom began to acquire Negro slaves, and when he died the Indians were faced with the problem of what to do with the now greatly multiplied Negro population, for which they had no real use. Finally they decided to use the slaves to clear the land and raise grain, so that they might breed and feed large numbers of Negroes for the wholesale market. With the money from the sale of slaves, Issetibbeha was able to go to France. He returned with some ludicrously elegant articles, among them a pair of slippers with red heels which his fat and indolent son, Mokketubbe, greatly coveted. Then Issetibbeha died and Mokketubbe became the Man. Now, in the present of the third section, the Indians approach Mokketubbe, squatting like a fat oriental potentate among his father's treasures, and remind him of his duty to lead the pursuit for the fugitive slave so that his father can be properly buried. The fourth section centers on the fleeing body servant who, after five days, is finally caught and, in the fifth section, brought back to the plantation to be sent after his late master.

"Red Leaves" exemplifies some of the finest aspects of Faulkner's narrative skill. Written in a lyrical style that can be both eloquently descriptive and simple and direct, it contrasts the decadent and dying Indian culture with the inarticulate desire for life of the primitive black man. Though there is no direct equation made between the imminent dispossession of the Indians by the white man and the almost moronic, luxury-corrupted figure of Mokketubbe, there is a certain implicit suggestion that the Indians have bought their own downfall with the white man's money

---

* Readers of all the stories of the Indians will note that two orders of descent are given: in "Red Leaves," Doom is the father of Issetibbeha and the grandfather of Mokketubbe; in "A Courtship," Doom (Ikkemotubbe) is the nephew of Issetibbeha and the cousin of Mokketubbe. In "The Old People" (in *Go Down, Moses*) the latter version of Doom's family history is used.

and the white man's values. Aside from the absurd and fleshy splendor of Mokketubbe, however, the Indians and their tradition are treated with an almost nostalgic sympathy that makes even more compelling the conflict of their interests and those of the black man.

RETREAT. Published in the *Saturday Evening Post*, October 13, 1934; see *The Unvanquished.*

A ROSE FOR EMILY. First published in *The Forum*, April 1930; reprinted in *These Thirteen* [1931] and *Collected Stories* [1950].

When Miss Emily Grierson was young, her domineering father drove away her suitors. Shortly after his death she was courted briefly by a Northern day laborer, Homer Barron, in spite of interference from her relatives, who were concerned solely with respectability. Barron disappeared and for forty years Miss Emily scarcely left her house. After her death at seventy-four, the townsfolk find an upstairs bedroom decked as a bridal boudoir. On the bed are the remains of a man, on the pillow beside him, a single strand of iron-gray hair.

"A Rose for Emily" has the Gothic atmosphere of a typical ghost story—the decaying Victorian mansion, the mystery created by Miss Emily's seclusion, and finally the macabre revelation in the upstairs bedroom—but it is also a study of a strangely pathetic, perhaps even tragic, character. The townsfolk, who had thought that the Griersons "held themselves a little too high for what they really were," felt smugly vindicated when Miss Emily seemed likely to remain a spinster; when her father died, word got around that "the house was all that was left to her; and in a way, people were glad. At last they could pity Miss Emily. Being left alone, and a pauper, she had become humanized."

The chief irony in the story lies in the contrast between the townspeople's envious attitude toward Miss Emily and the profound misery of her actual condition. Her neighbors can never quite forgive her seeming arrogance and feeling of superiority; yet, cheated of a chance for a "suitable" marriage, Miss Emily desperately sought love with an unworthy partner, murdered him rather than lose him, and thus doomed herself to even more hopeless isolation for the rest of her life. Driven from the world of the living by her acts, Miss Emily had only the dead to turn to. But the dead have no pity, and the townsfolk—with the reader—feel only horror at the discovery of murder so deliberately perpetrated and concealed, and a further horror at the suggestion of necrophilia.

SHALL NOT PERISH. First published in *Story*, July–August, 1943; reprinted in *Collected Stories* [1950].

Four months after the events related in "Two Soldiers," Pete Grier's family receives word that he has been killed. They set aside one day to grieve, and begin to watch the newspaper for news of other Yoknapatawpha County boys who have died for their country. When Major de Spain's boy is killed, the nine-year-old narrator and his mother go into Jefferson to see the bereaved father; Mrs. Grier tries to tell the bitter major the meaning of grief and to help him understand why men's sons must die in battle. The Griers, though they are poor country people, show a capacity for strength and endurance and understanding that the De Spains, in spite of their wealth and proud ancestry, are lacking.

SHINGLES FOR THE LORD. First published in *The Saturday Evening Post*, February 13, 1943; reprinted in *Collected Stories* [1950].

Res Grier is a bumbling but good-intentioned man whose poverty and ineptness is shown by his need to borrow tools for any chore he can't do with his own hands and feet. Because he has had to borrow a froe and maul, tools for splitting shingles, he is two hours late to help work on the church roof, and Solon Quick demands that Res make up the "six man-hour work-units" that his delay with the tools caused three men to lose. To avoid being publicly charged with the loss of the six hours, Res agrees to trade Solon his half-interest in a dog Solon wants to own. Res, however, has secretly traded with Tull, the other half-owner of the dog, six hours of work in exchange for Tull's interest in the animal. To fulfill his obligation to Tull, Res and his young son go to work stripping the old shingles from the church roof at night, but Res accidentally causes the lantern, swung from the roof, to fall into the church. The lantern explodes and burns. After Res has tripped and broken the water barrel (knocking himself out in the process), the other men arrive, but are too late to put out the fire. All present offer to contribute their time and labor to the raising of a new church, but Whitfield, the preacher, refuses to let Res touch the new building until he has proved that he is to be "trusted again with the powers and capacity of a man."

SKIRMISH AT SARTORIS. Published in *Scribner's Magazine*, April, 1935; see *The Unvanquished*.

SMOKE. Published in *Harper's Magazine*, April, 1932; reprinted in *Doctor Martino*; see *Knight's Gambit*.

SPOTTED HORSES. Published in *Scribner's Magazine*, June, 1931; revised to become the spotted-horse episode in *The Hamlet*.

THE TALL MEN. First published in *The Saturday Evening Post*, May 31, 1941; reprinted in *Collected Stories* [1950].

A state draft investigator comes to Yoknapatawpha County to serve a warrant on the McCallum twins, Anse and Lucius, who have failed to register for Selective Service. He arrives just after their father, Buddy Mc-Callum, has badly injured his leg. Buddy, learning that his boys are wanted by the government, tells them to go to Memphis immediately and enlist, at the same time instructing the doctor to amputate his leg, although there is no anesthetic available. The draft investigator, a man who sticks to the letter of the law, protests that he has come to serve a warrant to the boys and must take them back to Jefferson to answer the charge, but the town marshal subtly dissuades him, telling him the history of the McCallum family, and of their quiet pride, dignity, and strength.

THAT EVENING SUN. First published in American Mercury, March, 1931; reprinted in These Thirteen [1931] and Collected Stories [1950].

Narrated by Quentin Compson as a young child (later a central character in The Sound and the Fury and a narrator in Absalom, Absalom!), the story deals with a Negro washerwoman named Nancy, living in a cabin near the Compson house. Nancy cooks for the Compsons when Dilsey, their regular servant, is ill. She is also a prostitute, and is mortally afraid of Jesus, her estranged husband, who she believes is trying to kill her—apparently because she is pregnant by another man. The Compson children—Quentin, who is nine, and Caddy and Jason, his younger sister and brother—observe the action, but understand very little of its significance. The entire situation of the family—Mrs. Compson's whining querulousness and Mr. Compson's ineffectual attempts to placate her while trying to look out for Nancy—is briefly but subtly delineated.

Dilsey remains ill for some time, and the Compsons finally arrange a pallet in the kitchen for Nancy, who is afraid to go home to her cabin because she thinks that Jesus is lying in wait for her in the ditch. When Dilsey returns to work, Mrs. Compson refuses to let Nancy stay in the house for the night and Nancy, frightened but still clever, persuades the children to come to her cabin with her. She tells them a story and tries desperately to entertain them and keep them with her, but Jason is fretful and wants to go home, and the two older children are becoming uneasy. Finally, Mr. Compson arrives; he is sympathetic to Nancy's fears, but does not believe that she is in imminent danger. He takes the children away, and Nancy is so convinced that Jesus will get her no matter what she does that she does not even close the door.

Nancy's fate is not disclosed in this story, but there is a strong suggestion that she will actually be killed. She is resurrected to become a central character as Nancy Mannigoe in Requiem for a Nun (1951). It is ironic that in the short story the white family she loyally serves refuses to take her fears seriously and thus is partially responsible for her death, while in *Requiem* she sacrifices her own life so that her white employer, Temple Drake, might find some kind of moral salvation.

"That Evening Sun" is one of Faulkner's most anthologized stories; it displays some of the best elements of his fictional technique, particularly in the contrast between Nancy's calm horror of the death she knows awaits her and the children's total failure to sense that horror; they comment on her strange actions, but are untouched by the fear behind them. This is particularly brought out in the last sentences with Quentin's question, "Who will do our washing now, Father?" With the impersonal curiosity of childhood, he placidly accepts Nancy's expected death.

THAT WILL BE FINE. First published in *American Mercury*, July, 1935; reprinted in *Collected Stories* [1950].

The narrator, a young boy who does not understand the significance of the events he witnesses, is reminiscent of the young Jason Compson (*The Sound and the Fury*) in his single-minded interest in money.

The narrator's family is about to leave for nearby Mottstown to celebrate Christmas with Grandpa when it is discovered that Uncle Rodney has taken two thousand dollars worth of bonds from his company safe and forged his father's (Grandpa's) check to cover their value. Aunt Louisa, Uncle Rodney's sister, promises the sheriff that she will not let Rodney escape if the sheriff will defer arresting him until after Christmas. He is incarcerated in a Negro cabin on Grandpa's place for safekeeping, but the narrator, eager for a chance to acquire quarters, helps him escape from the cabin and tries to deliver a message to the woman Uncle Rodney is planning to run away with. The message, however, is intercepted by the woman's husband, who kills Uncle Rodney as the latter tries to keep his assignation. The narrator, seeing men carrying away the body, thinks that they are taking a side of beef to Grandpa for a Christmas present and remembers his earlier inspiration to get a present for Grandpa so that the old man will give him a quarter instead of the customary Christmas dime.

THERE WAS A QUEEN. First published in *Scribner's Magazine*, January, 1933; reprinted in *Doctor Martino* [1934] and *Collected Stories* [1950].

Returning to the Sartoris family some ten years after the events in *Sartoris* (1929), "There Was a Queen" centers on the contrast between the pride and dignity and sense of family of old Mrs. Virginia DuPre (Miss Jenny), the last of the Sartoris women, and the lack of these qualities in Narcissa Benbow Sartoris, the widow of Miss Jenny's great-great-nephew. Narcissa, after first insulting Miss Jenny by inviting a Yankee to the house for dinner, makes a mysterious two-day trip to Memphis, leaving her ten-year-old son Benbow (Bory) for the first time in his life. After her return, Narcissa tells Miss Jenny that her trip was connected with the anonymous and obscene letters she had received before her marriage, and had hidden but not destroyed. The letters were stolen the night of her marriage, and Narcissa was half-crazy at the thought of other people—men—reading such letters and knowing they were addressed to her. The thief, Byron Snopes, was never caught, but the Federal agent (the Yankee Narcissa invited to dinner) after him for bank robbery found the letters and finally came to Narcissa, thinking that she might know something of Snopes's whereabouts. To get the letters back from him, Narcissa went to Memphis and bargained with her body for their return. Her mysterious trip down to the pasture to sit in the creek with Bory, mentioned earlier in the story, was a kind of symbolic cleansing after this episode. When Miss Jenny has heard Narcissa's story she remains sitting by the window and does not come in to dinner. Elnora, the Negro servant, senses something wrong, and when she goes into the library she finds that Miss Jenny is dead.

TOMORROW. Published in *The Saturday Evening Post*, November 23, 1940; see *Knight's Gambit*.

TURNABOUT. First published in *The Saturday Evening Post*, March 5, 1932; reprinted in *Doctor Martino* [1934] and *Collected Stories* [1950]. Adapted for the screen by Faulkner as *Today We Live* [1933].

An eighteen-year-old British naval officer, Claude Hope, is picked up by an American pilot, Captain Bogard, after Hope, planning to sleep in the middle of a street, had caused a good deal of commotion among truck drivers and attracted the attention of the military police. Bogard and his companion, Lieutenant McGinnis, take the boy back to the airfield with them; their attitude toward him is protective but rather patronizing, for they think that he is only a green kid to whom war is a dandy game and whose job involves something harmless like running a launch around the harbor. They take him on a predawn bombing raid, which he enjoys with a complete childish delight—though he knows how to handle a machine gun well. He is completely enthusiastic over the pilots' skill and the danger involved in flying, particularly when, unknown to the pilots, one of their bombs snags on the underbody of the plane and is carried back to the airfield; by some miracle, it does not explode when the plane lands.

That morning, Bogard goes out with the English boy in his "launch"— a small, flat, very fast boat carrying one torpedo which is aimed by the boat itself; the boat must turn sharply after the torpedo has been released to avoid being run over by its own weapon. The English boy and his companion, Ronnie, run the boat with a skill and lighthearted indifference to danger that completely horrifies Bogard. After scooting blithely around ships and gunfire in an enemy harbor while they reset the torpedo (which has failed to take off properly), they finally fire the weapon at a freighter at almost point-blank range. Bogard, strained beyond the limit of his endurance, collapses and is sick.

After his return to shore, Bogard sends the boy a case of Scotch. About a month later he learns that Ronnie and Claude have failed to return from patrol one evening. Shortly afterward, Bogard makes a dangerous and unscheduled daylight raid behind enemy lines—a tribute to the valor of the two English boys; it is the nearest approximation he can make of Claude's and Ronnie's sea patrols into enemy waters.

TWO SOLDIERS. First published in *The Saturday Evening Post*, March 28, 1942; reprinted in *Collected Stories* [1950].

Pete Grier, a nineteen-year-old country boy from Frenchman's Bend, is not old enough to be drafted, but feels he must go to the war. He goes to Memphis to enlist. The following day his eight-year-old brother, the narrator, also leaves home for Memphis (a hundred miles away), where he plans to join the army and help Pete. He nearly gets into trouble with an unsympathetic soldier in the recruiting office, but Pete is finally brought to him and tells the boy that he must go and help his mother on the farm and look after Pete's ten acres. The boy's courage and determination and love for his older brother make him in spirit the soldier Pete is in fact.

UNCLE WILLY. First published in *American Mercury*, October, 1935; reprinted in *Collected Stories* [1950].

Uncle Willy Christian, the owner of Christian's Drugstore, is an elderly and kindly drug addict beloved by the young boys of Jefferson. The well-intentioned women of the town, however, get together with the minister to try to make him give up the habit; they finally send him off to an institution in Memphis. When he returns he breaks into the locked drug cabinet in the store; later—and even worse, as far as the righteous of the town are concerned—he marries an enormous and brassy woman, formerly a Memphis prostitute. The woman is bought off and sent back to Memphis, and Uncle Willy is declared mentally incompetent and sent back to the institution.

Sometime later, the young narrator receives a letter from Uncle Willy asking the boy to meet him at a certain bus stop in Memphis. The boy goes because Uncle Willy "was the finest man I ever knew, because he had had fun all his life in spite of what they had tried to do to him or with him, and I hoped that maybe if I could stay with him a while I could learn how to, so I could still have fun too when I had to get old." Having acquired a car and an airplane, Uncle Willy takes the narrator and Old Job, a Negro who had been his clerk in the drugstore, to a nearby town where they will stay until Uncle Willy learns to fly the plane. Old Job, however, fears that Uncle Willy will kill himself trying to learn to fly, and telephones to Jefferson to have the ladies come and save him. Just before the Jefferson contingent arrives, Uncle Willy manages to get the plane in the air; it crashes, and he is killed. The young narrator realizes that, in spite of adult disapproval, he has done right and has helped Uncle Willy, but knows with sorrow that he can never make the grownups understand.

THE UNVANQUISHED. Published in The Saturday Evening Post, November 14, 1936; see "Riposte in Tertio" in The Unvanquished.

VENDEE. Published in The Saturday Evening Post, December 5, 1936; see The Unvanquished.

VICTORY. First published in These Thirteen [1931]; reprinted in Collected Stories [1950].

A deeply ironic story, "Victory" deals with the career of a Scotch soldier who, soon after his enlistment, was sent to a penal battalion because he had not shaved on the morning of an inspection—this in spite of the fact that he was too young to shave. He returns to his former company and, during a raid on enemy lines, kills the sergeant-major who had been responsible for punishing him. He is given a citation for taking command and holding his position after all the non-commissioned officers had been killed. He rises to the rank of captain and after the war, instead of going back to his home in Scotland and following the family business, he takes a position in London in which he trades upon his distinguished appearance and his military rank. He loses his position when "conditions" become bad and is gradually reduced to the level of a beggar, though he meticulously maintains his appearance and his arrogant dignity.

THE WAIFS. Published in the Saturday Evening Post, May 4, 1957; included in The Town as the episode of the four vicious Snopes children.

WASH. First published in Harper's Magazine, February, 1934; reprinted in Doctor Martino [1934] and Collected Stories [1950].

One of Faulkner's best stories, "Wash" anticipates the subject of his later novel, Absalom, Absalom! (1936), which includes a revised version of the story (284–92) in its treatment of the rise and fall of Thomas Sutpen and the mythos of the South. "Wash" deals specifically with the death of Sutpen, although it is Wash Jones, Sutpen's poor-white handyman, whose disillusionment in Sutpen and the men like him—the brave, the honorable, the members of the Southern aristocracy who gallantly went off to fight in a lost cause—occupies the center of the stage. Having lost his son in battle and his wife as a result of the privations of wartime, Sutpen comes back to his ruined plantation and tries to make enough money to live by running,

with Jones's help, a roadside store. Jones respects and admires Sutpen—
"the Kernel"; though he is Sutpen's drinking companion, he knows his
place in the social hierarchy and does not try to capitalize on Sutpen's
friendship. When Sutpen seduces his fifteen-year-old granddaughter, Milly,
Wash is concerned but does not interfere, believing that Sutpen will do
right by anything he touches. However, Milly gives birth to a girl, and
Sutpen, crushed by his failure to get a male heir to continue his name, offers
Wash a merciless insult by his indifference to Milly and his infant daughter. This indifference is given an additional sting by the fact that Sutpen's
mare foaled a colt that same morning, and Sutpen seems more interested
in the male foal than in his own female child.

Wash, driven to despair by his realization that Sutpen is not the god
incarnate that he had believed him to be, kills him. He then waits patiently
for the body to be discovered and Sutpen's friends to come and take him to
jail. When they arrive, he murders Milly and the child, sets fire to the
tumble-down shack in which Sutpen had permitted them to live, and brings
on his own death by running at the waiting and armed men with a knife.

In *Absalom, Absalom!*, Sutpen's implicit comparison of Milly to a
brood mare and his similar failure to treat Wash as a human being capable
of admiration and disillusion and grief is given additional ironic emphasis
by the fact that Sutpen himself had come from a poor-white family and had
fought his way to his position in the Southern aristocracy as a result of an
unintentional snub given him by a Negro butler when he was a child.
Though the entire motivating force of his life was to achieve recognition as
an individual by the ruling class, he repeatedly failed to give others that
recognition, and thus inadvertently paved the way to the downfall of both
himself and the dynasty he had hoped to establish.

A Dictionary of Characters[*]

ALECK SANDER. The Negro companion of young Chick Mallison, and a minor character in *Intruder in the Dust*; also mentioned in *The Town*.

AMES, DALTON. The seducer of Caddy Compson, and a minor character in *The Sound and the Fury*.

ARMSTID, HENRY. A minor character in *As I Lay Dying*, *Light in August*, and *The Hamlet*; also mentioned in other novels and stories. The Armstid of *The Hamlet* is clearly a different character from his namesake in the two earlier novels; in *The Hamlet*, which takes place in the early years of the twentieth century, Armstid is a foolish and greedy man. He takes the money his gray and overworked wife has saved to buy shoes for their children and spends it on a wild Texas horse. No one can catch the horse, and Mrs. Armstid unsuccessfully sues Flem Snopes for the return of her money. Later Armstid becomes infected with buried-money fever and helps Ratliff and Bookwright buy the Old Frenchman Place from Flem Snopes. The results of this incident completely unbalance Armstid; in *The Town* he is mentioned as being locked up for life in the insane asylum at Jackson.

In *Light in August*, which takes place in the early 1930s, he is a good-hearted but somewhat weak man, and is henpecked by his domineering and sharp-tongued wife, here named Martha. He offers a ride to the pregnant Lena Grove, who has walked from Alabama to Misisssippi, and gives her food and shelter for the night.

AYERS, MAJOR. A minor character in *Mosquitoes*. A Briton, he is convinced that all Americans suffer from constipation, and is full of plans to market laxatives.

BASCOMB, MAURY. The brother of Mrs. Caroline Compson, and an alcoholic and mooching relative in *The Sound and the Fury*.

BEAUCHAMP FAMILY. See also McCaslin and Edmonds.

[*] Included are all major and most of the secondary characters in the novels, and characters who appear in two or more stories. For a complete listing of all characters mentioned in all of Faulkner's works, consult *Faulkner's People* by Robert W. Kirk and Marvin Klotz (University of California Press, Berkeley, Calif., 1963).

BEAUCHAMP, HENRY [1898–   ]. A son of Lucas Beauchamp, great-grandson of L. Q. C. McCaslin, and a minor character in "The Fire and the Hearth" in *Go Down, Moses.*

BEAUCHAMP, FONSIBA. The sister of James (Tennie's Jim) and Lucas Beauchamp, and a minor character in *Go Down, Moses.* Fonsiba marries a northern Negro and goes to live on a rundown farm in Arkansas.

BEAUCHAMP, HUBERT. Brother of Sophonsiba Beauchamp, uncle of Isaac McCaslin, and a character in "Was" and "The Bear" in *Go Down, Moses.* A half-humorous, half-pathetic man, Hubert loses his money after the Civil War and is reduced to "borrowing" from the cup he had set aside for Isaac McCaslin just after the boy's birth. The Beauchamp name becomes the family name of L. Q. C. McCaslin's Negro descendants after a Beauchamp slave marries McCaslin's mulatto son.

BEAUCHAMP, JAMES [TENNIE'S JIM] [1864–?]. The eldest son of Tennie Beauchamp and Tomey's Turl, the grandson on his father's side of L. Q. C. McCaslin, and a character in "The Old People" and "The Bear" in *Go Down, Moses.* He is a servant attached to the McCaslin-Edmonds family. On his twenty-first birthday he runs away from Mississippi to the North and is never heard from again.

BEAUCHAMP, LUCAS [1874–   ]. The part-Negro grandson of L. Q. C. McCaslin, and a character in "The Fire and the Hearth" in *Go Down, Moses,* and in *Intruder in the Dust.* Lucas is an independent, stubborn man who, though he can assume the mask of "niggerhood," "enveloping himself in an aura of timeless and stupid impassivity almost like a smell" (52, GDM), regards himself as a man first and only incidentally as a Negro. Lucas knows that the sheriff thinks of him only as a "nigger," but the sheriff does not know that Lucas believes the other man to be a redneck without "pride in his forbears nor hope for it in his descendants." (39) Like his white grandfather, Lucas is a kind of patriarch, proud, even arrogant; he is proud of his ancestor not as a white man, but as a man, precisely as he values himself. Because of his refusal to "act like a nigger," the townsfolk in *Intruder in the Dust* consider him uppity and stiffnecked. When Lucas is arrested for the murder of a white man and threatened with lynching, young Chick Mallison feels that "they're going to make a nigger out of him once in his life anyway." (23)

BEAUCHAMP, MOLLY WORSHAM. The wife of Lucas Beauchamp, and a character in "The Fire and the Hearth" and the title story of *Go Down, Moses.*

BEAUCHAMP, NATHALIE. The daughter of Lucas and Molly Beauchamp, and a minor character in "The Fire and the Hearth" in Go Down, Moses.

BEAUCHAMP, SAMUEL WORSHAM [BUTCH]. The grandson of old Molly Beauchamp; a tough young Negro murderer and a minor character in the title story of Go Down, Moses.

BEAUCHAMP, SOPHONSIBA. The sister of Hubert Beauchamp, wife of Uncle Buck McCaslin, mother of Isaac McCaslin, and a character in "Was" in Go Down, Moses. One of the best of Faulkner's minor comic characters, Miss Sophonsiba is an angular spinster who tries to translate reality into romance; she stoutly maintains that her brother Hubert is the true claimant to an English earldom, and she herself behaves with the romantic coyness of a young girl besieged by suitors. When the unwilling object of her flirtations, Uncle Buck McCaslin, accidentally stumbles into her bed one night, she raises a great hue and cry and demands that he marry her. On this occasion Uncle Buck escapes, but Sophonsiba later succeeds in capturing him.

BEAUCHAMP, TURL [TOMEY'S TURL or TERREL] [ca. 1833–   ]. The son of L. Q. C. McCaslin and McCaslin's mulatto daughter Tomey; a character in "Was," mentioned in the other stories in Go Down, Moses, and a character in The Town. Turl is the object of a mock foxhunt in "Was." Called in by Hubert Beauchamp to deal the cards in which Turl himself and his sweetheart Tennie, a Beauchamp slave, are part of the stakes, Turl deals Uncle Buddy the cards which incidentally save Uncle Buck from Miss Sophonsiba's clutches and, more important from Turl's point of view, change Tennie's ownership from the Beauchamp family to the McCaslin family. Turl later marries Tennie and fathers three children, James, Fonsiba, and Lucas, all of whom take the name of Beauchamp from Tennie.

In The Town and the short story "Centaur in Brass" Turl is considerably rejuvenated to play the part of a lusty young Negro who inadvertently helps spoil Flem Snopes' attempts to steal brass fittings from the town power plant.

BENBOW, HORACE [1886–   ]. Brother of Narcissa Benbow, husband of Belle Mitchell, and a character in Sartoris and Sanctuary. In Sartoris, Horace, just returned from the war, becomes involved with Belle Mitchell, a married woman with a young daughter. Though his sister Narcissa, to whom he is very close, objects strongly to his relationship with Belle, he marries her after her divorce. A lawyer, he is depicted as a literate, cultured man with a love of beautiful objects. Though essentially good, he is unable to assert himself or to escape from the influence of Narcissa and her conventional standards of morality and respectability. In *Sanctuary*, ten years later, Horace leaves Belle and attempts to defend a bootlegger wrongfully accused of murder. When the man is convicted and lynched, Horace, in defeat, goes back to an empty life with Belle.

BENBOW, NARCISSA [1893–   ]. Sister of Horace Benbow, wife of Bayard Sartoris, mother of Benbow Sartoris, and a character in *Sartoris*, *Sanctuary*, and the short story "There Was a Queen." In *Sartoris* Narcissa is the recipient of a number of anonymous obscene letters which she refuses to destroy and which, on the eve of her marriage to Bayard Sartoris, are stolen by Byron Snopes, their author. A placid, eminently respectable woman, she quarrels with her brother Horace over his marriage to a woman Narcissa despises as having a "backstairs nature." Though Narcissa herself appears to be the very epitome of virtue, her concern is solely with the surface appearance of morality. In *Sanctuary* she retorts to Horace that she doesn't care what he does, but she won't have him mixed up with a woman "people are talking about." In "There Was a Queen" her anonymous letters turn up in the hands of an FBI agent on the trail of Byron Snopes; Narcissa's true character is revealed when she spends a weekend in Memphis with the FBI man in order to get the letters back.

BINFORD, MR. The husband or consort of Miss Reba, landlord of her brothel, and a minor character in *The Reivers*. After his death he is deeply mourned by Miss Reba, who names one of her little dogs after him.

BLAND, GERALD. A minor character in *The Sound and the Fury*. Smooth, socially conscious, and somewhat supercilious, Bland brags to Quentin Compson about his conquests of women.

BON, CHARLES [1829–65]. Son of Eulalia Bon and Thomas Sutpen, half-brother of Judith and Henry Sutpen, and a character in *Absalom, Absalom!*. Though little is actually known about Bon, the narrators clothe the few facts of his life in elaborate speculations about both his personality and his motives; they variously imagine that he was raised in comparative wealth and idleness in New Orleans, that he may have been the agent (knowingly or otherwise) of his mother's supposed plot of revenge against Sutpen, and that he had an octoroon mistress by whom he had a young son. He arrives, when nearly thirty, at the University of Mississippi, where he meets young Henry Sutpen and becomes his intimate friend. He becomes engaged to his half-sister, Judith, but is finally killed by Henry before the marriage can take place.

BON, CHARLES ETIENNE SAINT-VALERY [1859–84]. Son of Charles Bon and an octoroon, father of Jim Bond, and a minor character in *Absalom, Absalom!*. Raised by Judith Sutpen and her mulatto half-sister after his mother's death, Etienne is white in appearance and physically delicate, but is clothed and treated as a Negro. As a young man he rejects his white blood entirely and calls himself Negro; he is sensitive and hostile, and becomes involved in racial fights which he usually instigates himself. Finally he marries a very black and apelike Negro woman, who bears him an idiot son named Jim Bond. Some aspects of his character are reminiscent of the white Negro Joe Christmas in *Light in August*.

BON, EULALIA. Daughter of a Haitian plantation owner, first wife of Thomas Sutpen, mother of Charles Bon, and a minor character in *Absalom, Absalom!*. Eulalia was offered as a wife to Sutpen, her father's overseer, after he had saved the family during a slave insurrection. Sometime after their son Charles was born, Sutpen discovered that his wife was not the daughter of a Spanish woman, as he had been told, but of a woman with some Negro blood. Sutpen divorced her and left her and the child with an equitable cash settlement. One of the narrators of *Absalom, Absalom!*, Shreve McCannon, suggests that Eulalia, wanting revenge on Sutpen, had raised Charles to be an instrument of his father's destruction.

BOND, JIM [1882–   ]. An idiot, great-grandson of Thomas Sutpen, grandson of Charles Bon, son of Etienne Bon, and a minor character in *Absalom, Absalom!*. Raised by Clytie, Sutpen's mulatto daughter, Jim Bond is Sutpen's last male descendant, the only remaining trace of his design to found a dynasty. After the burning of Sutpen's house in 1909, Jim is briefly heard howling in the ashes; he soon disappears and is never heard of again.

BOOKWRIGHT, HOMER. A country man living in Frenchman's Bend, frequently mentioned in the novels and stories but rarely playing a part of any significance. In *The Hamlet* he, with Ratliff and Armstid, falls for Flem Snopes' trick of salting the Old Frenchman Place with buried money. In "Tomorrow" (*Knight's Gambit*) he kills a handsome ne'er-do-well to prevent him from running away with his young daughter.

BUNCH, BYRON. A character in *Light in August*. Byron is a hard-working, quiet, self-effacing man, the only friend of the former clergyman Gail Hightower. When Byron meets Lena Grove, however, he is drawn into a web of events which finally force him to recognize the reality of human involvement.

BUNDREN, ADDIE. The wife of Anse Bundren, mother of Cash, Darl, Jewel, Dewey Dell, and Vardaman, and a character in *As I Lay Dying*. A strong, taciturn woman, Addie learns early that life was hard and that nothing can give it meaning except intense personal contact. Realizing that her husband is incapable of this, she has an affair with Whitfield, the preacher, who is the father of Jewel, her favorite child. Her attitude—love, hostility, or indifference—toward each of her children shapes their conceptions of themselves as they grow up, and determines the ways in which they react to her death.

BUNDREN, ANSE. The husband of Addie Bundren, father of Cash, Darl, Dewey Dell, and Vardaman, and a character in *As I Lay Dying*. A small farmer living just south of the Yoknapatawpha River in the Frenchman's Bend section, Anse is a well-meaning but weak man who is unwilling to be beholden to anyone, yet so ineffectual that his neighbors must constantly help him out. When Addie dies, his grief, though very shallow, is sincere, and he is rigidly faithful to a promise he has made her after their second son was born that he would bury her in Jefferson when she died.

BUNDREN, CASH [ca. 1900–]. Eldest son of Anse and Addie Bundren, and a character in *As I Lay Dying*. A carpenter, Cash is a fine, careful craftsman who takes pride in his work. As Addie is dying inside the house Cash works on her coffin, holding up boards for her approval as he shapes them; his painstaking work on the coffin is one expression of his affection for her. When the coffin and the wagon carrying it are swept into the flooded river, Cash suffers a broken leg which later becomes badly infected due to Anse's bungling attempts to set it; in spite of the great pain Cash is silent and uncomplaining. Loving music, he had saved money to buy a phonograph in Jefferson, but Anse takes the money from him to buy a pair of mules to replace those drowned in the river.

BUNDREN, DARL [ca. 1902–]. Second son of Anse and Addie Bundren, and a character in *As I Lay Dying*. An extremely sensitive and perceptive man, Darl suffers from his mother's emotional rejection of him, and is considered by the neighbors to be somewhat "queer." Of all the characters he is best able to intellectualize and verbalize his experience, and narrates nearly a third of the sections of the novel. The rivalry between him and Jewel, Addie's favorite, is intense but unspoken, as is the antagonism between Darl and Dewey Dell, a result of his knowledge that she is pregnant. The events of the funeral journey completely destroy his precarious mental balance, and at the end of the book he is sent off to the insane asylum in a state of extreme derangement.

BUNDREN, DEWEY DELL [ca. 1913–]. The only daughter of Anse and Addie Bundren, and a character in *As I Lay Dying*. An almost mindless female animal, Dewey Dell is less affected by her mother's death than are her brothers, and sees in it an excuse to get to Jefferson and acquire some abortion pills. It is as a result of her vindictive tale-telling that Darl is sent to the insane asylum.

BUNDREN, JEWEL [ca. 1912–   ]. The illegitimate son of Addie Bundren and Preacher Whitfield, and a character in *As I Lay Dying*. When he was fifteen, Jewel crept out every night for months to clear a section of land for a neighbor in exchange for a spotted horse, a descendant of the Texas horses brought into the county twenty-five years before by Flem Snopes. Jewel loves the horse, a symbol, according to Faulkner, of his alien position in the family. Though he does not openly show his love for his mother, he is the only one of the family who resents all the neighbors coming to watch her die. He justifies her faith in him when he fulfills her prophecy that he will save her from water and fire, and he lets Anse sell his horse for a pair of mules so that Addie's body can be taken to the cemetery in Jefferson. Like Addie, Jewel is a lover of action rather than words, and narrates only one section of the novel.

BUNDREN, VARDAMAN [ca. 1921–   ]. The youngest son of Addie and Anse Bundren, and a character in *As I Lay Dying*. Unable to cope with the fact of his mother's death, Vardaman associates the living Addie with an enormous fish he caught just before she died. He is afraid that she will suffocate when her coffin lid is nailed shut, and drills holes in the top so that she can breathe. Later, when her body is badly decomposed, he believes that the noises from inside the coffin indicate that Addie is speaking to him.

BURCH, LUCAS [ALIAS JOE BROWN]. A minor character in *Light in August*. A superficially attractive but weak and self-seeking man, Burch deserts his pregnant sweetheart Lena Grove and is the symbolic Judas who betrays his erstwhile friend and partner, Joe Christmas. His grasping eagerness for the reward money to which he thinks he is entitled, and his desire to see Christmas captured, make him an object of contempt even to those who believe Christmas to be guilty. However, despite his unsavory character, his word that Christmas is actually a Negro is accepted as good.

BURDEN, JOANNA. A character in *Light in August*. The spinster descendant of New Hampshire abolitionists, Joanna lives in an old house outside Jefferson, an alien in the town in which she was born. She believes that it is her mission to try to lift the black man up to the white man's level, and is burdened with a "black cross" of guilt (a guilt she believes every white child is born with) for the condition of the Negro. In her forties she has a passionate, almost perverted relationship with Joe Christmas, whom she claims as a Negro. Apparently this is an attempt to erase her white woman's guilt by offering herself as a sacrifice for violation by a Negro. When she reaches the menopause, however, her passion is redirected toward religious and social ends; she tries to change Joe into a "respectable" Negro, and finally urges him to pray with her. He refuses; she reveals that she intends to kill them both, but before she can shoot him he kills her with a razor.

CASPEY. A Negro servant attached to the Sartoris family in *Sartoris*. Caspey, just returned from the First World War, came back to Jefferson unwilling to accept an inferior status as a Negro, after having worked with labor crews in Europe. However, both the older Negroes at Sartoris and the white people disapprove of Caspey's ideas. Caspey himself is depicted as an insolent, troublemaking young buck with a strong streak of laziness in him. On the whole, he is a rather unsavory character. He is a spiritual, if not a blood, descendant of Loosh, the slave in *The Unvanquished* who wanted to be free. In "There Was a Queen," which takes place ten years after the events in *Sartoris*, Caspey is referred to as being in the penitentiary for stealing.

CHRISTIAN, UNCLE WILLY. A character in the short story "Uncle Willy" and *The Town*. The owner of Christian's Drugstore in Jefferson, Uncle Willy is a mild and harmless drug addict beloved by the young boys of the town, to whom he gives ice cream.

CHRISTMAS, JOE. A character in *Light in August*. Believing himself to be part Negro, Joe is antagonistic to Negroes and whites alike and spends his life both trying to find himself and to escape from himself. After his murder of Joanna Burden he is hunted down by the townsfolk and ritually sacrificed as the Negro murderer of a white woman. However, his death does not release the community of its guilt, for in death he achieves a kind of apotheosis and becomes not "the Negro" but "the man."

CLYTIE. See Sutpen, Clytemnestra.

COLDFIELD, ELLEN [1818–62]. A daughter of Goodhue Coldfield, sister of Rosa Coldfield, second wife of Thomas Sutpen, mother of Henry and Judith Sutpen, and a character in *Absalom, Absalom!*. Though later characterized by her sister as the victim of the demonic Sutpen, Ellen is apparently quite happy as the wife of Jefferson's biggest planter and mistress of its most impressive mansion. A voluble, childish woman, Ellen envisions a betrothal between her daughter Judith and Charles Bon even before the young people have met; after their meeting she boasts of the engagement around the town, though Charles has made no proposal. When Charles and Henry leave Sutpen's Hundred for good after Henry has quarreled with his father, Ellen is prostrated and takes to her bed. She dies two years later.

COLDFIELD, GOODHUE [d. 1864]. The father of Ellen and Rosa Coldfield, and a minor character in *Absalom, Absalom!*. Coldfield comes to Jefferson in 1828 and sets up a small store which is the sole support of himself and his family. A steward of the Methodist church, he is a piously respectable man with a good deal of moral strength, but rigid and uncompromising. In the 1830s he becomes involved in a money-making scheme with Thomas Sutpen; but, when it becomes apparent that the scheme will succeed, Coldfield withdraws and refuses to accept his share of what he feels is ill-gotten gain. When the Civil War begins, he protests by refusing to sell any goods to the military and even closing his store when troops are bivouacked near Jefferson. Eventually his store is looted, after which he nails himself up in the attic of his house and lives there for three years on food his daughter sends up on a rope. He dies in 1864 by starving himself to death.

COLDFIELD, ROSA [1845–1910]. A daughter of Goodhue Coldfield, sister of Ellen Coldfield Sutpen, aunt of Henry and Judith Sutpen, and a character in *Absalom, Absalom!*. Rosa speaks of herself as having been old even as a child, of never having had a girlhood. Frustrated and lonely from youth, she becomes an embittered spinster who feels the ruin of her life and happiness to be the fault of her brother-in-law, Thomas Sutpen, and makes her hatred of him the center of her empty existence. Never having had a life of her own, she at first lives vicariously through others: she suffers as she imagines her elder sister Ellen had suffered by being the wife of Sutpen, whom she calls a demon; she falls in love with her image of Charles Bon, her niece Judith's fiancé, and relives what she believes must be Judith's feelings about her approaching marriage. Despite her fear and hatred of Sutpen, she becomes engaged to marry him after Ellen's death; however, when he suggests that their marriage be conditional upon her bearing a male heir, she leaves Sutpen's Hundred in outrage. She spends the next forty-three years in poverty, wearing black as if widowed, but married to the past. In 1909 she begins to tell Sutpen's story—and her own—to Quentin Compson. Quentin helps her learn the end of the story of the Sutpen dynasty just before she dies.

COMPSON, BENJAMIN [1895–1935?]. The youngest child of Jason and Caroline Compson, and a character in *The Sound and the Fury*. Benjy, an idiot, narrates the first section of *The Sound and the Fury*, but he is revealed most clearly to the reader in the fourth section, where he is described by an omniscient narrator. Benjy was christened Maury, after his mother's brother, but when his idiocy became apparent his name was changed. He loves three things: his sister Caddy, who "smells like trees"; the pasture that his father sold to the golf club; and fire. When he is about eighteen he frightens a young girl on her way home from school; his brother Jason uses this incident as an excuse to have him castrated. Jason has him placed in the insane asylum in Jackson in 1933.

COMPSON, CANDACE [CADDY] [1891–   ]. Daughter of Jason and Caroline Compson, and a character in *The Sound and the Fury*. Although she is from one point of view the most important character in *The Sound and the Fury*, Caddy is seen—or, more frequently, remembered—only through the eyes of her brothers Benjy and Quentin, who love her, and Jason, who hates her. As a young girl, Caddy was seduced by Dalton Ames and there-after had a succession of lovers until she found herself pregnant and was hastily married to Sydney Herbert Head, an Indiana banker. She left Jefferson after the wedding, returned briefly a few months later to leave her infant daughter, and disappeared. She was then reported married to a motion-picture magnate in Hollywood, divorced, and last heard of as the mistress of a Nazi general.

COMPSON, CAROLINE [NEE BASCOMB] [d. 1933?]. The wife of Jason Compson III, mother of Quentin, Candace, Jason IV, and Benjy, sister of Maury Bascomb, and a minor character in "That Evening Sun" and *The Sound and the Fury*. A neurotic and whining woman, Mrs. Compson is insistent on the fact that she is a "lady," and is extremely concerned with appearances. Although she wants to appear to be a good mother, she has very little love for any of her children except Jason.

COMPSON, GENERAL JASON LYCURGUS II [d. 1900]. The father of Jason Compson III, a minor character in *Absalom, Absalom!*, and also mentioned in *Go Down, Moses* and *The Reivers*. Although a brigadier general in the Civil War, General Compson is not notably successful either in war or in civiilan life. He fails at Shiloh in 1862 and again at Resaca in 1864. As a member of Major de Spain's annual hunting parties in the Tallahatchie River Bottom, he cannot be trusted to find his way back to camp alone. However, he is the only friend of Thomas Sutpen and the only man to whom Sutpen made any confidences. General Compson tells Sutpen's story to his son Jason III, who in turn tells it to his son Quentin in *Absalom, Absalom!*.

COMPSON, JASON III [d. 1912]. The husband of Caroline Bascomb, father of Quentin, Candace, Jason IV, and Benjy, and a character in *The Sound and the Fury*, *Absalom, Absalom!*, and the short story "That Evening Sun."

COMPSON GENEALOGY

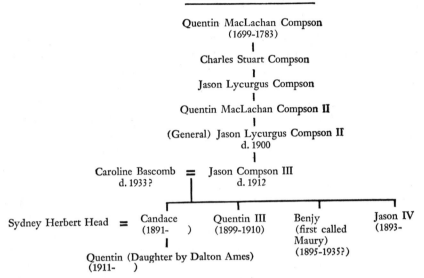

Quentin MacLachan Compson
(1699-1783)
|
Charles Stuart Compson
|
Jason Lycurgus Compson
|
Quentin MacLachan Compson II
|
(General) Jason Lycurgus Compson II
d. 1900
|
Caroline Bascomb   =   Jason Compson III
d. 1933?   d. 1912

Sydney Herbert Head   =   Candace   Quentin III   Benjy   Jason IV
(1891-   )   (1899-1910)   (first called   (1893-
| Maury)
Quentin (Daughter by Dalton Ames)   (1895-1935?)
(1911-   )

In the second section of *The Sound and the Fury* Mr. Compson, an aging ironist, is strongly contrasted with his son Quentin, who finds unbearable his father's belief that even pain and sorrow do not last. In *Absalom, Absalom!* Mr. Compson tells Quentin the story of Thomas Sutpen as he had heard it from his father, though his own personality colors his narrative and his speculations about the Sutpens. Though basically a well-intentioned man, he has been defeated by life and particularly by his whining, neurotic wife, and has retired into a kind of cynical detachment from the world, viewing life in terms of fatalism and mild pessimism.

COMPSON, JASON IV [1893-   ]. A son of Jason and Caroline Compson, narrator of the third section of *The Sound and the Fury*, and a minor character in *The Mansion*. A petty, avaricious man, Jason is perhaps the sanest of the Compsons and certainly the best adapted to survive in a money-oriented civilization. He systematically steals money sent to him by Caddy for her daughter's support, lies to his mother about the disposition of the money, and, judging all men by himself, trusts no one. Unemotional, highly logical, and respectful of the letter—but not the spirit—of the law, he bears a strong temperamental resemblance to Flem Snopes, with whom he locks economic horns in *The Mansion*. In the 1940s Jason tricks Flem into buying the Compson property in the expectation that the government will build an airfield on it; the airfield never materializes, but Flem, with typical shrewdness, makes even more money out of the property by subdividing it into small lots for veterans' housing.

COMPSON, QUENTIN III [1899–1910]. Eldest son of Jason and Caroline Compson, and narrator of the second section of *The Sound and the Fury* and a part of *Absalom, Absalom!*. A morbidly sensitive young man, Quentin tortures himself over his sister's loss of virtue and the supposed damage to the family honor. In 1909 he goes away to Harvard, where he tells his roommate, Shreve McCannon, the story of Thomas Sutpen as related in *Absalom, Absalom!*. He and Shreve reconstruct many of the missing links of the story as they imagine it might have happened; Quentin's contributions to the story reveal many of his own preoccupations with his sister, with honor, and with the idea of incest. The following spring his sister is hastily married, and Quentin is further tormented. Three months later he commits suicide.

COMPSON, QUENTIN [Miss]. The illegitimate daughter of Caddy Compson, and a character in the third and fourth sections of *The Sound and the Fury*. At seventeen she steals back the money her uncle Jason has misappropriated, runs away with a carnival pitchman, and is never heard of again.

CORPORAL, THE. A character in *A Fable*. The illegitimate son of a Balkan peasant woman and the man who was to become the Marshal, the Corporal is frequently identified with Christ by the parallelism of events in their lives. He is the leader of a mutinous regiment which refuses to carry out an attack and thus causes a temporary halt in the war. Though almost never named in the novel, he bears the name Dumont, taken from the Frenchman who married his elder sister, Marthe. His Christian name, Stefan, is probably an allusion to St. Stephen, the first Christian martyr.

DAMUDDY. The grandmother of the Compson children in *The Sound and the Fury*. Although she never appears as a living character, her funeral is an event of mysterious importance to her young grandchildren. Caddy climbs a tree and looks through the window to see what is going on.

DE SPAIN, MAJOR. Though a minor figure in many of the Yoknapatawpha County tales, Major de Spain is rarely brought into focus as a character. Sometime after the Civil War he acquires Thomas Sutpen's old fishing camp in the Tallahatchie River Bottom and establishes a hunting camp to which General Compson, the McCaslins, Boon Hogganbeck, and others go every November until the mid-1880s. His barn suffers at the hands of Ab Snopes in "Barn Burning."

DE SPAIN, MANFRED. Son of Major de Spain, and a character in *The Town*. In the beginning of *The Town*, De Spain, though mayor of Jefferson, appears to be a somewhat juvenile and hot-blooded man, the owner of a red racing car with a cut-out muffler; he is the rival of young Gavin Stevens for the attentions of Eula Varner Snopes. After a rather catastrophic scene at the Cotillion Club Christmas dance, at which Stevens and De Spain fight, De Spain settles down to a long-standing affair with Eula. Colonel Bayard Sartoris dies and De Spain succeeds him as president of the bank, with Eula's husband, Flem Snopes, as vice-president. Eight years later, Flem tries to force De Spain out of the bank; to prevent scandal, Eula kills herself, De Spain leaves town forever, and Flem takes over both the bank and the De Spain mansion.

DILSEY. The Compson's family cook, and a character in *The Sound and the Fury*, Dilsey is the embodiment of compassion and endurance, staying with the family even after Jason refuses to pay her, and providing a source of security and love for the idiot Benjy and young Miss Quentin. Dilsey is most clearly characterized in the fourth section of *The Sound and the Fury*.

DRAKE, TEMPLE [ca. 1913–   ]. A character in *Sanctuary* and *Requiem for a Nun*. A seventeen-year-old college student in *Sanctuary*, Temple is both irresponsible and provocative, flaunting herself before the men at Lee Goodwin's place even though she is afraid of what they might do to her. She allows herself to be abducted by Popeye and makes no attempt to escape from the brothel to which he takes her. By this passive acceptance of her plight she can feel that she is not responsible for what happens to her, and therefore not guilty of any wrongdoing. Eight years later, in *Requiem for a Nun*, she persists in believing herself innocent, and in separating her present blameless self—Mrs. Gowan Stevens—from the Temple Drake of her earlier experiences. Her attempts to gain a pardon for Nancy, the Negro nursemaid and murderer of her baby, end in Temple's final realization of her guilt and responsibility.

DUPRE, VIRGINIA SARTORIS [MISS JENNY] [1840–1930]. The sister of Colonel John Sartoris, a character in *The Unvanquished* ("An Odor of Verbena"), *Sartoris*, *Sanctuary*, and the short story "There Was a Queen." Miss Jenny, a young widow, came to Jefferson from the family home in Carolina in 1869 and remained with the Sartorises for the rest of her life. She is described as having eyes like her brother, Colonel John, except that hers were "very wise instead of intolerant." She is the only person to counsel her nephew Bayard against killing the man who shot his father. In *Sartoris* she perpetuates the legend of the glorious Sartoris past by retelling the story of the first Bayard, killed at Manassas, but she is the first to criticize other Sartorises for taking themselves and their tradition too seriously. Outspoken and frequently tart, Miss Jenny has few illusions about the Sartorises, yet she is completely loyal to them. She is realistic and thoroughly sensible, the only member of the family capable of deep affection, and a "lady of quality" in the fullest sense of the term. "There Was a Queen" recounts Miss Jenny's last days. She dies at ninety, as acute of mind and strong of character as ever.

EDMONDS FAMILY. See also Beauchamp and McCaslin.

EDMONDS, CAROTHERS [ROTH] [1898–   ]. Son of Zack Edmonds, great-great-great-grandson of L. Q. C. McCaslin, and a character in "The Fire and the Hearth" and "Delta Autumn" in Go Down, Moses. Though he is approximately the same age in both stories in which he appears, Roth seems to be weaker and more immature in "Delta Autumn" than in "The Fire and the Hearth." The latter story includes an account of his childhood realization that he is a white boy and his friend and almost foster brother, Henry Beauchamp, is a Negro. With Henry and his family, Roth sets the pattern that he will continue to follow in his future relationships with Negroes. In "Delta Autumn," he is presented as a somewhat cynical man, reckless and without much concern for others; he is, furthermore, a hunter who will kill does. He has had a son by a light-colored Negro woman who is, unknown to Roth, the granddaughter of James Beauchamp and the great-great-great-granddaughter of L. Q. C. McCaslin; thus, she stands in the same relation to the progenitor of the great McCaslin family as does Roth. His getting of an illegitimate child on her is a reenactment of his ancestor's seduction of his own mulatto daughter.

EDMONDS, MC CASLIN [CASS] [1850–?]. Great-grandson of L. Q. C. McCaslin, father of Zack Edmonds, second cousin of Isaac McCaslin, and a character in "Was" and in other stories in Go Down, Moses. A descendant of old McCaslin's daughter and thus on the distaff side of the family, Cass inherited the plantation only when Isaac McCaslin renounced his patrimony. Because Isaac was born in his father's old age and orphaned at twelve, Cass was a kind of second father to him, and supervised the nonwilderness aspects of his upbringing. Cass is frequently presented as a spokesman for the cause of reason and tradition, as in the fourth section of "The Bear," in which he tries to dissuade Ike from renouncing his patrimony.

EDMONDS, ZACHARY [ZACK] [1873–   ]. Son of McCaslin Edmonds, father of Carothers Edmonds, and a character in "The Fire and the Hearth" in Go Down, Moses. Zack and Lucas Beauchamp, his Negro cousin, are raised together and are almost like brothers; Zack, however, regards Lucas primarily as a Negro and treats him accordingly, until Lucas forces Zack to see him as a man with a man's rights and obligations.

EVERBE CORINTHIA [CORRIE]. A character in *The Reivers*. She is a good-hearted prostitute who reforms and marries Boon Hogganbeck. Another girl of the same name is a minor character in "The Leg."

FAIRCHILD, DAWSON. A character in *Mosquitoes*. He is a loquacious novelist, and was modeled after Sherwood Anderson.

FALLS, WILL [1825–192?]. A character in *Sartoris*. Falls is a friend of Colonel John Sartoris until the latter's death in the 1870s. As an old man, a pauper, he spends one day a week reminiscing about his old friend with Sartoris' son, Colonel Bayard, the president of the bank. When Colonel Bayard develops a wen on his cheek, Old Man Falls treats it with a home-made paste remedy, though the doctor claims that the paste will probably give Bayard blood poisoning. Miss Jenny and the doctor haul the protesting Bayard off to a specialist in Memphis; as Falls has predicted, the wen falls off at a touch.

FATHERS, SAM [1808–83]. A character in "The Old People" and "The Bear" in *Go Down, Moses*, and in the short story "A Justice." In the stories in *Go Down, Moses*, Sam is said to be the son of Ikkemotubbe, the Chickasaw chief, and a quadroon woman. Sold as a young child to L. Q. C. McCaslin, Sam grows up as a slave, but his innate dignity prevents both Negroes and whites from actually treating him as such. He works as a kind of carpenter and blacksmith on the plantation, but is essentially a hunter, a man of the wilderness; accordingly, he supervises the coming of age in the woods of both Cass Edmonds and Ike McCaslin in turn. He is identified with the wilderness in much the same way as is Old Ben, the great bear. When Old Ben is finally killed, Sam too chooses to die, and instructs Boon Hogganbeck, also of Chickasaw descent, to kill him and to give him the traditional Indian burial rites. In "A Justice" Sam is said to be the son of a Chickasaw named Crawfish-ford, or Craw-ford; when the black woman (who was married to a black man) who was the object of Craw-ford's attentions gave birth to a copper-colored son, Ikkemotubbe named the child Sam Had-Two-Fathers.

FRONY. Mother of Luster, and a minor character in *The Sound and the Fury*.

FROST, MARK. A poet, a minor character in *Mosquitoes*.

GILLIGAN, JOE. A character in *Soldier's Pay*. Gilligan meets Donald Mahon on a train, takes him home to Georgia, and looks after him.

GINOTTA, PETE.   A minor character in *Mosquitoes*.

GOODWIN, LEE.   A character in *Sanctuary*. A bootlegger living at the Old Frenchman Place, Goodwin is arrested and tried for the murder of a feeble-minded white man. He is basically a good man, but his weakness and his unwillingness to accuse the real murderer, for fear of retribution, leads to a mockery of justice and his own terrible death at the hands of a mob.

GOODWIN, RUBY.   A character in *Sanctuary*. The common-law wife of Lee Goodwin, Ruby is looked upon as a criminal and an outcast by the people of Jefferson. Though she is a former prostitute and has led a far from respectable life, she is faithful and loyal to Goodwin, and is one of the few characters in the novel with any real potentiality for good. She is implicitly contrasted with the superficially respectable but hypocritical and self-righteous women of Jefferson.

GORDON.   A sculptor, a character in *Mosquitoes*.

GOWRIE, CRAWFORD.   A thief and a murderer, a minor character in *Intruder in the Dust*.

GOWRIE, NUB.   The paterfamilias of the Gowrie hill clan, a minor character in *Intruder in the Dust*.

GOWRIE, VINSON.   His murder is the beginning of the events in *Intruder in the Dust*.

GRAGNON, GENERAL.   A character in *A Fable*. A division commander, Gragnon condemns both his division and himself to death because of the division's mutiny.

GRIER FAMILY, THE.   A family of country people living in Frenchman's Bend, warm, sympathetic, and, though poor, dignified. In "Shingles for the Lord," a humorous story, Res, the father of the family, is seen as a bumbling, comic figure whose complicated and farcical attempts to preserve his dignity result only in his further and more public shaming of himself by his own ineptitude. "Two Soldiers" deals with nineteen-year-old Pete and his eight-year-old brother and their courageous and touching desire to defend their country. "Shall Not Perish," a sequel to the previous story, shows the quiet wisdom and endurance of the family in their acceptance of Pete's death in battle.

GRIMM, PERCY.   A minor character in *Light in August*. A militant patriot,

Grimm is a fanatic who embodies the inhuman destructiveness of racism and superpatriotism. He eagerly leads the pursuit of Joe Christmas, a supposed Negro accused of murdering a white woman.

HABERSHAM, MISS EUNICE [see also WORSHAM]. A character in *Intruder in the Dust*. A spinster of nearly eighty, Miss Habersham is the last descendant of one of the original founders of Jefferson. When Lucas Beauchamp is threatened with lynching for the murder of a white man, Miss Habersham helps young Chick Mallison and his Negro companion Aleck Sander prove Lucas innocent. She appears briefly at the end of *The Town*.

HARRISS, MELISANDRE BACKUS. A character in the title story in *Knight's Gambit*, mentioned also in *The Town* and *The Mansion*. Melisandre is the daughter of a widower who spends his time sitting on the gallery of his house reading the Latin poets and drinking weak whiskey and sodas. In her teens, she becomes secretly engaged to Gavin Stevens. Gavin goes to Germany to school and remains in Europe during the First World War; while he is gone Melisandre marries a New Orleans bootlegger named Harriss, by whom she has two children. After the death of her father, Harriss transforms the Backus property into a kind of horse farm, and, at his death of his "thirty-eight-caliber occupational disease," Melisandre is left a very wealthy woman. In *Knight's Gambit* Gavin Stevens prevents her hot-tempered son Max from causing the death of Captain Gualdres, their Argentinian house guest, and shortly afterwards marries Melisandre. She appears briefly as Gavin's wife in *The Mansion*.

HAWK, DRUSILLA [b. ca. 1842; departed Jefferson for Alabama, 1874]. Niece of Rosa Millard, second wife of Colonel John Sartoris, and a minor character in *The Unvanquished*. A masculine, aggressive girl, Drusilla runs away from her home in Alabama to spend the last years of the war fighting with Colonel Sartoris' troop, and returns with him to Jefferson when the war is over. When Colonel Sartoris is killed by his former business partner, Drusilla tries to inspire his son Bayard with vengeance and her own love of violent, passionate action.

HEAD, SYDNEY HERBERT. An Indiana banker, briefly married to Caddy Compson in *The Sound and the Fury*.

HIGHTOWER, GAIL. A character in *Light in August*. As a child and a young man, Hightower had been deeply moved by tales told by his father and a Negro woman of his grandfather's death in the Civil War. As a result, Hightower becomes a kind of ghost of his grandfather, reliving in his imagination the day of his grandfather's seemingly glorious end when the elder man raided a henhouse in Jefferson and was killed, in all likelihood by a Confederate soldier's wife. Hightower studies for the ministry, and, with great effort, arranges in the seminary to be sent to the church in Jefferson, the scene of his grandfather's death. His congregation, however, is first puzzled, then alarmed and outraged that his sermons are full of galloping cavalry. When his wife commits suicide, driven to distraction by his immersion in the past, he is finally forced to resign his pastorate. He continues to live in Jefferson as a recluse, befriended only by Byron Bunch. When, through Byron, he is forced to become involved in the Joe Christmas tragedy, he comes to the realization that he has failed his wife, as well as his parishioners, in committing himself to the past, and that he is responsible for his wife's death.

HINES, EUPHEUS [DOC].   A character in *Light in August*. A religious fanatic, Hines believes that he is an instrument ordained by God to bring about the destruction of "Satan's spawn"—Hines's grandson, Joe Christmas. Hines kills his daughter's lover, a Mexican rumored to have Negro blood; later, by refusing to admit a doctor when his daughter is giving birth, he indirectly causes her death. Some months afterward he leaves his baby grandson in a Memphis orphanage, where he himself works as a janitor. He watches the boy for five years, hinting to him that he is a "nigger." Some thirty years later, when Joe Christmas is arrested for murder, Hines tries to organize a mob to lynch him.

HINES, MRS.   The wife of Doc Hines and a minor character in *Light in August*. Mrs. Hines tries to persuade Hightower to help save her grandson, Joe Christmas. Gavin Stevens speculates that she may have visited Joe in jail and urged him to try to escape.

HOGGANBECK, BOON.   A character in "The Old People" and "The Bear" in *Go Down, Moses*, and in *The Reivers*. Boon's grandmother was a Chickasaw Indian woman, but the rest of his ancestors being white, he is considered to be a white man. Tall, muscular, and ugly, he has hardly more than the mind of a child, but nevertheless a strong sense of loyalty, particularly to the McCaslins and to Major de Spain. He deeply loves Lion, the great savage hunting dog, and risks his life to save him when the bear Old Ben has grabbed the dog. Though he loves the hunt, he is incapable of hitting the broad side of a barn with a gun, and is notorious for having shot a passing Negro woman while emptying his gun at a Negro man. In *The Reivers* he is attached to the Priest branch of the McCaslin family, and takes Boss Priest's car for a wild trip to Memphis with young Lucius Priest and the Negro Ned McCaslin.

HOGGANBECK, DAVID.   A character in "A Courtship." Probably the grandfather of Boon Hogganbeck, he is the pilot of a steamboat that made a yearly visit up the river to the Chickasaw plantation. On one occasion he and Ikkemotubbe compete for the attentions of Herman Basket's beautiful sister.

HOGGANBECK, LUCIUS.   The son of Boon Hogganbeck and Everbe Corinthia, and a minor character in The Town.

HOLMES, JACK.   A stunt parachutist, a character in Pylon.

HOUSTON, JACK.   A character in The Hamlet and The Mansion. A proud man, independent and almost arrogant, Houston is set apart from the countryfolk of Frenchman's Bend by both his demeanor and his relative prosperity. In many ways he is a symbol of strong and unfettered masculinity—an equation that is intensified by the stallion he rides and the hound that accompanies him. His arrogance and his seemingly deliberate baiting of Mink Snopes over the matter of the pasturage fee for Mink's strayed yearling lead Mink to ambush and murder him. The Mansion gives a longer and more detailed version of this incident.

IKKEMOTUBBE.   A character in "A Courtship," "A Justice," "Red Leaves," and mentioned in "The Old People" (the latter in Go Down, Moses). Accounts of Ikkemotubbe's history are various and inconsistent. Most agree, however, that he was the last great Chickasaw chief of the area that was to become Yoknapatawpha County, and that he came into the chieftainship through craft rather than right. In "A Courtship" he is a young man competing with David Hogganbeck, a young white steamboat pilot, for the attentions of a lovely Indian girl. When both contestants lose the girl to a less athletic but more insidious suitor, they leave the Plantation for New Orleans, where Ikkemotubbe remains for seven years. In New Orleans he passes as the chief of his People, traditionally known as the Man, and thus acquires the name of "Doom" (from the French du homme). When he returns to the Plantation he is a man who knows what he wants and will not be crossed; he brings with him strong medicine with which he persuades the rightful Man to abdicate so that he can assume the chieftainship. In some of the stories he is reputed to be the father of Sam Fathers, the great hunter of Go Down, Moses.

JAMESON, DOROTHY.   A minor character in Mosquitoes.

JIGGS.   A mechanic attached to the Shumann-Holmes family, and a minor character in Pylon.

JONES, JANUARIUS. A lascivious, satyrlike man who pursues females in *Soldier's Pay*.

JONES, MILLY [1853–69]. The granddaughter of Wash Jones, and a minor character in "Wash" and in *Absalom, Absalom!*. Milly is seduced by Thomas Sutpen, who desperately wants a male heir to carry on his name; when Milly gives birth to a daughter, however, he is cruelly indifferent to her and the child. Mortified and disillusioned by Sutpen's treatment of the girl, Jones kills him, and then Milly and her infant.

JONES, WASH [ca. 1807–69]. A character in "Wash" and *Absalom, Absalom!*. A poor white whom Thomas Sutpen has permitted to live in his abandoned fishing camp, Jones is Sutpen's handyman and sometime drinking companion. Because of Sutpen's thoughtless indifference to Jones's granddaughter, who has just given birth to Sutpen's daughter, Jones kills him. When the posse comes to take him to jail, Jones kills his granddaughter and her infant and provokes his own death at the hands of the other men. His character is a mixture of pride and servility, laziness and loyalty. It is precisely his unexceptionableness, the quality that makes him the epitome of the common poor white, that make his final disillusionment in his idolized hero Sutpen so moving and so terrible.

KAUFFMAN, JULIUS. A minor character in *Mosquitoes*.

LALLEMONT, GENERAL. A character in *A Fable*, the only friend of division commander General Gragnon.

LITTLEJOHN, MRS. The owner of a boardinghouse in Frenchman's Bend, a minor character in *The Hamlet*.

LEVINE, DAVID. A character in *A Fable*. A young British airman, Levine wants a chance to become an heroic flyer.

LOOSH. A Negro slave of the Sartoris family, a character in *The Unvanquished*. At the very beginning of the book Loosh's attitude toward the fall of Vicksburg and Corinth and his baiting of young Bayard and Ringo mark him as different from the other Negroes, who are steadfastly loyal to their white owners. Loosh is elated by the information that General Sherman is coming to free all the Negroes, and is thus implicitly identified with the horde of semihysterical former slaves who leave their homes to drown themselves trying to cross "Jordan." Portrayed as a subtly unsympathetic character about whom the Sartorises are in some undefined way suspicious, Loosh justifies their suspicions when he shows the invading Yankees where the family silver was buried, and then, having been freed, leaves the plantation.

LOWE, JULIAN. A minor character in *Soldier's Pay*. Julian develops an adolescent crush on Mrs. Margaret Powers, but in spite of his protestations of eternal love, his callow devotion soon fades.

LUSTER. The grandson of Dilsey, and the nurse boy of the idiot Benjy Compson in *The Sound and the Fury*.

MAC CALLUM FAMILY, THE [also spelled MC CALLUM]. A father and his six sons appearing in *Sartoris* and the short story "The Tall Men," and mentioned in other of the Yoknapatawpha County novels. The MacCallums are hill farmers living in the northeast part of the county eighteen miles from Jefferson. It is to their farm that young Bayard Sartoris retreats for a kind of breathing space after accidentally killing his grandfather. Though poor and uneducated, the MacCallums have a large measure of natural dignity, and live in unaggressive content. The family includes the following:

Buddy [1899–   ]. The youngest son, named Virginius for his father but always called by his nickname. Buddy runs away to join the Army at seventeen and serves in Europe, where he is awarded what he calls a "charm" for doing something that does not seem significant to him but which "severely annoyed" the enemy. Taciturn and almost completely indifferent to physical discomfort, Buddy is content to hunt and farm and is at peace with himself. In "The Tall Men," which takes place ca. 1940, Buddy (the only brother to marry) is the father of twins, Anse and Lucius, who are served a warrant by the state draft investigator for having failed to register for the draft.

Henry [1869–   ]. The second son. Plump and placid, Henry is the most domestic of all the MacCallums. He supervises the kitchen and brews the family whiskey according to a recipe handed down for generations.

Jackson [1867–   ]. The eldest son. He tries to revolutionize hunting by breeding a vixen to a hound, hoping for pups with a hound's wind and a fox's smartness. He is described as a "sort of shy and impractical Cincinnatus."

Lee [188?–   ]. The fifth son. The most taciturn of all the MacCallums, Lee is a good tenor and was "much in demand at Sunday singings." Shy and moody, he often goes out alone to tramp around the countryside.

Rafe [1875–   ]. Christened Raphael Semmes and twin of Stuart. A horseman, Rafe is easy of manner and the only one who "by any stretch of the imagination could have been called loquacious." He has a brief part in the title story of *Knight's Gambit*.

Stuart [1875–   ]. Twin of Rafe. Stuart is a good farmer and trader, and has a sizable bank account.

Virginius [named Anse in "The Tall Men"] [1845–1925?]. The pater-familias. In 1861 he walks from Mississippi to Virginia to fight with the Stonewall brigade. At the end of the war he walks back to Mississippi, builds a house, and marries. Never having accepted the South's defeat in the Civil War, he is enraged when Buddy joins the Union army in 1916. As a result, Buddy's army career and his medal are never mentioned in the house.

MC CANNON, SHREVLIN [SHREVE] [1890–   ]. The Harvard roommate of Quentin Compson, and a minor character in *The Sound and the Fury* and *Absalom, Absalom!*. A Canadian, Shreve asks Quentin to tell him about the South, and Quentin begins the story of Thomas Sutpen recounted in *Absalom, Absalom!*. Shreve listens to part of the Sutpen saga, contributes his own version of a part of it, and, with Quentin, reconstructs the relationship between Henry Sutpen and Charles Bon.

MC CARRON, HOAKE. A character in *The Hamlet* and *The Mansion*, lover of Eula Varner, and father of Linda Snopes. There are several different versions of McCarron's seduction of Eula given in *The Hamlet, The Town*, and *The Mansion*. Basic to all of them is the story that McCarron, a dashing young man with the smartest buggy in town, courts Eula to the jealousy and despair of several of her would-be suitors, who ambush the couple one night. Eula helps McCarron beat off the attackers, and later that evening becomes pregnant by him. In *The Hamlet* McCarron leaves town immediately after Eula's pregnancy is known; in *The Mansion* she refuses to marry him and sends him away. He also appears in *The Mansion* as a New York newspaperman who is brought by Gavin Stevens to meet Linda—McCarron's daughter—at her wedding.

MC CASLIN FAMILY. See also Edmonds and Beauchamp.

MC CASLIN, AMODEUS [UNCLE BUDDY] [1799–1879] and MC CASLIN, THEOPHILUS [UNCLE BUCK] [1799–1879]. The twin sons of L. Q. C. McCaslin. Uncle Buck, the husband of Sophonsiba Beauchamp and the father of Isaac Mc-Caslin, is a central character in "Was" and appears or is referred to in many of the other stories in *Go Down, Moses*, and is an important character in the "Vendee" chapter of *The Unvanquished*. After the death of their father, the twins move out of the nearly-completed plantation house and into a cabin which they have built themselves. They are described in *The Unvanquished* as being ahead of their time because of their views on the ownership of the land; they believe that "land did not belong to people but that people belonged to the land" (45) and that the earth would not permit men to live on it if they behaved, or used it, improperly. They also disapprove of slavery and free their father's slaves, allowing each to work out the price paid for him and thus buy his freedom. Once freed, however, the former slaves refuse to leave the plantation. The twins try to keep their Negroes from running loose at night and causing trouble all over the county by driving all that can be found into the plantation house at sunset and putting a nail into the front yard—in spite of the fact that the windows are not glassed and there is no back door at all. Any Negro caught and housed at sundown is honor-bound to escape from the house only while the door is being shut, and to be back in the house when one of the twins removes the nail the following morning. In the beginning of the Civil War, the brothers try to join Colonel Sartoris' troop, but are told that they are too old. They threaten to raise their own company if Colonel Sartoris will not take them, but finally compromise when the Colonel agrees to take one of them. Uncle Buddy receives the honor by winning a poker game from Uncle Buck. In Go Down, Moses, it is Uncle Buck who goes to the war, spending four years with General Nathaniel Bedford Forrest.

MC CASLIN, ISAAC [IKE OR UNCLE IKE] [1867–1947]. Son of Uncle Buck McCaslin and Sophonsiba Beauchamp, and a character in "The Old People," "The Bear," and "Delta Autumn," all in Go Down, Moses. He is briefly mentioned in The Mansion and The Reivers. The last white male descendant of old Carothers bearing the name McCaslin, Ike refuses to inherit the plantation because he believes that land belongs to all men in common and that it has been cursed by being held in private ownership. He has chosen, through his relationship with old Sam Fathers, wilderness values in opposition to the values of civilization, and lives a simple, ascetic life, the most important part of which is spent in hunting. He becomes a carpenter, goes to live in Jefferson, and marries, but his wife wants him to claim the plantation to which he has renounced his right. When he makes it plain that he will never accept his inheritance, she refuses to have any further sexual relationship with him, and he is left childless at her death. He is mentioned in The Mansion and The Reivers as owning a hardware store on the square.

MC CASLIN, LUCIUS QUINTUS CAROTHERS [1772–1837]. Founder of the McCaslin family in Yoknapatawpha County. Born in Carolina, McCaslin migrated to Mississippi sometime in the early nineteenth century and acquired a large grant of land from Ikkemotubbe, the Chickasaw chief of the area. He was the father of three legitimate children, the twins Amodeus (Uncle Buddy) and Theophilus (Uncle Buck) and a daughter, and of two illegitimate children by his Negro slaves: Tomasima, or Tomey, the daughter of

Eunice, and Terrel, or Tomey's Turl, his son by his daughter Tomey. He provided a legacy of one thousand dollars for his part-Negro son (which Turl did not accept), and his legitimate sons Uncle Buck and Uncle Buddy increased the legacy to one thousand dollars each for Turl's three children, James, Fonsiba, and Lucas Beauchamp.

MC CASLIN, NED.   A Negro attached to the Priest family, and a character in *The Reivers*.

MC CORD.   A newspaperman, a minor character in *The Wild Palms*.

MC EACHERN, SIMON.   A character in *Light in August*. A rigid, Calvinistic Presbyterian, McEachern adopted Joe Christmas when the child was five years old. Though his treatment of Joe is harsh and cold, the boy at least feels that his foster father's beatings are predictable and reasonable, whereas he hates Mrs. McEachern's weak attempts at kindness and affection.

MAC GOWAN, SKEETS.   A minor character in *As I Lay Dying*, *The Town*, and *The Mansion*. A clerk in Christian's Drugstore in Jefferson, MacGowan pretends to be a pharmacist when Dewey Dell Bundren comes to try to buy abortion pills. He gives her some fake medicine and tells her to come back at night for the rest of the treatment. In *The Mansion* he is described as "a young man with swagger and dash to him . . . with a considerable following of fourteen and fifteen-year-old girls."

MAGDA.   See Marthe.

MAHON, DONALD.   A central character in *Soldier's Pay*, he returns home to die after the war.

MALLISON, CHARLES [CHICK].   The nephew of Gavin Stevens, and a character in *Intruder in the Dust*, *Knight's Gambit*, *The Town*, and *The Mansion*. In *Intruder in the Dust* sixteen-year-old Chick digs up a white man's grave in an attempt to substantiate the story of Lucas Beauchamp, who is accused of murdering the dead man. In *Knight's Gambit* he narrates "Monk," "Tomorrow," and "An Error in Chemistry," and is a character in the title story. He narrates a large part of *The Town*, usually retelling events that happened before he was born or in his early childhood, and thus frequently speaks more for the people of Jefferson as a whole than for himself as an individual. The Snopes saga is seen through his eyes as a child growing up in the latter part of *The Town* and in his sections in *The Mansion*. Since he is more often a narrator than a character in his own right, he does not have a well-defined and consistent personality throughout the stories in

McCASLIN GENEALOGY

white wife = Lucius Quintus Carothers McCaslin (1772-1837) = Eunice (Negro) d. 1832

daughter = Edmonds	Sophonsiba Beauchamp = Theophilus "Uncle Buck" (1799-1879)	Amodeus "Uncle Buddy" (1799-1879)	Tomasina, "Tomey" (1810-1833) daughter

male Edmonds

Isaac McCaslin (1867-1947)

Tomey's Turl "Terrel Beauchamp" b. 1833 = Tennie Beauchamp

"Cass" McCaslin Edmonds b. 1850

James "Tennie's Jim" b. 1864

Fonsiba b. 1869

3 children who died in infancy

L. Q. C. Priest* b. 1846 = Sarah Edmonds

Zachary "Zack" Edmonds b. 1873

granddaughter = George Wilkins

Lucas Beauchamp b. 1874 = Molly Worsham b. 1874

Maury Priest = Alison Lessup

Carothers "Roth" Edmonds b. 1898

Henry b. 1898

daughter

Nat

Samuel "Butch" Beauchamp (1914-1940)

Lucius b. 1894

Alexander b. 1904?

Maury

son

*distant kinsman of
L. Q. C. McCaslin

which he appears. Thus, in *Intruder in the Dust* he is an almost idealized adolescent struggling with the choice between what his society considers to be right and what he senses is a deeper moral obligation; in *The Mansion*, however, he is a flippant, pseudosophisticated young man who seems almost totally unrelated to the boy-hero of the earlier book.

MANNIGOE, NANCY.   A character in "That Evening Sun" and *Requiem for a Nun*. In "That Evening Sun" Nancy is a Negro servant attached to the Compson family; she lives in terror of her husband, who has threatened to kill her. In *Requiem for a Nun* Nancy (apparently murdered in the earlier story) is resurrected to play the part of the "dopefiend nigger whore" whom Temple Drake (Mrs. Gowan Stevens) takes out of the gutter to be a nursemaid to her children. Like many of Faulkner's Negro characters, Nancy, the "Nun" of the title, is deeply perceptive, sacrificing, and loyal; she murders Temple's baby—and thus knowingly sacrifices her own life— in order to force Temple to face the truth about herself and, in so doing, to achieve some kind of moral salvation.

MARSHAL, THE.   A character in *A Fable*. The supreme commander of the Allied Forces, the Marshal is a figure representing Authority and in some ways Jehovah. He is the father of the Corporal.

MARTHE.   The half-sister of the Corporal, and a character in *A Fable*. Marthe had been responsible for her older but feeble-minded sister and for her infant half-brother since she was nine years old. Of middle European origin, she married a Frenchman named Dumont in order to get her half-brother to France. During part of her life she is called Magda.

MARYA.   The sister of Marthe, half-sister of the Corporal, and a minor character in *A Fable*. In spite—or because—of her feeblemindedness, Marya has an intuitive understanding that approaches the preternatural. In one of the final scenes of the novel she recognizes the Runner and his companion, the Corporal's betrayer; she understands the object of the Runner's visit, and consoles the other with the knowledge that he doesn't have "much longer to despair."

MAURIER, MRS. PATRICIA.   A cultivator of artists, she organizes the yachting party that is the setting for most of *Mosquitoes*.

MILLARD, ROSA [GRANNY] [?–1864].   The mother-in-law of Colonel John Sartoris, grandmother of Bayard Sartoris, and a main character in *The Unvanquished* and the short story "My Grandmother Millard and the Battle of Harrykin Creek." One of Faulkner's most admirable female characters,

Rosa Millard raises Bayard and his Negro companion Ringo from very early childhood, teaching them, by her example, respect for truth and honesty. After the Union army has been through the county and most of the poorer residents are on the verge of starvation, Miss Rosa becomes involved in "requisitioning" Yankee army mules. Though done in a good cause, it is nonetheless stealing in her eyes, and she makes a public confession of her sins in church. Later, she attempts to get four thoroughbred horses from Grumby, a lawless poor white with a raiding commission; though she knows Grumby is dangerous, she is convinced that no Southerner will harm an old woman, and goes to him alone. Grumby, having no Southern respect for old ladies, kills her.

MITCHELL, BELLE. A minor character in *Sartoris* and mentioned in *Sanctuary.* Belle divorces her husband to marry the lawyer Horace Benbow. The marriage is unhappy, and Horace tries unsuccessfully to leave her.

MITCHELL, LITTLE BELLE. The daughter of Belle Mitchell and the step-daughter of Horace Benbow, and a minor character in *Sartoris* and *Sanctuary.*

MONSIEUR TOOLEYMON. See Sutterfield, Reverend Toby.

MOSELEY. A minor character in *As I Lay Dying.* Moseley operates a pharmacy in Mottson, where the Bundrens have to go in order to reach Jefferson. Dewey Dell tries to buy abortion pills, but Moseley, a righteous man, indignantly refuses to sell her anything.

OTIS. A minor character in *The Reivers.* A noxious insect of a child, Otis is fifteen but looks ten, and is even more retarded in his moral development. He thoroughly upsets the household of Miss Reba when he comes to visit his relative Everbe Corinthia.

PEABODY, LUCIUS QUINTUS [LOOSH]. A minor character in *Sartoris* and *As I Lay Dying.* A descendant of the Dr. Peabody who was one of the early settlers in Jefferson, Loosh Peabody is an enormously fat and amiable man of 87 at the time of the main events related in *Sartoris.* His shabby office and informal behavior are contrasted with the impeccably sterile professional manner of the new doctor in town—a contrast which shows the new doctor to be superior in asepsis, Loosh in generosity, friendliness, and perhaps general ability. Loosh maintains that he cannot afford to retire because he has to feed a quantity of Negroes that he has had around his place so long that he cannot get rid of them. In *As I Lay Dying,* Peabody (rejuvenated to about age 70) is sent for by Anse Bundren to look at his dying wife,

Addie. Their youngest child, Vardaman, connects Peabody's arrival with his mother's death and drives away Peabody's team. Near the end of the book Peabody treats the eldest son, Cash, for a badly broken leg that Anse has tried to set with cement.

PETE.   Brother of Red and a minor character in *Requiem for a Nun*. Pete tries to blackmail Temple Drake Stevens with letters she had written to his dead brother.

POPEYE.   A character in *Sanctuary*, also mentioned in *Requiem for a Nun*. The vicious and amoral son of a syphilitic, Popeye represents the evil and conscienceless aspects of the modern mechanized world. He is afraid of nature and natural objects—animals, trees, etc.—and is described in terms of metallic or otherwise lifeless things. He is "unnatural" both literally (he has several physical abnormalities) and figuratively, and is completely corrupt and devoid of normal human feelings.

POWERS, MRS. MARGARET.   A widow, a central character in *Soldier's Pay*. She cares for, and finally marries, the dying Donald Mahon.

PRIEST, LUCIUS.   The narrator of *The Reivers*.

PRIEST, LUCIUS [BOSS].   Grandfather of young Lucius Priest, and a minor character in *The Reivers*.

QUARTERMASTER GENERAL, THE.   A character in *A Fable*. A Norman, he attended school with the man who was to become the Marshal, and was his only friend. Despite his loyalty to the Marshal, he attempts to resign his generalship when he learns how the military leaders have ended the Runner's attempt to bring about a more permanent armistice.

QUICK, SOLON [LON].   A country man living in Frenchman's Bend, Quick (usually named Lon, sometimes Ben or Uncle Ben) appears in minor roles in many of the county tales. He sells Jewel Bundren a spotted horse in *As I Lay Dying*; he is the owner-driver of the Jefferson-Frenchman's Bend bus in "Shall Not Perish" and he is referred to as the constable of Frenchman's Bend in *The Mansion*. As Uncle Ben Quick, he sells Ratliff fifty goats in *The Hamlet*, and is referred to as the owner of a sawmill in Frenchman's Bend.

RATLIFF, V. K. [VLADIMIR KYRILYTCH].   A character in "A Bear Hunt," *The Hamlet*, *The Town*, and *The Mansion*. Ratliff is the descendant of one of the original founders of Jefferson, V. K. Ratcliffe, who in turn was descended from one Vladimir Kyrilytch, a member of a hired German regiment in the American Revolution. Ratliff is a sewing-machine salesman, regularly covering four counties and thus observing all that is of interest in the area. His sister keeps house for him in Jefferson when he is not traveling, and with Grover Cleveland Winbush he owns a small restaurant in town. Perceptive and loquacious, he narrates many of the sections in the Snopes trilogy, though he infrequently takes part in the action himself. He is perhaps Faulkner's most successful narrator-character: as an observer of human nature he is both shrewd and compassionate, sufficiently detached to recount with irony and dry humor the activities of others, and sufficiently involved to become a fully delineated character in his own right. In *Sartoris* he appears briefly under the name of Suratt.

REBA, MISS.   See Rivers, Reba.

RED.   A minor character in *Sanctuary*. The lover of Temple Drake, as proxy for the impotent Popeye, Red is murdered by Popeye for trying to see Temple alone. The description of Red's gangland funeral is an excellent example of Faulkner's use of grotesque and macabre humor.

REDMOND, BEN [or REDLAW].   A character mentioned in *The Unvanquished*, *Sartoris*, and the prose sections of *Requiem for a Nun*. A Northerner who comes to Jefferson at the end of the Civil War, Redmond enters a business partnership with Colonel John Sartoris. He later becomes Sartoris' enemy and eventually kills him. Redmond's career is modeled on that of R. J. Thurmond, the former business partner and killer of Colonel William C. Falkner, the author's great-grandfather and the model for Colonel Sartoris.

RIDER.   A young Negro, the central character in "Pantaloon in Black" in *Go Down, Moses*.

RINGO [MARENGO] [1850–?].   A Negro companion of Bayard Sartoris, and a character in *The Unvanquished*. Raised together from infancy, Ringo and Bayard Sartoris treat each other almost as equals during their boyhood and seem mutually unaware of the social distinctions between them. Ringo draws maps and otherwise helps Rosa Millard to "requisition" mules from the Union army. When she is murdered by the leader of a lawless band of poor whites, he goes with Bayard and Uncle Buck McCaslin on the manhunt for the killer, and, when they have cornered the man, helps Bayard to kill him. Ringo is one of Faulkner's most attractive Negro characters; however, probably because he is only seen as a boy or a very young man, he does not have the depth of a Dilsey or a Lucas Beauchamp. He is similar, in many respects, to young Henry Beauchamp in "The Fire and the Hearth" (*Go Down, Moses*), or to Aleck Sander in *Intruder in the Dust*.

RITTENMEYER, CHARLOTTE.   A young married woman who leaves her husband to go away with a young interne, and a central character in *The Wild Palms*. Believing that the modern world has no room for love, she and Harry Wilbourne travel all over the country looking for a place that will allow their love to grow.

RITTENMEYER, FRANCIS [RAT].   Husband of Charlotte Rittenmeyer and a minor character in *The Wild Palms*.

RIVERS, REBA [MISS REBA].   A minor character in *Sanctuary*, *The Mansion*, and *The Reivers*. The madam of a Memphis brothel, Miss Reba is fat, warm-hearted, and inclined to be maudlin after too much gin, but withal practical and efficient. Her sections in *Sanctuary* and *The Reivers* are among the best pieces of Faulkner's comic writing.

ROBYN, PAT.   The niece of Mrs. Maurier, and a central character in *Mosquitoes*.

ROBYN, THEODORE [GUS or JOSH].   The twin brother of Pat Robyn, nephew of Mrs. Maurier, and a minor character in *Mosquitoes*.

RUNNER, THE.   A character in *A Fable*. Formerly a commissioned officer, the Runner chose to return to the ranks as a private. He tries to carry on the Corporal's attempt to bring about an armistice.

SAMSON.   A minor character in *As I Lay Dying*. When the Bundrens are unable to cross the river over his washed-out bridge, Samson advises them to bury Addie in nearby New Hope and volunteers assistance, but Anse is determined to cary out his promise to bury her in Jefferson.

SARTORIS, BAYARD [1] [1838–62].   The brother of Colonel John Sartoris, mentioned in *Sartoris*. Called "not so much a black sheep as a nuisance," Bayard becomes a heroic figure to the family after his death, though its cause is inglorious in the extreme. On a lighthearted raiding party, Jeb Stuart, Bayard, and a few others break up a Union camp at breakfast and capture a major. When the major ironically comments that Stuart has not captured their anchovies, Bayard dashes back to the camp—and is shot by a frightened cook.

SARTORIS, BAYARD [2] [1850–1919].   The son of Colonel John Sartoris, grandfather of "young" Bayard Sartoris, and a main character in *Sartoris* and *The Unvanquished*. In the stories in *The Unvanquished*, Bayard is first seen as a boy of twelve playing at war and shooting—more or less by accident—the horse from underneath a Union soldier. At fifteen he and Ringo, his Negro companion, track down and kill a vicious man named Grumby, who has murdered his grandmother. In the last story, "An Odor of Verbena," Bayard refuses to avenge his father's death at the hands of his former business partner, and thereby repudiates the Sartoris tradition of violence.

In *Sartoris*, Bayard (bearing the honorary title of Colonel inherited from his father) is in his late sixties, growing deaf and rather ineffectual. Still acting as president of the bank, he is fussed over by his aunt, Miss Jenny, as though he were a child, and he is unable to command enough respect from young Bayard to forbid him from speeding and general hellraising. Finally young Bayard runs the car over a cliff while his grandfather is riding with him, and the old man dies of a heart attack.

SARTORIS, BAYARD [3] [1893–1920].   Grandson of Colonel Bayard Sartoris, husband of Narcissa Benbow, father of Benbow Sartoris, and a main character in *Sartoris* and in the short story "Ad Astra." Bayard suffers from an overwhelming death wish, the result of his twin's death in war and his own inability to adjust to life. An immature and thoroughly selfish young man, he is incapable of love and responsive only to the thrills involved in dangerous pranks. When his grandfather is killed as a result of Bayard's reckless driving, the young man leaves home, but continues his search for destruction. Some months later he is killed testing an airplane.

SARTORIS, COLONEL JOHN [1823–74?–76?].   Brother of Virginia (Miss Jenny) Sartoris DuPre, father of Colonel Bayard Sartoris, great-grandfather of "young" Bayard Sartoris, and a character in *The Unvanquished* and *Sartoris*, also mentioned in many of the other novels and stories. Colonel John Sartoris was modeled on Faulkner's great-grandfather, Colonel William C. Falkner, who was also a Civil War hero and a railroad-builder. Like his fictional counterpart, Colonel Falkner led a violent, colorful life and met his death at the hand of his former business partner.

Jefferson's leading citizen and one of its most enterprising builders, Colonel Sartoris is a proud, intolerant man to whom family and preservation of the ideals of the ante-bellum South are of first importance. Near the end of a life in which he has done too much killing, he comes to a realization that he must do a little "moral housecleaning," and accordingly meets unarmed the man who is to kill him.* In all the novels in which he

* In *The Unvanquished* Colonel Sartoris is killed in 1874; in *Sartoris* the date on his tombstone is 1876.

SARTORIS GENEALOGY

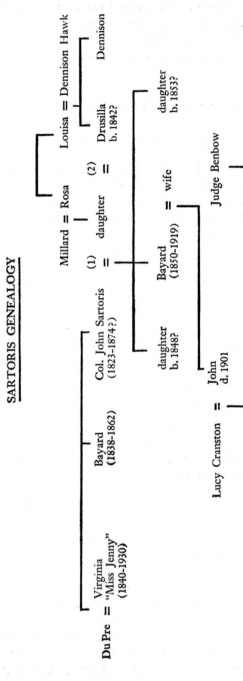

appears he is never seen directly, but always from a romantic distance—through the eyes of a child (in *The Unvanquished*) or the mists of memory (in *Sartoris*). As a result, he is a figure somewhat larger than life, and makes up in idealized attractiveness what he lacks in depth of characterization.

SARTORIS, JENNY.   See DuPre, Virginia Sartoris.

SARTORIS, JOHN [1823–74].   See Sartoris, Colonel John.

SARTORIS, JOHN [JOHNNY] [1893–1918].   Twin brother of "young" Bayard Sartoris, and a character in "All the Dead Pilots," also mentioned in *Sartoris*. Though described as a daredevil and something of a troublemaker (he was sent to Princeton because he and Bayard had perpetrated too many pranks at the University of Virginia), Johnny is spoken of by the MacCallums as high-spirited and warmly affectionate; he seems to have been less moody and more considerate than his twin. He is killed in aerial combat when he rashly attacks a group of more powerful German planes. Miss Jenny says of him that he used the war just as a "good excuse to get himself killed."

SAUNDERS, CECILY.   The fiancée of Donald Mahon, and a character in *Soldier's Pay*.

SENTRY, THE.   A character in *A Fable*. A cockney horse groom in America before the war, he became a Mason and was baptized into the Baptist church by his companion, the lay preacher Tobe Sutterfield. During the war he gained the loyalty and sympathy of the men in his battalion by initiating them into the Masonic brotherhood, and ran a kind of gambling-insurance-and-loan company for them.

SHUMANN, JACKIE.   The young son of Laverne Shumann, and a minor character in *Pylon*.

SHUMANN, LAVERNE.   The shared wife of a pair of fliers, and a character in *Pylon*.

SHUMANN, ROGER.   A racing pilot, a central character in *Pylon*.

SNOPES, ABNER [AB].   A character in *The Unvanquished*, the short story "Barn Burning," and *The Hamlet*. The Yoknapatawpha County progenitor of the numerous Snopes family, Ab first appears in the county during the Civil War as a horse and mule trader. He is said to have gotten his limp by being shot in the foot by Colonel Sartoris while attempting to steal horses from a Confederate picket line. He is a mercenary, vicious poor white, and is largely responsible for Rosa Millard's death at the hands of the leader of a band of lawless poor whites in *The Unvanquished*. In "Barn Burning," which takes place some thirty years later, his streak of viciousness is apparent in his habit of burning his landlords' barns in revenge for what he considers his unfair treatment at their hands. He is described as having a "wolflike independence and even courage when the advantage was at least neutral which impressed strangers, as if they got from his latent ravening ferocity not so much a sense of dependability as a feeling that his ferocious conviction in the rightness of his own actions would be of advantage to all whose interest lay with his." In *The Hamlet* V. K. Ratliff explains that Ab's pusillanimity is not the result of "natural meanness"; he has been soured by his experiences, particularly by being beaten in a horse-trading contest with one Pat Stamper. In *The Town* he is mentioned as a harmless eccentric who grows watermelons with which to entice town boys so he can drive them out of his yard with rocks.

SNOPES, BYRON. A character in *Sartoris*, also mentioned in *The Town*. With the help of Colonel Bayard Sartoris, Byron is sent to business college in Memphis; he returns to Jefferson and works as a clerk in Colonel Sartoris' bank. He writes anonymous and obscene letters to Narcissa Benbow, soon to marry Colonel Sartoris' grandson, and, on the night of her wedding, steals back the packet of letters, robs the bank, and flees to Texas. Several years later he sends his four children, the offspring of an Apache squaw, to his cousin Flem. The children perpetrate various dark deeds, among them the killing and eating of a valuable Pekinese dog, and Flem, after paying for the dog, sends them to their cousins in Frenchman's Bend. The Snopeses there, however, are equally unable to cope with the children, and send them back to Jefferson to be shipped on to El Paso.

SNOPES, CLARENCE EGGLESTONE. The son of I. O. Snopes and his second (bigamous) wife, and a character in *Sanctuary* and *The Mansion*. Clarence is a wild youth who generally upsets the community of Frenchman's Bend until Will Varner makes him constable. Through Varner's influence he is elected to the upper house of the state legislature. Clarence, however, finds it necessary to go to the capitol, Jackson, by way of Memphis, where he is well known in the local brothels, particularly at a house staffed by Negro women. In *Sanctuary* he finds his young cousin Virgil living in Miss Reba's brothel under the impression that it is a boardinghouse; this episode is elaborated in *The Mansion*. In the latter book, Clarence decides to run for Congress, but, before he can announce his candidacy, he is victimized by

SNOPES GENEALOGY

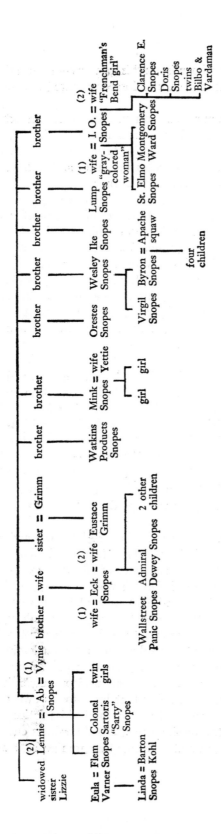

a group of dogs who mistake his trousers for a nearby dog-thicket. As a result of this contretemps, he is forced to retire from politics.

SNOPES, COLONEL SARTORIS [SARTY].   Son of Ab Snopes, and a character in "Barn Burning." The boy Sarty is one of the few sympathetic Snopeses. Forced to choose between loyalty to his villainous father and his sense of right and justice, Sarty chooses the latter and warns the owner of a barn that the elder Snopes is about to burn.

SNOPES, DORIS.   The youngest brother of Senator Clarence Snopes and the son of I. O. Snopes and his second (bigamous) wife, and a minor character in *The Town* and *The Mansion*. Doris has the "mentality of a child and the moral principles of a wolverine." (368, T) He "adopts" his half-Indian cousins, the children of Byron Snopes and an Apache squaw, when they are deported from Jefferson for extreme mischief and sent to Frenchman's Bend. Doris claims he is going to train them to hunt in a pack, but soon he, too, suffers at their hands, and is found tied to a tree around which a stack of wood is burning.

SNOPES, ECK.   Father of Wallstreet Panic Snopes, and a character in *The Hamlet* and *The Town*. Believed to be not a true Snopes because of his honesty, industry, and kindness, Eck arrives in Frenchman's Bend soon after his cousin Flem and operates the blacksmith shop that his cousin I. O. has leased from Flem. In *The Town* he runs the restaurant Flem acquired from V. K. Ratliff, until Flem fires him for being too honest. He then gets a job as a night watchman at the depot oil tank; four years later he climbs into the tank with a lantern seeking a lost child, and is killed when the oil fumes ignite and explode.

SNOPES, FLEM [ca. 1880–1946].   Son of Ab Snopes, and a character in "Barn Burning," "Centaur in Brass," *The Hamlet*, *The Town* and *The Mansion*. The shrewdest and most avaricious of all the Snopes clan, Flem works his way from the clerkship of Varner's store in Frenchman's Bend to the presidency of the Merchants and Farmers Bank in Jefferson, and from the status of a landless poor white to that of a wealthy and apparently respectable man. Described as having eyes the color of stagnant water, Flem is a two-dimensional villain, utterly inhuman in his singleminded pursuit first of money and then of respectability. He is sexually impotent, and completely indifferent to human ties and obligations. Ironically, it is his refusal to come to the aid of his cousin Mink that leads to his own end. He has a strict respect for the letter of the law, and, unlike his relatives, never involves himself in anything technically illegal. His shrewdness enables him to take advantage of situations and of people that are ripe, as it were, to fall into his hands; he seldom initiates plots to others' undoing, but simply steps in and offers to let folks (as Ratliff expresses it) "bare their backsides to him." In *The Hamlet* his villainy is seen in comic relief, for his success is largely a result of the greed and self-seeking of others. In *The Town*, however, he uses his wife and her daughter as pawns in his game of finance, and becomes both more reprehensible and less well delineated as a comic figure.

SNOPES, IKE. A character in *The Hamlet*. An idiot, Ike is the ward of his cousin Flem, but is cared for by Mrs. Littlejohn and does some work in her boardinghouse. He falls in love with Jack Houston's cow and finally runs away with her. He is caught by Houston, who is ready to give the cow to him, but Mrs. Littlejohn pays for the animal with money left with her for Ike by V. K. Ratliff. When Ike's affair with the cow becomes literally a public spectacle through the agency of his cousin Lump, Ratliff intervenes and persuades I. O. Snopes that something must be done about it. I. O. gets the other Snopeses together and they decide that the cow must be killed and fed to Ike to cure him of his unnatural passion. The burden of the animal's purchase falls on Eck Snopes, who, being a compassionate man, later gives the bereaved idiot a wooden image of his cow to console him.

SNOPES, I. O. The bigamous husband of a "gray-colored woman" and a Frenchman's Bend girl, and the father of Montgomery Ward and St. Elmo by the first, and of Clarence, Doris, and the twins Bilbo and Vardaman by the second; a character in the short story "Mule in the Yard," also appearing in *The Hamlet* and *The Town*. In *The Hamlet*, I. O. arrives in Frenchman's Bend in the wake of Flem Snopes and becomes the manager of the blacksmith shop—this in spite of the fact that he is afraid of horses and mules and that his assistant, Eck Snopes, who does most of the actual work, knows nothing about blacksmithing. I. O., given to the incessant and non-sensical stringing together of proverbs, becomes the village schoolmaster for a time. In *The Town* he runs the Jefferson restaurant that Flem has acquired from V. K. Ratliff, and later takes over the old Commercial Hotel, which he changes to the "Snopes Hotel," eventually moving the restaurant into it. He becomes involved with Lonzo Hait in a scheme of leaving mules on a blind railroad curve at night and collecting money from the railroad claims adjuster for their sudden death (this incident is recounted in "Mule in the Yard"). Finally Flem buys I. O.'s remaining mules, on the condition that I. O. move back to Frenchman's Bend and never own another business in Jefferson.

SNOPES, LINDA [1908–]. Daughter of Eula Varner and Hoake McCarron, and a character in *The Town* and *The Mansion*. In *The Town* Linda, still in her teens, is courted by Gavin Stevens, a lawyer nearly twice her age who is attracted to her partially because he had been hopelessly in love with her mother. Linda believes that Flem Snopes, her mother's husband, is her father; after her mother commits suicide to prevent her eighteen-year-long affair with Manfred de Spain from becoming a scandal, Linda goes away to New York City, where she lives with Barton Kohl, a Jewish sculptor. She marries him just before leaving with him for Spain, where they are to fight with the Loyalists in the Spanish Civil War. He is killed in a plane crash and Linda is later deafened by an exploding shell. Returning to Jefferson, she tries to improve conditions in the Negro schools and is branded a Jew, a Communist, and a nigger-lover. She goes to work in a shipyard in Pascagoula and does not return to Jefferson until after the war. She arranges to have Mink Snopes, who has sworn to kill Flem for an old slight, pardoned from the penitentiary on the condition that, if he accepts the pardon and one thousand dollars a year, he will never enter Mississippi again. Actually, Linda is counting on the fact that Mink will return to revenge himself on Flem, and in so doing revenge her mother's death.

SNOPES, LUMP [LAUNCELOT].   A character in *The Hamlet*. Flem's successor as clerk in Varner's store, Lump takes a plank out of the wall of the stable so the men can watch the idiot Ike Snopes's affair with his cow. When his cousin Mink murders Jack Houston, Lump tries to persuade him to take him to the place where the body is hidden in order to get the fifty dollars Lump is convinced Houston was carrying when he was killed. When Mrs. Armstid sues Flem Snopes for the money the Texan horse auctioneer has promised that Flem would return to her, Lump perjures himself in swearing that he saw Flem give Mrs. Armstid's money back to the Texan, who has left town.

SNOPES, MINK [1883–   ].   A character in *The Hamlet* and *The Mansion*. In *The Hamlet*, Mink allows his scrub yearling to stray into Jack Houston's pasture; Houston refuses to return the animal unless Mink pays him a three-dollar pasturage fee. In revenge Mink ambushes and kills Houston and hides his body in a hollow tree stump in the swamp. After he has been apprehended by the sheriff he repeatedly tries to send a message to his cousin Flem in Frenchman's Bend, believing that Flem must help him whether he wants to or not, because of their kinship. Flem, however, is noticeably absent from Mink's trial, and Mink vows revenge. He is sentenced to life in Parchman Penitentiary. In *The Mansion*, just before he becomes eligible for parole, he is persuaded to try to escape by his cousin Montgomery Ward Snopes, an agent of Flem's. Caught and given an additional twenty years, Mink serves all but the last two and fulfills his vow of vengeance against Flem as soon as he is released. *The Mansion* treats Mink's

killing of Houston in greater length than *The Hamlet*, giving Mink somewhat more reason for his sense of outrage: he works nights on Houston's
fences to pay for the increased value of his cow, which is estimated to be
thirty-seven dollars, since she has been well fed during the winter and bred
by a pedigreed bull; after Mink has worked out half the value of the cow,
the price agreed that he should pay, Houston adds a one-dollar pound fee
and Mink, outraged at this, ambushes him.

SNOPES, MONTGOMERY WARD.   Son of I. O. Snopes by his first wife, half-
brother of Clarence Snopes, and a character in *The Town* and *The Mansion*. In about 1915 Montgomery Ward goes to France with Gavin
Stevens * to work for the Y.M.C.A. He comes back from the war wearing
long hair, a beard, and a Basque beret, and opens a photography shop
called "Atelier Monty." In 1923 Gavin and the sheriff discover that the
photography shop is a blind for Montgomery Ward's real business—selling
pornography. Monty protests that the sheriff dare not prosecute for lack
of evidence and for fear of incriminating many of Jefferson's leading citizens, but Flem Snopes intervenes by planting bootleg whiskey in the studio
and Monty is sent to Parchman Penitentiary. In *The Mansion*, threatened
by Flem with prosecution on a federal charge of sending pornography
through the mails, Monty persuades Mink Snopes, in Parchman for murder, to try to escape, then tips off the guards so that Mink's escape is foiled.

SNOPES, ORESTES.   A character in *The Mansion*. The last Snopes to arrive
in Jefferson, Res moves into the remodeled carriage house on what was
formerly the Compson property, now owned by his cousin Flem. He raises
a few scrub cattle and hogs, principally to annoy his crotchety neighbor,
Mr. Meadowfill, into selling him his small corner of the Compson property, so that Res can resell it to an oil company to build a service station.
Res nearly succeeds in killing old man Meadowfill with a homemade
booby trap—for which the blame would naturally fall on Meadowfill's
son-in-law, a war veteran—but his attempt is thwarted by Gavin Stevens.

SNOPES, VIRGIL.   Son of Wesley Snopes, and a minor character in *Sanctuary*
and *The Mansion*. With his friend Fonzo Winbush, Virgil goes to Memphis to attend barber college. They mistake Miss Reba Rivers' brothel for
a boardinghouse and live there in complete innocence for two months until Senator Clarence Snopes arrives on the scene and enlightens them.
Virgil proves to have a remarkable capacity for women, and Clarence sets
up a small business betting skeptics that Virgil can satisfy two prostitutes
in a row.

* In *Sartoris* Montgomery Ward is mentioned as doing Y.M.C.A. work in Europe with
Horace Benbow.

SNOPES, WALLSTREET PANIC.   Son of Eck Snopes, and a character in *The Hamlet* and *The Town*. In *The Hamlet*, Wallstreet Panic is a small child who, in his enthusiasm over the wild spotted horses being auctioned, refuses to stay out of the way and narrowly escapes being trampled. In *The Town*, his family moves to Jefferson when he is twelve; he begins school and completes his education through high school in a few years. By the age of nineteen he is managing the grocery store in which he had worked while in school. Eventually he comes to own a wholesale warehouse and a chain of grocery stores. Like his father, he is a Snopes in name only, and is hard-working and honest; though successful in business, he is not avaricious. He marries a Jefferson girl who abhors the idea of Snopesism but refuses to change their name because she wants to live it down.

SNOPES, WATKINS PRODUCTS.   A character in *The Mansion*. A carpenter, Wat remodels the De Spain mansion for his cousin Flem and later does over the Compson carriage house for his cousin Orestes to live in.

SNOPES, WESLEY.   Father of Byron and Virgil Snopes, and mentioned in *The Hamlet* and *The Town*. Wes looks like a schoolmaster, but soon busies himself acting as a revival singing teacher—until he is caught with a fourteen-year-old girl pupil and run out of town on a rail.

STEINBAUER, JENNY.   A character in *Mosquitoes*. She is an idly voluptuous girl who in many ways prefigures Faulkner's later, more skilled use of the earth-mother character in Lena Grove and Eula Varner.

STEVENS, GAVIN.   A character in the short story "Hair" (in *These Thirteen*), in *Light in August*, in the title story of *Go Down, Moses*, in *Intruder in the Dust*, in *Knight's Gambit*, in *Requiem for a Nun*, in *The Town*, and in *The Mansion*. Faulkner's most ubiquitous character, Stevens is a lawyer (frequently a county attorney) and an intellectual, with degrees from Harvard and Heidelberg, but he is also a man who understands country people and can speak with them in their own idiom. A descendant of one of the original settlers of Jefferson and the son of Judge Lemuel Stevens, Gavin makes his home with his married sister, her husband, and their son, and is a mentor and guide as well as uncle to young Chick, who usually appears in the novels as Stevens' young assistant and occasionally as his interpreter. Suffering from a lifelong attraction to adolescent girls, Gavin becomes secretly engaged to young Melisandre Backus before he goes to Heidelberg, but she marries another man in his absence. He becomes infatuated with Eula Varner Snopes in *The Town* and is devoted to her through her lifetime. He transfers part of his affection to her young daughter, Linda, and tries to save her (she is a Snopes in name only) from

Snopesism by encouraging her to leave Jefferson and go away to school. In *The Mansion* he maintains a platonic relationship with Linda, now widowed and deafened, and he finally marries the widowed and wealthy Melisandre Backus Harriss (his marriage is also mentioned in the title story of *Knight's Gambit*).

In *Intruder in the Dust* he, like the rest of the citizens of Jefferson, believes Lucas Beauchamp guilty of murdering a white man until Chick finds another body in the grave. In *Requiem for a Nun* he forces Temple Drake to admit to herself—as well as to her husband—her guilt and moral responsibility for the death of her baby, killed by a Negro nursemaid to prevent Temple from running away with the brother of her former lover and thus destroying her home.

Stevens is frequently considered to be a persona of Faulkner himself, though it is far more likely that he is a mask or an antiself, in view of the fact that Stevens is first and foremost a man of reason and logic, whereas Faulkner frequently protested that it was people, rather than ideas, in which he himself was primarily interested. As an intellectual, Stevens is a speaker rather than an actor, an observer of the lives of others rather than a participant. A reasonable and rational man, he is frequently incapable of understnding the irrational aspects of human behavior. He is in some senses an idealized figure—Faulkner clearly admires him and is inclined to be perhaps too uncritical of him—of the intelligent, civilized man who maintains an almost perfect equilibrium between his status as a public servant, a member of society in good standing, and his purely personal inclinations and beliefs. As a character, he is somewhat similar to Faulkner's earlier creation of the sympathetic but emotionally rather inept lawyer Horace Benbow (see *Sanctuary*).

STEVENS, GOWAN [ca. 1909–   ]. A cousin * of Gavin Stevens, and a character in *Sanctuary*, *Requiem for a Nun*, and *The Town*. In *Sanctuary* Gowan is a drunken cavalier who, having been taught to drink like a gentleman at school in Virginia, believes that his ability to hold his liquor is an index of his manhood. After catastrophic experiences, he swears off alcohol, and later marries Temple Drake in an attempt to make up for his earlier conduct. As her husband in *Requiem for a Nun* he is a relatively stable man, but without any great force of character. In *The Town* he appears briefly as a teen-age boy who observes the rivalry between Gavin Stevens and Manfred de Spain and later passes on information about it to his young cousin, Chick Mallison.

* The actual relationship of Gowan to the rest of the Stevens family is vague; he is probably a second cousin of Gavin Stevens. Though in *Requiem for a Nun* Gowan refers to his elder relative as Uncle Gavin, the "uncle" may be a courtesy title given in deference to Gavin's age.

STEVENS GENEALOGY

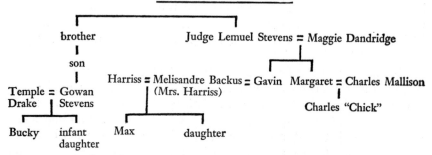

SURATT, V. K.   [see also RATLIFF, V. K.], a minor character in *Sartoris*. A sew-ing-machine salesman, Suratt takes Bayard Sartoris, just patched up from a bad fall from a horse, out to his place in Frenchman's Bend where he has a cache of whiskey. In the later novels Suratt's name is changed to Ratliff.

SUTPEN, CLYTEMNESTRA [CLYTIE] [1834–1909].   Daughter of Thomas Sut-pen and a Negro slave, half-sister of Judith and Henry Sutpen, and a minor character in *Absalom, Absalom!*. Though remaining with Judith after the war in a quasi-slave capacity, Clytie is apparently aware of her relationship to the Sutpen family. After Judith and Charles Etienne Bon die of yellow fever, Clytie stays on and cares for young Jim Bond, an idiot mulatto and the great-grandson of Sutpen through Charles Bon. When Henry Sutpen comes home in about 1905 after forty years of hiding, Clytie hides him in the plantation house and cares for him when he becomes ill. In 1909 Henry's presence is discovered by Miss Rosa Coldfield; when she sends an ambulance for Henry, Clytie mistakenly thinks it will take Henry to jail for killing Charles Bon over fifty years before. To save Henry from hang-ing, she sets fire to the house over both their heads.

SUTPEN, HENRY [1839–1909].   Son of Ellen Coldfield and Thomas Sutpen, sister of Judith Sutpen, half-brother of Charles Bon, and a character in *Absalom, Absalom!*. At the University of Mississippi Henry becomes an intimate friend of Charles Bon, not knowing that Bon is his half-brother. When Sutpen forbids Bon's marriage to Judith, Henry renounces his father and leaves home with Charles, accompanying him to New Orleans and then to the Civil War. At the end of the war Henry kills Charles at the gate to the plantation to prevent his marrying Judith. He disappears and is not heard of again until his aunt, Miss Rosa Coldfield, discovers him ill and hiding in the dilapidated plantation house in 1909. He dies when the servant Clytie burns the house to save him from hanging.

SUTPEN, JUDITH [1841–84].   Daughter of Ellen Coldfield and Thomas

SUTPEN GENEALOGY

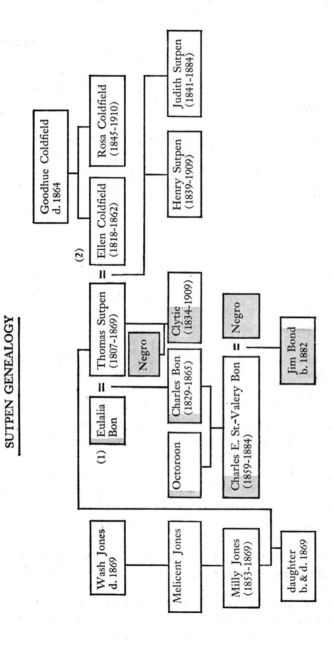

Sutpen, and a character in *Absalom, Absalom!*. Engaged to Charles Bon, her unacknowledged half-brother, Judith is widowed before she is ever a bride when her brother Henry kills Charles to prevent him from marrying her. Some years later, Judith arranges for Charles's octoroon mistress and little boy to visit his grave, and later, hearing that the octoroon has died, brings Charles's young son back to Sutpen's Hundred. When as a young man Charles's son contracts yellow fever, Judith nurses him until both die of the disease.

SUTPEN, THOMAS [1807–69]. Husband of Eulalia and father of Charles Bon, father of Clytie by a Negro slave, husband of Ellen Coldfield and father of Henry and Judith Sutpen, and the central character in *Absalom, Absalom!*. The son of a poor-white mountaineer, Sutpen as a boy was shocked at being treated as an inferior at an elegant plantation house. Concluding that the aristocracy can only be combated with their own weapons —wealth, lands, and family—he sets out to achieve them, and conceives a "grand design" to become the founder of a great Southern dynasty. He wants sons to inherit his name and position, so he divorces his first wife when he learns that she has Negro blood. Forced to start over again, he comes to Jefferson in the early 1830s and marries Ellen Coldfield, by whom he has two children, Henry and Judith.

Shortly before the outbreak of the Civil War young Henry Sutpen becomes a friend of Charles Bon, Sutpen's unacknowledged son by his first wife. Sutpen believes that he is acting morally, and in the interests of his "design," when he refuses to recognize Charles as his son, but as a result of Sutpen's seemingly groundless refusal to let Judith marry Charles, Henry repudiates his birthright and goes with Charles to New Orleans. Finally, at the end of the war, Henry kills Charles and flees, taking with him Sutpen's hope of grandchildren to carry on his name. In an attempt to provide himself with a new male heir Sutpen becomes engaged to his young sister-in-law, Rosa Coldfield, but makes the mistake of suggesting that their marriage not take place until she has proved that she can bear him a son; scandalized, she leaves the plantation. He then seduces the fifteen-year-old granddaughter of his poor-white handyman, Wash Jones, but the girl gives birth to a daughter. Jones, mortified and disillusioned at Sutpen's attitude toward the girl and her baby, kills him.

SUTTERFIELD, REVEREND TOBE. A character in *A Fable*. A Negro stable hand and lay preacher, he becomes the head of Les Amis Myriades et Anonymes à la France de Tout le Monde, a society for peace endowed by a wealthy American widow. He is also known as "Monsieur Tooleymon."

TALLIAFERRO, ERNEST. A character in *Mosquitoes*. He is a foolish, garrulous man who fancies himself something of a dandy with women.

TENNIE'S JIM. See Beauchamp, James.

TOMEY'S TURL or TERREL. See Beauchamp, Turl.

TOMMY. A character in *Sanctuary*. A feeble-minded white man living with the bootlegger Lee Goodwin at the Old Frenchman Place, Tommy is good-natured and kind; he is murdered by Popeye while trying to protect Temple Drake.

T. P. A minor character in *The Sound and the Fury*. He was Benjy Compson's nurse boy from about 1910 until the mid-1920's.

TULL, CORA. Wife of Vernon Tull, and a minor character in *As I Lay Dying* and *The Hamlet*. In *As I Lay Dying* Cora is a comic figure, the apotheosis of conventional piety. She frequently exhorts her friend and neighbor, Addie Bundren, to lay aside her pride and repent her sins, but Addie refuses, believing that to people like Cora sin was just a word, and that therefore salvation was just a word too. Cora, convinced of the rightness of her beliefs, talks incessantly, unaware of the emptiness of her life behind her words. In *The Hamlet* she unsuccessfully sues Flem Snopes for damages sustained when one of Flem's wild spotted horses collides with the Tull wagon.

TULL, VERNON. Husband of Cora Tull, a neighbor of the Bundren family, and a minor character in *As I Lay Dying*, *The Hamlet*, and "Shingles for the Lord." In *As I Lay Dying* Tull, the Bundrens' nearest neighbor, is the narrator of six sections; his position of close neighbor makes him an important outside observer of the family. He describes actions, but unlike his wife never makes judgments. Like the other neighbors, he offers Anse the use of his team and wagon, which Anse refuses. After the Bundrens discover that Samson's bridge is out they return to Tull's and cross his ford. In *The Hamlet* he is one of the three country people who falls for Flem Snopes's trick of salting the Old Frenchman Place with buried money.

VARNER, EULA [1889–1927]. Youngest child of Will Varner, wife of Flem Snopes, mother of Linda Snopes, and a character in *The Hamlet* and *The Town*. A physically precocious child, passive and sensual even as a young girl, Eula is at first presented as a kind of vegetable Helen of Troy, placid to the point of immobility, unselfconscious and seemingly unaware of the turmoil she stirs up in any male who chances to see her. At seventeen, she is courted by, among others, a young man named Hoake McCarron, by whom she becomes pregnant. McCarron leaves town, and Eula is married to Flem Snopes; her daughter, Linda, is born during their year-long Texas honeymoon. In *The Town* Eula becomes the mistress of Manfred de Spain, first the mayor and later a bank president in Jefferson; her husband is impotent and she and De Spain are adulterously faithful for eighteen years. She kills herself to prevent scandal when Flem tries to force De Spain out of the presidency of the bank.

VARNER, JODY. Son of Will Varner and a character in *The Hamlet*. A corpulent man in his thirties, Jody clerks in his father's store until Flem Snopes arrives on the scene. In an attempt to protect the Varner barns from the threat of Flem's barn-burning father, Jody tries to trick the Snopeses out of their crop, but is taken in his own trap. A comic character, Jody is typical of those who, though appearing respectable and reasonably law-abiding, feel that the semblance of respectability is as good as the real thing and that anything one can get away with is right action. It is he, and others like him, who inadvertently aid Flem in his rise to power.

VARNER, WILL [UNCLE BILLY]. Father of Jody and Eula Varner, and a minor character in *The Hamlet*, *The Town*, and *The Mansion*. The wealthiest and most powerful man in Frenchman's Bend, Varner owns most of the land in the area, as well as the cotton gin, grist mill, blacksmith shop, and village store. When his daughter Eula becomes pregnant, he marries her to Flem Snopes, unloading the worthless Old Frenchman Place as part of Eula's dowry. One of the cofounders and major stockholders of Colonel Sartoris' bank in Jefferson, he uses his influence to get Flem the vice-presidency of the bank, and is later forced to help Flem get Manfred de Spain, the president, out of office and Flem installed in his place. He is described as being "anything in the world but unmoral since his were the strictest of simple moral standards: that whatever Will Varner decided to do was right, and anybody in the way had damned well better beware." (276, T) In *The Mansion* he takes part in a plot to prevent Clarence Snopes, a Mississippi State Senator whose office is due to Varner's influence, from announcing himself as a candidate for Congress, and succeeds in eliminating him from politics altogether.

VERSH. A minor character in *The Sound and the Fury*. Versh was Benjy Compson's nurse boy until ca. 1910.

WEST, DAVID. A minor character in *Mosquitoes*. David, a steward on Mrs.

Maurier's yacht, falls in love with Pat Robyn and attempts to elope with her to Mandeville.

WHITFIELD, PREACHER.   One-time lover of Addie Bundren, father of Jewel Bundren, and a minor character in *As I Lay Dying*. Some twenty years before the novel takes place Whitfield had been the lover of Addie Bundren, who had turned to him after discovering that there was no real emotional contact between herself and her husband. In Addie's mind Whitfield is a strong and vital man who knows the reality of love and is not misled by empty phrases. When he hears she is dying, he wrestles with his conscience and decides that he should confess his sin to the deceived husband. Addie dies, however, before he can reach the Bundren farm, and Whitfield interprets this to mean that God has accepted his intention to confess for the deed itself; he says nothing to Anse. Whitfield is occasionally mentioned in several of the novels and stories but rarely appears as an important character. In "Shingles for the Lord" he is the minister of the Frenchman's Bend Methodist Church. He performs an emergency wedding in the story "Tomorrow" in *Knight's Gambit*. In *The Hamlet* he is described as "a harsh, stupid, honest, superstitious, and an upright man." (205)

WILBOURNE, HARRY.   A central character in *The Wild Palms*. He is a rigid, puritanistic young interne who tries to reject his background and live only for love.

WILKINS, GEORGE.   A minor character in "The Fire and the Hearth" in *Go Down, Moses*. Wilkins encroaches on Lucas Beauchamp's whiskey-still territory and eventually causes Lucas to be arrested.

WINBUSH, GROVER CLEVELAND.   A character in *The Town*. With V. K. Ratliff, Winbush owns a backstreet restaurant in Jefferson, but soon after Ratliff sells his interest to Flem Snopes, Winbush is weaseled out of his share. He becomes the night marshal, a job he holds until he cannot be found on the night of a robbery and it comes out that he has been frequenting Montgomery Ward Snopes's pornography studio.

WISEMAN, EVA.   A minor character in *Mosquitoes*.

WORSHAM, MISS EUNICE.   A character in the title story of *Go Down, Moses*. Raised with the Negro Molly Worsham Beauchamp almost as with a sister, Miss Worsham comes to Molly's aid and helps her have her grandson, executed for murder in Chicago, brought home and given a proper burial. In *Intruder in the Dust* Miss Worsham appears again, but is named Miss Eunice Habersham.

FAULKNER'S LIFE has not yet become the subject of a full-length and thoroughly researched biography; there are, however, a number of shorter pieces—three small books, Ward L. Miner's *The World of William Faulkner* (1952), Robert Coughlan's *The Private World of William Faulkner* (1953), John Faulkner's *My Brother Bill* (1963), and a variety of articles, introductions, and brief biographical résumés in critical studies. Unfortunately, the biographical material in the majority of these books has been collected at second hand from earlier sources; as a result, Faulkner biography tends to be at best contradictory in regard to small details, vague in spots, and sometimes howlingly apocryphal, notably on the subjects of his more than twenty-year-long alliance with Hollywood, his fondness for good bourbon, and his unwillingness to be impressed with visiting celebrities. Faulkner himself is responsible for a good part of the current misinformation about him, for he seems to have delighted in improving on the bare facts of his existence as much as in inventing the tales that have made him famous. Reportedly a prolific fabricator of stories from childhood, he jealously ensured the privacy of his personal life by creating for himself a public image—and, from a biographical point of view at least, succeeded only too well. Not only are the mere facts of his private life—particularly from the time of his first commercial success with *Sanctuary* in 1931 until his winning of the Nobel Prize in 1950—largely unavailable to the public, but a considerable number of the available facts, including Faulkner's own comments on his life, must be taken with a large grain of salt.

Of Faulkner's twenty novels, fifteen are set in Yoknapatawpha County; of his major works—*The Sound and the Fury, As I Lay Dying, Light in August, Absalom, Absalom!, The Hamlet, Go Down, Moses,* and *A Fable*—all but *A Fable* take place in his "mythical kingdom," a fabulous section of northern Mississippi that is recognizably patterned after Lafayette County, of which Oxford, Faulkner's home during almost all his life, is the county seat. Ward L. Miner, in his study of Yoknapatawpha County vis-à-vis the actual county of Lafayette, has pointed out the parallels and contrasts between them; certainly Faulkner assimilated and used the quasi-legendary material of Lafayette County's past and present, transforming it and its people into the raw material for his own legend of the South, infusing it with a mythic power beyond reality and creating a world that transcends its prototype to become a microcosm reflecting the universal struggle of man in conflict with his environment, his fellows, or his heart. The sources of Faulkner's legend were all around him, though it took him thirty years to discover the potential literary wealth amid which he had grown up. Not until he began *Sartoris* (1929), his third novel, did he begin to realize that "my own little postage stamp of native soil was worth writing about and that I would never live long enough to exhaust it, and that by sublimating the actual into the apocryphal I would have complete liberty to use whatever talent I might have to its absolute top." (*Three Decades of Criticism*, p. 82.)

The legends of Faulkner's ancestry thus have more than simple biographical relevance. "When I was a little boy," he said once, "there'd be sometimes twenty or thirty people in the house, mostly relatives . . . some maybe coming for overnight and staying on for months, swapping stories about the family and about the past, while I sat in a corner and listened. That's where I got my books." (Quoted by Robert N. Linscott in *Esquire*, July, 1963).

Originally from Carolina, the Faulkner family * emigrated first to Tennessee, where William Cuthbert Faulkner, the novelist's great-grandfather, was born in 1825. At about fourteen young Faulkner left home for Mississippi and went to live with his uncle, John Wesley Thompson, in Ripley (Tippah County), about fifty miles northeast of Oxford. At the outbreak of the Mexican War he joined the "Tippah Volunteers" and was elected lieutenant, but was never actually involved in combat. After the war he read law in his uncle's office, and in 1847 married Holland Pearce, from Knoxville, who later died bearing his first son, named John Wesley Thompson for Faulkner's uncle.

In 1849 began the first of several incidents that were to make W. C. Faulkner's life as bloodily colorful and complicated as that of any character of fiction. Apparently one Robert Hindman applied for membership in a local secret society and heard (what may not have been the case) that Faulkner had spoken against him. Hindman confronted Faulkner, pulling a pistol which failed to fire the first two times he pulled the trigger; before he could fire again, Faulkner stabbed and killed him.† Faulkner was tried and acquitted on the grounds that he had acted in self-defense. As soon as the trial was over, however, he was attacked outside the courthouse by Hindman's younger brother, and in the ensuing fracas Faulkner killed one

* The information on Faulkner's family history is largely based on Robert Cantwell's introduction to *Sartoris* (Signet edition, first printing July, 1953) and his essay "The Faulkners: Recollections of a Gifted Family," included in *Three Decades of Criticism*.
† Robert Cantwell (in his "Recollections") believes that evidence strongly suggests a plot by unknowns to incite Hindman to a murderous rage, provide him with a malfunctioning gun, and therefore practically guarantee his death at the hands of his attempted victim.

of Hindman's friends. Faulkner was tried and acquitted once again. Following the trial there was one more incident involving young Hindman, but it did not end in bloodshed. Feeling ran high and bitter, and the town was split in its sympathies during the more than two-year-long period that the feud continued. Finally Hindman challenged Faulkner to a duel, but a peacemaking friend intervened and it was called off at the last moment. Hindman moved to Arkansas, and shortly thereafter Faulkner met and married Elizabeth Vance—according to the family legend, the little girl, now grown up, who had given fourteen-year-old William a cup of water, and whom he had thereupon promised to marry, when he first arrived in Ripley looking for his uncle.

At the outbreak of the Civil War Faulkner organized a volunteer regiment and, as its colonel, led it to the first battle of Manassas. At the yearly election of officers, however, the regiment deposed him and elected another man colonel. In a pique, Colonel Faulkner rode back to Ripley and raised another outfit. After the war he entered a partnership with Richard J. Thurmond, * a banker and lawyer, in order to build a railroad—the Ripley, Ship Island, and Kentucky, which was completed in 1872 and ran between Ripley and Middelton, Tennessee. Colonel Faulkner had become by the mid-1870s one of the most influential and powerful citizens of Ripley. Besides the railroad, he had a thriving law practice, a military and political record (he had helped establish the "Know Nothing" party in Mississippi before the war), a large plantation, and a grist mill, cotton mill, and sawmill. About this time, having heard that "some no-good people" named Faulkner were living in a nearby town, the colonel dropped the "u" from his name to avoid confusion. In 1880 the building that housed the Ripley *Advertiser* burned, and, in order to get the paper going again, Colonel Falkner advanced money and began to write a book to be serialized to help promotion. The *Advertiser* flourished, and the serial, *The White Rose of Memphis*, was published in book form, going through thirty-five editions before it finally went out of print (it was reissued, with a preface by Robert Cantwell, in 1953). Falkner also wrote another novel, *The Little Brick Church*, a volume dealing with his European travels, and various essays.

Toward the end of the 1880s Colonel Falkner had extended his railroad southward, and wanted eventually to bring it to Gulfport. Thurmond apparently disagreed with his plan, and their disagreement (both men seem to have been hot-tempered and stubborn) became a bitter feud. Finally Thurmond offered to sell his interest at a price so high that, even though the colonel was a wealthy man, he was obliged to borrow and mortgage frantically to raise the money. In 1889, soon after this incident, Falkner ran

* Cantwell gives Thurmond's first initials as "J.H."—a puzzling circumstance, inasmuch as he quotes Colonel Faulkner addressing Thurmond as "Dick."

for the state legislature; Thurmond ran against him, lost, and shot Falkner, who died the next day. Thurmond was tried but acquitted, on the evidence of witnesses who said that Falkner had drawn first. Although there are conflicting stories, it seems almost certain that Falkner, who normally carried a gun, was unarmed on that day, and was completely surprised by Thurmond's attack on him.

After Colonel Falkner's death, John, his son by his first wife, moved to Oxford with his wife, the former Sallie Murry. John inherited the title of colonel, becoming known as the "young Colonel." His youngest son, Murry, married Maud Butler and moved to New Albany, about thirty miles from Oxford.

The young Colonel, who was apparently a somewhat paler version of his colorful father, extended the railroad and became president of the First National Bank of Oxford, of which he later lost control (he then withdrew all his money and carried it in a bucket to the rival bank across the square).* His youngest son, Murry, lived a very placid life. He was a conductor on the family railroad, then went into the livery-stable business, the hardware business, and finally became secretary and business manager of the University of Mississippi.

The son of Murry and Maud Butler Falkner, William was born in New Albany on September 25, 1897, and was a small child when the family moved to Oxford. A quiet boy who liked to read, he was a notorious spinner of tall tales and, according to legend, replied to his third-grade teacher when asked what he wanted to be when he grew up, "I want to be a writer like my great-grandaddy." His schooling was erratic; according to most sources, he attended school only intermittently after he began to work in his grandfather's bank, and left high school completely after the tenth grade. When he was in his teens he began to write poetry and was taken under the literary wing of Phil Stone, the son of one of Oxford's oldest families and a graduate of Yale studying law at the University of Mississippi. Stone thought that William's verses showed talent, encouraged and directed his reading, and was very probably—and certainly according to Stone himself—one of the most important influences in the shaping of his career.

Thanks to the excellent work of Carvel Collins in compiling and reissuing Faulkner's earliest known work for the University of Mississippi newspaper, *The Mississippian* (see *Early Prose and Poetry*) and for the New Orleans *Times-Picayune* (see *New Orleans Sketches*), a great deal of the misinformation concerning Faulkner's life between 1918 and 1926 has been

* Cf. the episode in *The Town* in which Flem Snopes, in an attempt to start a panic at Manfred de Spain's bank, withdraws all his money and carries it in a bucket across the square to the rival bank.

cleared up. Contrary to popular legend, fostered by Faulkner himself, he did not enlist in the Royal Canadian Air Force (Canada had no air force in the First World War), nor did he ever fly in combat. On July 8, 1918, he left Oxford for Toronto, Canada, where he entered flight training in Britain's Royal Air Force; he was made an honorary second lieutenant on December 22, 1918, a month after the armistice. However, Faulkner's legendarizing of his air force career has more than once gone into print as gospel truth. According to Anthony Buttitta (*The Saturday Review of Literature*, May 21, 1928), formerly editor of *Contempo*, in which some of Faulkner's early work was published, Faulkner was transferred to Oxford, England, where he was in training as a noncommissioned officer for more than a year, taking some courses at Oxford in his spare time. He was made a lieutenant in the R.A.F., sent to France as an observer, and crashed twice and was wounded once. Marshall J. Smith, in an earlier article (*The Bookman*, Dec., 1931) quotes Faulkner as reporting essentially the same story— obviously pure invention amusedly handed out by Faulkner to improve on a rather undramatic air force career.

Faulkner continued to write poetry, and on August 6, 1919, *New Republic* published "L'Apres-Midi d'un Faune," his first piece of writing known to have appeared in print. *Ole Miss*, the University of Mississippi annual, had published some of Faulkner's drawings, done in a style suggestive of John Held, in the yearbooks for 1916–17 and 1917–18. The question of who put the "u" back in Faulkner's last name (dropped by Faulkner's great-grandfather and not reinstated by the family) may as well be parenthetically answered here, inasmuch as "L'Apres-Midi d' un Faune" was signed by one William *Faulkner*—this in 1919. Thereafter, he used both spellings of the name until approximately 1921; after that year he consistently signed himself "Faulkner." There is thus no validity in the oftenrepeated story that, when *The Marble Faun* was published in 1924, a printer's error resulted in the mispelling of the author's name from Falkner to Faulkner—a change that Faulkner supposedly adopted at that time.

In September of 1919, Faulkner registered as a special student at the University of Mississippi, enrolling in French, Spanish, and a survey course in English literature. He began to publish poems in *The Mississippian*, the university newspaper; in November his first published short story, "Landing in Luck," appeared in the paper. It dealt with a young air force cadet in flight training in Canada and was a creditable, competent piece of work. Faulkner continued to contribute poems during the spring semester, and the following fall again enrolled at the university, but withdrew in November. *The Mississippian* retained his name as one of its "Contributing Editors" and continued to publish his poems, articles, and reviews, through December, 1922.

On an invitation from Stark Young, whom he had known at Oxford,

Faulkner left for New York City, probably in hopes of making some contacts in the publishing world. Nothing of that sort materialized, but he made at least one fortunate acquaintance: Elizabeth Prall, who was later the wife of Sherwood Anderson. Young lived in a room in Miss Prall's house, and Faulkner shared Young's quarters for a time. Faulkner held a series of odd jobs—among them clerking in a bookstore of which Miss Prall was manager—but accomplished little in the way of meeting friendly editors and publishers and returned to Oxford late in 1921. He took an examination for the temporary postmastership of the university post office, and was permanently appointed to the position in March of 1922. However, his tendency to read while on duty—according to some sources, he included the mail as part of his reading material, finding personal letters a rich source for future fiction—and generally to neglect the distribution and handling of mail began to elicit complaints, and on October 31, 1924, he resigned from his position.

The end of his postmastership rather neatly marks the end of one period of his life, a period that might be considered a preapprenticeship to the craft of an artist in which Faulkner had not found himself artistically —indeed, had not even any real conception of the direction in which his talent could be most fully realized. Whether or not he ever seriously considered himself a graphic artist is difficult to determine; his drawings show both talent and wit, but little originality. His poetry, which he certainly did take seriously, is also imitative, rather thickly populated with nymphs, fauns, and other pastoral creatures, and tends to err on the side of overrich language; yet occasionally, as in "Study," he achieves a voice and a stance that is his own, a subtle mixture of linguistic sensitivity and wit:

> Somewhere a slender voiceless breeze will go
> Unlinking the shivering poplars' arms, and brakes
> With sleeves simply crossed where waters flow;
> A sunless stream quiet and deep, that slakes
> The thirsty alders pausing there at dawn.
> (Hush, now, hush. Where was I? Jonson)
>
> Somewhere a candle's guttering gold
> Weaves a tapestry upon a cottage wall
> And her gold hair, simple fold on fold,
> While I can think of nothing else at all
> Except the sunset in her eyes' still pool.
> (Work, work, you fool!—)
>
> Somewhere a blackbird lost within a wood
> Whistles through its golden wired throat;
> Some ways are white with birches in a hood

Of silver shaken by his mellow note,
Trembling gaspingly as though in fear;
Where the timid violet first appear.

(Muted dreams for them, for me
Bitter science. Exams are near
And my thoughts uncontrollably
Wander, and I cannot hear
The voice telling me that work I must,
For everything will be the same when I am dead
A thousand years. I wish I were a bust
All head.)

The unevenness of his poetry, however, is evident from only a few lines of "Naiad's Song," published in *The Mississippian* a few months earlier than "Study."

Come ye sorrowful and keep
Tryst with us here in wedded sleep,
The silent noon lies over us
And shaken ripples cover us,
Our arms are soft as is the stream.
Come keep with us our slumbrous dream
Disheartened ones, if ye are sad,
If ye are in a garment clad
Of sorrow, come with us to sleep
In undulations dim and deep;
Where sunlight spreads and quivering lies
To draw in golden reveries
Its fingers through our glistered hair,
Finding profound contentment there.

This poem, imitative in content and unremarkable in style, hardly foreshadows a brilliant poetic career. However, like most of his poetry, it indicates the depth and direction of his reading and of his literary taste in general. In his teens a devotee of Swinburne, he later came to the Elizabethans, Shakespeare, Spenser, Shelley, and Keats—standard fare for any student of literature—and, significantly, recognized a potential greatness in the new literary lights of the twenties. He wrote articles in praise of Eugene O'Neill, Conrad Aiken, and Joseph Hergesheimer, and took pot shots at the "American critic," who "Takes the piece under examination for an instrument upon which to run difficult arpeggios of cleverness. . . . His trade becomes mental gymnastics . . . holding the yokelry enravished, not

with what he says, but how he says it." (110, EP&P) He was strongly influ-
enced by the French symbolist movement, particularly by Paul Verlaine,
four of whose poems Faulkner "adapted." Actually, Faulkner's poems from
Verlaine are verse translations that, except for an occasional error, are very
close to a literal translation from the French.

The fruit of this five-year period of apprenticeship appeared in December of 1924 with the publication of Faulkner's first book, a collection of
poems entitled *The Marble Faun*. It included a preface by Phil Stone,
whose financial and other assistance had largely been responsible for its
publication.

Faulkner had decided by this time to leave Mississippi. It is possible
that he visited New Orleans in order to meet Sherwood Anderson, now living there with his wife, the former Elizabeth Prall, whom Faulkner had
known in New York. At any rate, in January of 1925 he left Oxford for
New Orleans. He intended to sail from there for Europe, but for some
reason the European jaunt was postponed and he settled in the Vieux
Carré for about six months. He began writing sketches for the Sunday
feature section of the New Orleans *Times-Picayune* and for *The Double
Dealer*, a "little magazine" published in New Orleans, in which one of
Faulkner's poems had appeared in 1922. One of the best of the little magazines published by the literary avant-garde during the twenties, *The Double
Dealer* was strongly aware of new currents in American literature. It published the early work of many then-unknown writers, among them Hart
Crane, Sherwood Anderson, Ernest Hemingway, Robert Penn Warren,
Thornton Wilder, and Edmund Wilson. As the center of much of the
literary life in New Orleans, *The Double Dealer* provided Faulkner with
the acquaintance of many of its editors and contributors, and undoubtedly
sharpened his awareness of the literary revolution taking place around him
and to which he himself was to contribute so greatly.

In addition to his contacts through *The Double Dealer*, Faulkner had
an invaluable associate in Sherwood Anderson, who returned to New
Orleans in March after an absence of a few months. In 1925 Anderson was
nearly forty, already an established writer, whose *Winesburg, Ohio* (1919)
had found a good deal of popularity and literary acclaim. Faulkner had
read, and been greatly impressed with, Anderson's work, considering his
short story "I'm a Fool" one of the two best short stories he had ever read.
The other was Conrad's *Heart of Darkness*. (Collins, NOS, 18) According
to both Faulkner and Anderson, it was the older man who was responsible
for turning Faulkner's interest away from poetry toward fiction. Writing in
the *Atlantic* in 1953, Faulkner commented on Anderson's life and work
habits: ". . . here was a man who would be in seclusion all forenoon—
working. Then in the afternoon he would appear and we would walk about
the city, talking. Then in the evening we would meet again, with a bottle

now, and now we would really talk. . . . Then tomorrow forenoon and he would be secluded again—working; whereupon I said to myself, 'If this is what it takes to be a novelist, then that's the life for me.' " According to legend, Faulkner thereupon disappeared for six weeks to write his first novel, *Soldier's Pay*. Anderson agreed to place it with his publisher, Horace Liveright, as long as he, Anderson, did not have to read it. However it came about, Liveright listened to Anderson's recommendation, read the manuscript, and agreed to buy it. The novel appeared in 1926, received some favorable critical attention, but sold poorly.

Faulkner's friendship with Anderson had at least one other important result, for their excursions together as members of yachting parties on Lake Ponchartrain became the material from which Faulkner drew his second novel, *Mosquitoes* (1927), in which Anderson appears as the novelist Dawson Fairchild. Aside from being the most successfully delineated character in the novel, Fairchild tells a series of tall tales of the swamps—according to Faulkner, stories that he and Anderson cooked up. Though brief, they are among the best pieces of writing in the book. A satire on literary life and literary lion hunters in New Orleans, *Mosquitoes* is the work of a promising writer, but not in itself a particularly good novel. It reflects the influence particularly of Aldous Huxley, whose social satire was brilliant, acid, and popular among young writers and intellectuals. However, though its style was one not well suited to Faulkner's talents, its main theme—that talk has been substituted for action, that words have become only dead shadows of the actualities they represent—recurs again and again in his major novels.

With his friend William Spratling, an artist, Faulkner collaborated on a little book of caricatures of residents of the French Quarter called *Sherwood Anderson and other Famous Creoles* (1926). Faulkner wrote the introduction in a parody of Anderson's style, and this, unfortunately, offended Anderson and terminated their friendship for many years. Despite this incident, however, Anderson continued to speak warmly of Faulkner's talent. Faulkner, in 1929, dedicated *Sartoris* to his former mentor, remembering that it was through Anderson's kindness that he was first published, and believing "that this book will give him no reason to regret that fact."

Faulkner himself claims to have worked for a bootlegger during his stay in New Orleans. This colorful bit of Faulknerana may not have much basis in fact, inasmuch as he himself dates his rum-running days between 1921 and 1923—years during which, according to more reliable evidence, he was in Oxford. However, one may discount the years he gives as a reasonable lapse of memory, and enjoy the story:

> I ran a launch from New Orleans across Pontchartrain down the industrial canal out into the Gulf where the schooner from Cuba would bring the

raw alcohol and bury it on a sand-spit and we'd dig it up and bring it back to the bootlegger and his mother—she was an Italian, she was a nice little old lady, and she was the expert, she would turn it into Scotch with a little creosote, and bourbon. We had the labels, the bottles, everything—it was quite a business. (21, F IN U)

His flight training as a cadet in the R.A.F. provided him with a long-lived interest in flying—an interest that is reflected in his short stories about war pilots and in *Pylon*, a novel dealing with stunt fliers. According to Robert Coughlan, on one occasion Faulkner did some wing-walking for a flying circus near New Orleans. Though he did not mention the location, Faulkner related having done some "barnstorming in the early days after the War, when aeroplanes were not too usual and people would pay a hundred dollars to be taken for a short ride in one." (68, F IN U) Later, in Oxford, Faulkner kept a plane, and is reported (*News-Week*, March 30, 1935) to have run a flying circus at the Memphis airport.

In July of 1925 Faulkner and Spratling embarked for Europe on the freighter *West Ivis*. They landed in Genoa, spending some time in Italy, Switzerland, and Paris. Faulkner was still writing poetry, as well as sketches for the *Times-Picayune*, and, while in Paris, was reportedly working on a novel. He returned to the United States toward the end of 1925, and went back to Oxford, where, according to the information he gave to the New Orleans *Item* the following autumn, he spent the spring working as a professional golfer at the Oxford country club and, among other things, shot a hole in one. During the summer he worked in a lumber mill, and then on fishing boats on the Mississippi coast (probably Pascagoula) where he worked nights on *Mosquitoes*. The novel was published early in 1927 and sold even less well than *Soldier's Pay*. Liveright, who had contracted for three novels, felt unable to accept another book and broke the contract.

Faulkner returned to Oxford, where he supported himself intermittently at such odd jobs as carpentering and house painting. In 1929, though he had no steady job and his prospects of becoming financially successful as a writer were poor, he married Estelle Oldham Franklin, whom he had known since childhood and who had recently returned to Oxford with her two children from a previous marriage. In January of that year Harcourt, Brace and Company had published *Sartoris*, Faulkner's first novel to deal with his mythical Yoknapatawpha County. *Sartoris* is a good novel, if not a great one. The difference between it and his two previous books is remarkable, and perhaps can only be explained by the fact that, with *Sartoris*, Faulkner stopped imitating and began to speak in his own voice, to write from the heart rather than from the head. *Sartoris* has none of the weary sophistication of *Soldier's Pay*, nor the superficial slickness and interminable talk of *Mosquitoes*. It is structurally weak, and the writing tends to be perhaps overromantic in spots, but it has a conviction and latent power that foreshadows the immense stature of the novels that were to follow almost immediately upon its heels. It is certainly indicative of the magnitude of Faulkner's genius that, after five years of trying on poetry for size and another five of unsuccessfully borrowing other writers' novelistic styles, he should, so rapidly and with such certainty, find himself as a novelist and proceed to write *The Sound and the Fury*, one of the foremost American novels of the twentieth century. Published in October of 1929, *The Sound and the Fury* is indisputably the work of a master craftsman, of a mature artist with a depth of vision and originality equaled by no other contemporary American novelist. Yet, except for a small wave of excitement in literary circles, the book received little popular attention.

With *Sartoris*, Faulkner found his theme, the development of which would fill fifteen novels and many short stories, and still not be exhausted. Writing of his own land, of a tradition and a people of which he was a part, he was no longer obviously imitative of other successful young writers, no longer struggling to find a subject and a style suitable to his individual and phenomenal talent. *Sartoris*, of all his novels, draws most heavily on his own personal background. Colonel John Sartoris was obviously modeled on Colonel William C. Falkner, for the major incidents in both their careers are the same: both failed to be reelected as colonel of their first Civil War troop and came home to raise another; both were leading citizens and railroad builders; both met their deaths at the hands of business partners. It is difficult to determine if there was a similarity of personality, and perhaps not particularly important. It is interesting, though, that both figures— certainly Colonel Sartoris, and very probably, at least, Colonel Falkner —were romanticized by their descendants to the degree that, whatever their personal failings, their deeds became the materials for family myth.

Following *Sartoris* there came a creative period in Faulkner's life that is unmatched in the history of American fiction; between 1929 and 1936 Faulkner published six novels, two collections of short stories, and wrote a large part of *The Hamlet* (not published until 1940). Of the novels—*The Sound and the Fury* (1929), *As I Lay Dying* (1930), *Sanctuary* (1931), *Light in August* (1932), *Pylon* (1935), *Absalom, Absalom!* (1936)—all but *Pylon* are set in Yoknapatawpha County, and all but *Pylon* and *Sanctuary* are major works of a mature writer.

There are many structural flaws in *Sartoris*, almost none in *The Sound and the Fury*, written at almost the same time. *As I Lay Dying* was written in six weeks and needed almost no revision; like the preceding novel, it was perfectly conceived, almost perfectly executed. *Sanctuary*, though admittedly not up to the standard of the rest of his work, has unduly suffered from Faulkner's comment that he wrote it purely to make money and selected the most "horrific tale [he] could imagine." The original story (written before *As I Lay Dying*) may indeed have been horrific, but Faulkner, seeing it in galleys, decided that after all it would not do, that he could not insult the integrity of *The Sound and the Fury* and *As I Lay Dying* by allowing *Sanctuary* to appear in its original form. The galleys, which have been preserved, indicate the extent of his revisions. Faulkner rewrote the book almost in its entirety, changing the order of many of the sequences and adding a good deal. However, author's corrections in galleys involved resetting and additional printing expense, and Faulkner paid in cold cash for the pleasure of rewriting *Sanctuary*. *Light in August* is among his best work, but *Pylon* (though admired in Europe) is generally considered by American critics to be a failure. It was written after he had begun *Absalom, Absalom!*; having troubles with the latter, he wrote *Pylon* "to get away from it for awhile." Strangely enough, *Absalom, Absalom!* is very possibly his best novel; *Pylon* is almost certainly his worst.

During the summer of 1929 Faulkner worked firing boilers in the university power plant, where he wrote *As I Lay Dying* during the slack hours between midnight and 4:00 A.M., using an overturned wheelbarrow as a table. The publication of *Sanctuary* in 1931 brought him his first popular success, for even his revised version contained enough elements of the sensational to ensure moralistic cries of horror and consequent high sales. From a relatively unknown author with a following only among a handful of intellectuals he became the man of the moment and was suddenly very much in demand. In no time he was spirited off to Hollywood to write scripts; besides writing film versions of *Sanctuary*, the short story "Turnabout" (filmed as *Today We Live*), and *Intruder in the Dust* (novel, 1948; film, 1949), he worked on other pictures for Hollywood off and on over a period of more than twenty years. Though his connection with Hollywood was mutually profitable, Faulkner had little love for movieland life and considered his script work purely a financial necessity. He had bought a house dating back to before the Civil War which was badly in need of expensive repairs, and he was supporting (prior to 1935, when his brother Dean was killed in it) a small plane, so his expenses were anything but light. Except for his trips to Hollywood, and a few short excursions to New York, Faulkner spent most of his time in Oxford, as much as possible out of the public eye.

Between 1936 and 1950 Faulkner did relatively little writing. He wrote "An Odor of Verbena" and tacked it on to six stories published in magazines between 1934 and 1936 to form *The Unvanquished* (1938). He went back to a group of stories published between 1931 and 1939 and rewrote them to form *The Hamlet* (1940). In 1942 he published *Go Down, Moses*, a series of short stories unified in theme and subject matter, and in 1948 *Intruder in the Dust*, the central character of which had appeared in *Go Down, Moses*. *Knight's Gambit* (1949) is a collection of short stories (all but one previously published) involving Gavin Stevens and Chick Mallison, characters from *Intruder in the Dust*. After the bombing of Pearl Harbor in 1941, Faulkner conceived the idea central to *A Fable* (1954), upon which he worked intermittently from 1944 until 1953. His only major work to be set outside of Yoknapatawpha County, and his most abstract and philosophical treatment of themes common to his earlier major novels, *A Fable* is generally regarded as an important statement of Faulkner's beliefs, but a book whose complexity tends to defeat its own purpose. Of the novels on which he worked during these years, only *The Hamlet*, *Go Down, Moses*, and *A Fable* come even close to the excellence of his earlier works.

With the exception of a few articles (by George Marion O'Donnell, Warren Beck, and Conrad Aiken), early criticism of Faulkner's work was largely unfavorable, even by critics who ought to have known better. By the mid-forties all of his books except *Sanctuary* were out of print. In 1945, however, Malcolm Cowley collected and edited a selection of his work for the Viking *Portable* series, and Cowley's judicious job of editing and introducing became the genesis of a Faulkner revival—a rare thing to happen to a living author. Faulkner's winning of the Nobel Prize for 1949 (awarded 1950) and his deservedly famous acceptance speech completed the ascent toward fame Cowley's work had begun for him, and Faulkner found himself squarely in the public eye—the last place on earth, it seemed, he wished to be.

Following the Nobel Prize, Faulkner was suddenly overwhelmed with recognition. In 1951 he was presented with L'Òrdre National de la Légion d'Honneur by the French consul in New Orleans. In the same year he was awarded the National Book Award for his *Collected Stories*. In May of 1952 he went to Paris for a meeting of writers at the Salle Gaveau in connection with the festival Oeuvres du XXe Siècle, when he was warmly and enthusiastically greeted. April 2, 1953, saw the first production of a Faulkner work on television; the Lux Video Theater presented Faulkner's own adaptation of his short story "The Brooch." Since that time adaptations of many of Faulkner's stories and novels have been for television—"Wild Stallion," adapted from the title story of *Knight's Gambit*, on July 7, 1955; *The Sound and the Fury*, on December 6, 1955; *As I Lay Dying*, on October 7, 1956; "Ad Astra" on September 7, 1958; "The Tall Men," on September 14, 1958; "Old Man," on November 20, 1958; "Tomorrow" (from *Knight's Gambit*), on March 7, 1960.

In 1955 Faulkner was awarded the Pulitzer Prize and the National Book Award for *A Fable*. In August of the same year he visited Japan as a participant in the Summer Seminar in American Literature at Nagano, conducted under the auspices of the U. S. Department of State. (See Robert Jelliffe, *Faulkner at Nagano*.) He published *Big Woods*, a collection of four hunting stories, three of which had previously appeared elsewhere. *Requiem for a Nun*, which had appeared in 1951 as a sequel to *Sanctuary*, was adapted for the stage by Albert Camus and opened in Paris on September 20, 1956. Ruth Ford's adaptation, largely based on that of Camus, opened in New York on January 28, 1959. Aside from *A Fable*, Faulkner's most important book during the fifties was *The Mansion* (1959), the concluding volume of the Snopes trilogy begun with *The Hamlet*. The second volume, *The Town*, had appeared in 1957, but is of considerably lesser stature. His last work, *The Reivers* (1962), is in the humorous vein of *The Hamlet* and, though an excellent comic novel, is largely without deeper significance. Faulkner was posthumously awarded the Pulitzer Prize for *The Reivers* in May of 1963, nearly a year after his death from a heart attack on July 6, 1962.

Faulkner, like Addie Bundren in *As I Lay Dying*, was "always a very private" person. Preferring to live the quiet life of a gentleman farmer in Oxford, he avoided publicity to such a degree that his very unwillingness to accept his position as a literary personage has become famous. Faulknerana is full of legends of his refusal to receive visiting celebrities because of a "previous engagement to hunt a coon" (Coughlan, *Private World*, 83)—reportedly his reply to the ballerina Alicia Markova when she sent word that she wished to meet him. He had a distressing tendency to talk determinedly of the joys of raising horses to academicians who were expiring with eagerness to have him comment on literature. Perhaps even more current than these stories are tales of his fondness and amazing capacity for good bourbon, among them an anecdote related by a young friend and hunting companion, who reports that Faulkner would bring along two fifths of bourbon for a day's hunting expedition, finish the first by noon, the second by sundown—and still get his young friends home by dark.

Though he gave a relatively large number of interviews during the fifties and made at least eight speeches, his public comments have consisted primarily of rephrasings of the ideas contained in his Nobel Prize address:

> I feel that this award was not made to me as a man but to my work— a life's work in the agony and sweat of the human spirit, not for glory and least of all for profit, but to create out of the materials of the human spirit something which did not exist before. So this award is only mine in trust. It will not be difficult to find a dedication for the money part of it commensurate with the purpose and significance of its origin. But I would like to do the same with the acclaim too, by using this moment as a pinnacle from which I might be listened to by the young men and women already dedicated to the same anguish and travail, among whom is already that one who will some day stand here where I am standing.

Our tragedy today is a general and universal physical fear so long sustained by now that we can even bear it. There are no longer problems of the spirit. There is only the question: When will I be blown up? Because of this, the young man or woman writing today has forgotten the problems of the human heart in conflict with itself which alone can make good writing because only that is worth writing about, worth the agony and the sweat.

He must learn them again. He must teach himself that the basest of all things is to be afraid; and, teaching himself that, forget it forever, leaving no room in his workshop for anything but the old verities and truths of the heart, the old universal truths lacking which any story is ephemeral and doomed—love and honor and pity and pride and compassion and sacrifice. Until he does so he labors under a curse. He writes not of love but of lust, of defeats in which nobody loses anything of value, of victories without hope and worst of all without pity or compassion. His griefs grieve on no universal bones, leaving no scars. He writes not of the heart but of the glands.

Until he relearns these things he will write as though he stood among and watched the end of man. I decline to accept the end of man. It is easy enough to say that man is immortal simply because he will endure; that when the last ding-dong of doom has clanged and faded from the last worthless rock hanging tideless in the last red and dying evening, that even then there will still be one more sound: that of his puny inexhaustible voice, still talking. I refuse to accept this. I believe that man will not merely endure: he will prevail. He is immortal, not because he alone among creatures has an inexhaustible voice, but because he has a soul, a spirit capable of compassion and sacrifice and endurance. The poet's, the writer's, duty is to write about these things. It is his privilege to help man endure by lifting his heart, by reminding him of the courage and honor and hope and pride and compassion and pity and sacrifice which have been the glory of his past. The poet's voice need not merely be the record of man, it can be one of the props, the pillars to help him endure and prevail.

The best source of Faulkner's opinions on literature (his own included) and on several questions of current interest is *Faulkner in the University* (edited by Frederick L. Gwynn and Joseph L. Blotner, 1959), transcriptions of tape-recorded sessions with classes and other university groups made while Faulkner was writer in residence at the University of Virginia during 1957 and 1958.

Critical studies of Faulkner's work met the sudden upsurge of interest in his books that followed the Nobel Prize. The first book-length study to appear was *William Faulkner: A Critical Appraisal* by Harry M. Campbell and Reuel M. Foster, published in 1951. Several others followed (see bibliography for complete listings), and work on Faulkner continues to appear. By far the best Faulkner criticism to date is Olga Vickery's *The Novels of*

William Faulkner: A Critical Interpretation (1959). An excellent selection of critical articles and reviews (including an extensive bibliography) is contained in *William Faulkner: Three Decades of Criticism*, edited by Frederick J. Hoffman and Olga W. Vickery, 1960).

All of Faulkner's novels are readily available, most of them in inexpensive paperback editions; after his winning of the Nobel Prize, even his deservedly neglected *Mosquitoes* and *Soldier's Pay* were exhumed from their twenty-five-year-long rest in the dim realm of out-of-print books. His two volumes of poems, *The Marble Faun* (1924) and *A Green Bough* (1933), have never been reissued, nor are the privately printed stories "Idyll in the Desert" (1931) and "Miss Zilphia Gant" (1932) available except in special collections in libraries. *Salmagundi* (1932), also not reprinted, contains material originally published in *The Double Dealer*. In 1953 and 1955, respectively, William Van O'Connor edited collections of Faulkner's sketches for the New Orleans *Times-Picayune* under the titles *Mirrors of Chartres Street* and *Jealousy and Episode: Two Stories by William Faulkner*. A complete collection of Faulkner's work for the *Times-Picayune*, as well as a group of sketches from one issue of *The Double Dealer*, appeared in 1958 as *New Orleans Sketches*, for which the editor, Carvel Collins, supplied a valuable introduction. In 1962 Collins edited, with an introduction, Faulkner's *Early Prose and Poetry*, a collection of drawings, poems, and articles from 1917 to 1925, most of which appeared in two University of Mississippi publications, the *Ole Miss* annual and *The Mississippian*.

Selected Bibliography

WORKS BY FAULKNER

ABSALOM, ABSALOM! (novel). New York, Random House, 1936; New York, The Modern Library, Inc. (Random House), 1955.

AS I LAY DYING (novel). New York, Cape and Smith, 1930; New York, The Modern Library, Inc. (Random House), 1946 (with The Sound and the Fury).

BIG WOODS (four hunting stories). New York, Random House, 1955.

COLLECTED STORIES. New York, Random House, 1950.

DOCTOR MARTINO AND OTHER STORIES. New York, Harrison Smith & Robert Haas, Inc., 1934.

EARLY PROSE AND POETRY (compiled and edited by Carvel Collins). Boston, Atlantic-Little, Brown & Company, 1962. Faulkner's earliest published writing, most of which originally appeared in the University of Mississippi student newspaper; with a valuable introduction by the editor.

A FABLE (novel). New York, Random House, 1954.

GO DOWN, MOSES (seven related short stories). New York, Random House, 1942; New York, The Modern Library, Inc. (Random House), 1955; England, Penguin Books, Ltd., 1960.

A GREEN BOUGH (poems). New York, Harrison Smith & Robert Haas, Inc., 1933.

THE HAMLET (first volume of the Snopes trilogy). New York, Random House, 1940; New York, The Modern Library, Inc. (Random House), 1956; New York, Vintage Books (Random House).

INTRUDER IN THE DUST (novel). New York, Random House, 1948; New York, Signet Books (New American Library of World Literature, Inc.), 1950.

KNIGHT'S GAMBIT (six slightly related short stories). New York, Random House, 1949; New York, Signet Books (New American Library of World Literature, Inc.), 1950.

LIGHT IN AUGUST (novel). New York, Harrison Smith & Robert Haas, 1932; New York, The Modern Library, Inc. (Random House), 1950.

THE MANSION (third volume of the Snopes trilogy). New York, Random House, 1959.

THE MARBLE FAUN (poems). Boston, Four Seas Company, 1924.

MOSQUITOES (novel). New York, Boni & Liveright, 1927; New York, Dell Books (Dell Publishing Company, Inc.), 1962.

NEW ORLEANS SKETCHES (compiled and edited by Carvel Collins). New Brunswick, N. J., Rutgers University Press, 1958; New York, Grove Press, 1961. An interesting collection of Faulkner's early writing for the New Orleans *Times-Picayune* and the "little magazine" *The Double Dealer*; with a good introduction.

PYLON (novel). New York, Harrison Smith & Robert Haas, Inc., 1935; New York, Signet Books (New American Library of World Literature, Inc.), 1951.

THE REIVERS (novel). New York, Random House, 1962.

REQUIEM FOR A NUN (play with narrative interludes, a sequel to Sanctuary). New York, Random House, 1951; New York, Signet Books (New American Library of World Literature, Inc.), 1954 (with Sanctuary).

SANCTUARY (novel). New York, Cape and Smith, 1931; New York, The Modern Library, Inc. (Random House), 1932; New York, Signet Books (New American Library of World Literature, Inc.), 1954 (with Requiem for a Nun).

SARTORIS (novel). New York, Harcourt, Brace & Company, 1929; New York, Signet Books (New American Library of World Literature, Inc.), 1953.

SOLDIER'S PAY (novel). New York, Boni & Liveright, 1926; New York, Signet Books (New American Library of World Literature, Inc.), 1951.

THE SOUND AND THE FURY (novel). New York, Cape and Smith, 1929; New York, The Modern Library, Inc. (Random House), 1946 (with a new appendix by the author, and in the same volume with As I Lay Dying).

THESE THIRTEEN (short stories). New York, Cape and Smith, 1931.

THE TOWN (second volume of the Snopes trilogy). New York, Random House, 1957; New York, Vintage Books (Random House), 1961.

THE UNVANQUISHED (seven related short stories). New York, Random House, 1938; New York, Signet Books (New American Library of World Literature, Inc.), 1959.

THE VIKING PORTABLE FAULKNER (edited by Malcolm Cowley). New York, The Viking Press, Inc., 1954. An excellent collection of Faulkner's best short novels and stories; with good introductory material.

THE WILD PALMS (double novel). New York, Random House, 1939; New York, Signet Books (New American Library of World Literature, Inc.), 1954 (The Wild Palms and The [sic] Old Man).

STUDIES OF FAULKNER

BECK, WARREN. Man in Motion: Faulkner's Trilogy. Madison, Wis., University of Wisconsin Press, 1961. A book-length study of The Hamlet, The Town, and The Mansion.

BROOKS, CLEANTH. William Faulkner: The Yoknapatawpha Country. New Haven, Conn., Yale University Press, 1963. A detailed study of the Yoknapatawpha County novels, emphasizing the relation of the individual and the community, the discovery of evil, and the theme of honor. Recommended.

COUGHLAN, ROBERT. The Private World of William Faulkner. New York, Harper & Brothers, 1954. An informal biography, interesting primarily for its anecdotal material, but undocumented and not always accurate.

FAULKNER, JOHN. My Brother Bill: An Affectionate Reminiscence. New York, Trident Press Book (Simon and Schuster), 1963. An amusing, anecdotal biography, particularly good for a picture of Faulkner's childhood.

GWYNN, FREDERICK L., and JOSEPH L. BLOTNER, editors. Faulkner in the University: Class Conferences at the University of Virginia, 1957–58. Charlottesville, Va., University of Virginia Press, 1959. A rich source of Faulkner's opinions on his work, on other writers, and on some current questions.

HOFFMAN, FREDERICK J. William Faulkner. (Twayne's United States Authors Series.) New York, Twayne Publishers, Inc., 1961.

HOFFMAN, FREDERICK J., and OLGA W. VICKERY, editors. William Faulkner: Three Decades of Criticism. East Lansing, Mich., Michigan State University Press, 1960. An excellent collection of the most important Faulkner criticism to appear in magazines; with a valuable introduction and extensive bibliography by the editors.

HOWE, IRVING. William Faulkner: A Critical Study. New York, Vintage Books (Random House), 1962. An expanded and revised edition of a work that first appeared in 1952, and (in its revised form) one of the better critical studies now available.

JELLIFFE, ROBERT A., editor. Faulkner at Nagano. Tokyo, Kenkyusha Ltd., 1956. Transcripts of Faulkner's addresses and meetings with students in Japan.

MALIN, IRVING. William Faulkner, An Interpretation. Stanford, Calif., Stanford University Press, 1957.

MILLGATE, MICHAEL. William Faulkner. New York, Grove Press, 1961. A brief biography and survey of Faulkner's work.

MINER, WARD L. The World of William Faulkner. Durham, N. C., Duke University Press, 1952. A study of the mythical Yoknapatawpha County in its relation to its prototype, Lafayette County, Mississippi.

O'CONNOR, WILLIAM VAN. William Faulkner. (University of Minnesota Pamphlets of American Writers.) Minneapolis, Minn., University of Minnesota Press, 1959. A very brief survey of Faulkner's life and writings.

—— The Tangled Fire of William Faulkner. Minneapolis, Minn., University of Minneosta Press, 1954.

SLATOFF, WALTER J. Quest for Failure: A Study of William Faulkner. Ithaca, N. Y., Cornell University Press, 1960. A detailed analysis of Faulkner's use of antithetical conditions in both style and subject matter, with attention given to the major novels.

SWIGGART, PETER. The Art of Faulkner's Novels. Austin, Texas, University of Texas Press, 1963. An analysis of Faulkner's use of "puritans" and "primitives" in his novels.

THOMPSON, LAWRANCE. William Faulkner: An Introduction and Interpretation. New York, Barnes & Noble, Inc., 1963. A sound, readable study of eight of Faulkner's novels. Recommended to the student.

VICKERY, OLGA W. The Novels of William Faulkner: A Critical Interpretation. Baton Rouge, La., Louisiana State University Press, 1959. The most nearly definitive of all Faulkner studies to date; a lucid and perceptive analysis of all the novels. Highly recommended.

WAGGONER, HYATT H. William Faulkner: From Jefferson to the World. Lexington, Ky., University of Kentucky Press, 1959.

Index